The House Connection

The House Connection

How to Read the Houses in an Astrological Chart

Karen Hamaker-Zondag

SAMUEL WEISER, INC.

York Beach, Maine

First published in 1994 by
Samuel Weiser, Inc.
P. O. Box 612
York Beach, Maine 03910–0612

Translated by Transcript, Ltd.

Library of Congress Cataloging-in-Publication Data

Hamaker-Zondag, Karen.
   [Huisheren en huizenverbanden. English]
   The house connection : how to read the houses in an astrological
chart / by Karen Hamaker-Zondag.
      p.   cm.
   Includes bibliographical references and index.
   1. Houses (Astrology)   I. Title
BF1716.H35513 1994
133.5'3--dc20   93–45898
                                   CIP

ISBN 0–87728–769–4
BJ

Typeset in 10 point Garamond

Printed in the United States of America

99 98 97
10 9 8 7 6 5 4 3 2

The paper used in this publication meets the minimum requirements
of the American National Standard for Permanence of Paper for
Printed Library Materials Z39.48-1984.

To all my pupils

Table of Contents

List of Charts and Figures

• • •

Astrological Signs and Symbols *

Sign	Symbol	Day Ruler / Night Ruler		Element	Cross
Aries	♈	Mars	♂	Fire	Cardinal
		Pluto	♇		
Taurus	♉	Venus	♀	Earth	Fixed
		—			
Gemini	♊	Mercury	☿	Air	Mutable
		—			
Cancer	♋	Moon	☽	Water	Cardinal
		—			
Leo	♌	Sun	☉	Fire	Fixed
		—			
Virgo	♍	Mercury	☿	Earth	Mutable
		—			
Libra	♎	Venus	♀	Air	Cardinal
		—			
Scorpio	♏	Pluto	♇	Water	Fixed
		Mars	♂		
Sagittarius	♐	Jupiter	♃	Fire	Mutable
		Neptune	♆		
Capricorn	♑	Saturn	♄	Earth	Cardinal
		Uranus	♅		
Aquarius	♒	Uranus	♅	Air	Fixed
		Saturn	♄		
Pisces	♓	Neptune	♆	Water	Mutable
		Jupiter	♃		

*The reader should note that this author uses European glyphs for the planets. Pub.

Foreword

House rulers and house connections are important when looking at a horoscope. Morin de Villefranche described this in some detail in his *Astrologia Gallica: Book 21.* He embroidered the scanty outline of the subject as it was known in his time. The study of house rulers appears as early as Ptolemy, and Cardanus occupied himself with it, to name but two exponents of the art. However, Morin appears to have been the first to make a systematic approach, but he lived in an era when the human psyche was still very much unexplored territory. Therefore, many of his pronouncements and interpretations, which usually relate to external characteristics and circumstances, look rather antiquated today. Astrology is now becoming increasingly psychological in its expression and this is why I have written this book.

House rulers and house connections provide us with a wider and deeper perspective of the chart, and supply answers to all kinds of questions that might otherwise remain a mystery. For example, it is often said that with Jupiter in the 2nd house the native will enjoy a good income. So how is it that there are people with Jupiter in the 2nd house who time and again suffer financial reverses? Generally speaking, the cause seems to be that the rulers of the 2nd houses are involved in difficult aspects and house connections, so that the promise of Jupiter in the 2nd cannot be realized except after many setbacks and a great deal of hard work. And there are numerous other examples we could mention that would show how necessary it is to take the house connections and house rulers into account when interpreting the chart.

I have been working with house connections ever since I began my astrological studies, and this book is the distillate of my findings. Nothing could persuade me to omit this particular facet of interpretation, and I am in full agreement with the spontaneous comment of a student who once said, "If you overlooked the house rulers and house connections or did not know how to deal with them, you would not be able to derive one quarter of the information from the chart you derive from it now." I hope to present a systematic account of how to work with this very important technique.

Again, as always, my thanks to my husband Hans, who is an unfailing source of support and constructive criticism for he read every line of the manuscript, commenting wherever he thought necessary. His efforts have made the work much easier to read and understand. It is invaluable to have him to turn to behind the scenes.

Amstelveen,
Karen Hamaker-Zondag

Other books by Karen Hamaker-Zondag

Aspects and Personality

Elements and Crosses as the Basis of the Horoscope

Handbook of Horary Astrology

Houses and Personality Development

Psychological Astrology

The Twelfth House

• • •

Foundations of Personality (1994)
(Combines *Elements and Crosses as the Basis
of the Horoscope* and *Houses and Personality
Development* into one volume to provide a
complete foundation for horoscope interpretation.)

PART I

THEORY

1

Types of Ruler

Rulers of Signs

Each planet, through its nature and properties, has a special relationship with a certain sign and it is known as the ruler (or dispositor) of that sign. Some planets rule two signs. On the other hand, some signs have two rulers, a day ruler and a night ruler. This is the result of the discovery of the trans-Saturnian planets (Uranus, Neptune, and Pluto) which now have to be included in the system of rulers or dispositors.

The day ruler (or dispositor) is the principal ruler of a sign. The night ruler (or dispositor), the second ruler, is certainly important for a sign, but its role is subordinate to that of the day ruler. The word "night" has nothing to do with the "dark side" of such a planet, and even less to do with nighttime: all it indicates is that the planet comes in second place.[1]

Astrologers are pretty well agreed on where to assign both the classical and the trans-Saturnian planets; Pluto is the only bone of

---

[1]However, there may originally have been more in it than that, because Sibly says (*Science of Astrology*, 1784, p. 133): "Jupiter . . . has allotted for his houses . . . Sagittary and Pisces . . . Pisces his night house, is in trine to Cancer, the house of the nocturnal luminary, and Sagittary, his day-house, in trine to Leo, the house of the diurnal luminary." *Translator's note*

contention. Most astrologers place Pluto in Scorpio, a minority place it in Aries, removing Mars from Aries and giving it to Scorpio.

On looking at the rulerships more closely (see Table 1 on page 6), we see that they have a systematic basis. This becomes clear if we arrange the zodiac signs in a certain way, starting with Leo, ruled by the Sun, and Cancer, ruled by the Moon. The Sun and Moon stand respectively for male and female, day and night, creative (yang) and receptive (yin), also for conscious and unconscious. They are known as the "lights" of the horoscope, and are the most significant factors in interpretation. By using the Sun and Moon and their signs as our foundation, it is possible for us to understand figure 1.

By placing the signs as they are shown in figure 1, we can make sense of the rulership arrangement assigned to the classical planets from Mercury to Saturn inclusive. This distribution of rulerships held

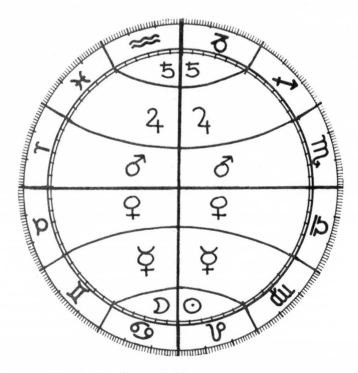

Figure 1. The classical dispositorships.

good until the discovery of Uranus. A vertical line is drawn from the Sun and Moon to Saturn. Plainly this represents the psychological structure of the human being in symbolic form. The psyche consists of a conscious and an unconscious part (Sun and Moon), and we come through our contacts (Mercury), through our emotional relationships and the sense of security they afford (Venus), through our activities and our ego-function (Mars), and through our philosophy of life and our religious expansion (Jupiter), to a certain measure of our self-demarcation and assumption of responsibility (Saturn). In my book describing the nature and functioning of the planets, I have already discussed this quite fully.[2]

By adding the more recently discovered trans-Saturnian planets to figure 1, we find that the ascending vertical line curves back down to the bottom of the diagram in a way that is reminiscent of the uroboros, the serpent swallowing its own tail. The recurrent line is shown in figure 2 (page 6). Here Uranus rules Aquarius; but, as we can see in Table 1, it is the night ruler of Capricorn. The former ruler of Aquarius, Saturn, is now demoted to become night ruler of the sign, but retains its primacy as day ruler of Capricorn. In fact, Capricorn and Aquarius are ruled by the same two planets, but one planet takes pride of place in one sign and the other planet takes pride of place in the other. The day ruler is always the stronger of the two rulers, and this is the one we shall concentrate on in the following pages.

The same thing is true of Sagittarius and Pisces: Neptune is now acknowledged as ruler of Pisces, with the sign's former sole ruler, Jupiter, pushed into second place as the night ruler; but Jupiter has retained its position as the main ruler, or day ruler, of Sagittarius, of which Neptune is now the night ruler.

Pluto has become ruler of Scorpio, leaving Mars to become the night ruler of the sign. But Mars remains day ruler of Aries while Pluto is its night ruler.

The remaining signs, the pairs Taurus/Libra, Gemini/Virgo and Cancer/Leo, have to make do with sharing one ruler per pair; except for Cancer and Leo, which do have their own individual rulers, but no night ruler. Thus the system appears to be incomplete; but this makes sense, because the development of human beings is still far from complete. Just as in the last two centuries three planets have been discovered that have heralded a period of stormy developments, so in

---

[2]See *Planetary Symbolism in the Horoscope* (York Beach, ME: Samuel Weiser, 1985).

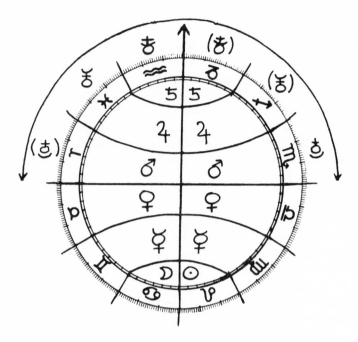

Figure 2. The classical and trans-Saturnian dispositorships.

Table 1. Signs and their Rulers.

Sign	Day Ruler	Night Ruler
Aries	Mars	—
Taurus	Venus	—
Gemini	Mercury	—
Cancer	Moon	—
Leo	Sun	—
Virgo	Mercury	—
Libra	Venus	—
Scorpio	Pluto	Mars
Sagittarius	Jupiter	Neptune
Capricorn	Saturn	Uranus
Aquarius	Uranus	Saturn
Pisces	Neptune	Jupiter

the future others now unknown may be discovered or, perhaps, we may gain a better conception of heavenly bodies we already know.

For example, there is a belt of asteroids circling the Sun, and according to some authorities, these asteroids consist of the broken fragments of what was once a planet. Other astrologers think that this belt of asteroids should be assigned to Virgo; still others think that some asteroids belong to Virgo and others to Libra. Opinions are still very much divided on the matter. A recently found member of the Sun's family is the planetary fragment Chiron, with an orbit between those of Saturn and Uranus. Chiron was discovered in 1977, and its possible influence has been studied by astrologers all over the world. The research is not yet unanimous, but a strong body of opinion provisionally assigns this fragment to Libra. And there are other signs that the system of dispositorships may be extended and further refined in the future, especially as astronomers suspect that there is another planet somewhere beyond Pluto.

However, it does not matter too much, for our purposes, whether or not there are planets still to be discovered. Only at the moment when a planet is observed or observable in the heavens, is it thought to manifest its influence on the earthly plane. "That which is above is as that which is below, and that which is below is as that which is above."[3] What is found to have material existence in the sky will perceptibly affect the earth.

Rulers of Houses

Each house begins in a certain sign; the cusp of the house stands in this sign. The signs of the various cusps depend on the moment of birth. This is decisive for our house divisions. For example, let's consider the case of someone born with a Leo Ascendant. What this means is that the cusp of the 1st house lies in the sign of Leo. The house ruler is the planet that is the (day) ruler of the sign on the cusp of the given house. Since the Sun rules Leo, it also rules the 1st house in our example. The Sun here is the lord, or ruler, of house 1.

If Scorpio was the sign on the Ascendant, then Pluto, the day ruler (or day dispositor) of Scorpio, would have been the ruler of the

---

[3]Quoted from *The Emerald Table of Hermes*. Mary Anne Atwood's translation in *A Suggestive Enquiry* (Belfast, 1918). *Tr.*

1st house. The other house cusps, too, begin in certain signs. When, for example, cusp 6 (the beginning of the sixth house) lies in Sagittarius, then Jupiter, the day ruler of Sagittarius, is the ruler of house 6.

As stated earlier, some signs have more than one ruler; they have an additional (though less important) night ruler. The question that arises is how far this second planet plays a role as house ruler. Experience teaches that such a second ruler does indeed have a role to play; but, in every case, it is overshadowed by the day ruler of the sign standing on the cusp of the house. The best thing to do with the night ruler is to look to it for extra information, but to attach much less importance to it.

Quite often, a house that begins in a certain sign contains the whole of the following sign and ends in the sign after that. The sign that does not contain a house cusp is called intercepted. Not all charts have intercepted signs, but many do. In Chart 1, the 6th house begins in Sagittarius and the 7th house begins in Aquarius. This means that the intermediate sign, Capricorn, lies wholly in the 6th house and is therefore intercepted. When a sign is intercepted, the influence of its (day) ruler is not lost, but it is co-ruler of the house within which it lies. In our example, the 6th house has two rulers, namely Jupiter (from Sagittarius) and Saturn (from Capricorn). *But, even so, we must not forget that the main ruler is always the planet that rules the sign standing on the cusp, even if the cusp is in the last degree of that sign.* In our example, Jupiter is the main ruler of the 6th house and Saturn is the somewhat less important co-ruler. However, we must certainly not ignore the information provided by Saturn, for a co-ruler can often supply significant subsidiary details.

At this point, some confusion can occur. We are looking at the main ruler and co-ruler of a house. In our example, Sagittarius and Capricorn both rule the 6th house and they both have night rulers (Neptune and Uranus respectively). These play no role of importance here. What we are talking about are *house* rulers (main rulers and co-rulers), not sign rulers (day and night rulers).

It can happen that a house begins halfway through a sign. Say, for example, that the 11th house starts at 16° Taurus. This means that the remaining fourteen degrees of Taurus fall in the 11th house, while the first sixteen degrees of this sign, that is to say the larger number, are still in the 10th house. For this reason, we might think that Venus, the day dispositor of Taurus, not only rules over the 11th house (which begins in Taurus) but has something to say about the 10th house. The

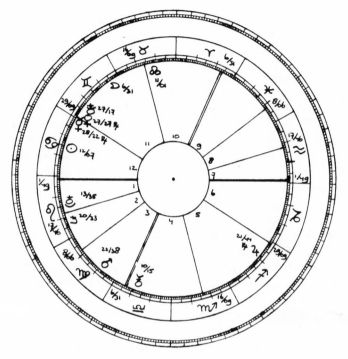

Chart 1. A natal chart. Registered time of birth: July 4, 1948, clocktime 6:15 hrs. Blokker, Holland.

idea is very plausible, but it is a big mistake. *The ruler of a house is always determined by the sign in which the house begins and, should the case arise, by the sign that is intercepted in the house.*

On examining Chart 1, we find the following house rulers:

Ruler of 1: Sun
Ruler of 2: Sun
Ruler of 3: Mercury
Ruler of 4: Venus
Ruler of 5: Pluto
Ruler of 6: Jupiter and Saturn (co-ruler of 6)
Ruler of 7: Uranus
Ruler of 8: Uranus

Ruler of 9: Neptune
Ruler of 10: Mars
Ruler of 11: Venus
Ruler of 12: Mercury and the Moon (co-ruler of 12)

Thus all the planets take part as house rulers. As we see, there are planets ruling over more than one house, and there are those that share their dispositorship or rulership over a house with some other planet. Because the house rulerships are determined by the relationships of the houses to the signs, only some of us will have the Sun as ruler of the 1st and Mars as ruler of the 10th. So there are considerable differences. And here is the great value of working with house rulers: they give extremely individual indications.

Because none of the planets (except the Moon) travel particularly fast, everybody born on the day for which Chart 1 was cast will have a conjunction of Venus, Mercury, and Uranus. In fact, the aspect lasts a number of days, although (of course) its nearness to being exact varies. Now, although many people will share the aspect — and the character potential that goes with it — only some of them will have Venus as ruler of the 4th and the 11th. Others, born at some other time of day, or in another part of the world (or both), could have Venus as ruler of the 2nd and the 9th for instance.

The house a given planet rules makes a big difference when you interpret a chart. A house ruler, by its aspects and by its placements in sign and house, makes an indelible mark on the house over which it rules. Therefore, in Chart 1, the placement of Venus says something not only about how Venus expresses herself as a planet (that is to say about the need for harmony, balance, and emotional contacts), but also (as she is ruler of the 4th and the 11th) about domestic affairs and the native's inner emotional basis (house 4) as well as attitudes regarding friends and people of similar tastes and interests (house 11). So a planet always performs a twofold function in a horoscope: it expresses its own characteristics, and it rules one or more specific areas of life.

How House Rulers Function

Since a house ruler can tell us so much, it will be prudent to take a close look at its functioning with a view to establishing rules for interpretation. The first thing to consider is if a house ruler's sole influence is on external circumstances. This question has to be asked because we know that the houses in the horoscope are said to represent various circumstances of life, and it is natural to suppose that the house rulers must have a similar influence on our circumstances. However, by restricting the role of a house ruler to circumstances, we fail to go far enough. My many years of practical experience have painted me another picture.

The houses of the horoscope represent not only external circumstances but also our (generally unconscious) expectation patterns and needs. Since it is impossible to divorce internal and external, we can just as reasonably find *in the houses* some developments in character due to life's experiences as we can reasonably find character traits in the planets *in the signs*. The houses have *also* to do with desire patterns, and this makes it possible to interpret them psychologically (as already explained in my earlier book on the nature and background of the houses).[4] The ruler of a house is not just an indicator of the circumstances in which the things promised by that house must take shape, it is also an indicator of the native's inclinations and of the effect these will have on his or her character.

Working with progressions confirms this. There are a number of techniques used by astrologers to move planets in the natal chart so that the chart becomes a dynamic picture of the life of the individual. Making these legitimate alterations in the positions of the natal planets enables us to find analogies to inner development and external happenings. When a progressed planet forms a temporary aspect with some other planet, the planets concerned make their influence felt not only according to their own planetary nature but also according to their significance as dispositors of one or more houses. Certain areas of life (the houses) will be involved in the aspects of progressed planets. An interpretation confined to external events implies that progressed aspects always relate to things that affect us from the outside, and this is certainly not true in practice. Progressions of house rulers, for example, are often linked with inner developments, showing that our situations and circumstances are closely connected with our inner needs and normal expectations.

---

[4] See my book *Houses and Personality Development* (York Beach, ME: Samuel Weiser, 1988). If you don't have a copy of this book, note that it will be reissued in a double volume (also including *Elements and Crosses as the Basis of the Horoscope*) under the title *Foundations of Personality* in the fall of 1994.

Like the planets, the house rulers can be interpreted psychologically, as may easily be demonstrated by an example. Mercury is the planet that tells us something about the way a person speaks, makes contacts, thinks, does business, etc., and, in a similar fashion, the ruler of the 3rd house tells us about the way the person expresses the area of life covering such things as contacts, information, conversation, and thought. That being so, because a difficult temporary progressed aspect between *Mercury* and Neptune can go with temporary learning problems, clouding of thought and an unusually active dream life, we need not be surprised that the same sort of thing could happen with a comparable aspect between *the 3rd house ruler* and Neptune.

A horoscope is replete with so many interpretative factors that the mode in which a planet will express itself is very varied. The different possibilities arise from the planet's many placement options in sign and house. So the effect of Mercury will change from chart to chart, even though, as a planet, its psychological meaning remains the same. By considering the house rulerships, we gain additional information as to the terrain in which a planet deploys its forces. As we have just observed, the 3rd house displays an obvious relationship to the planet Mercury. It always has something to say about our manner of gathering information, thinking, communicating, and associating. The role played by the ruler of the 3rd house in our chart, *regardless of what planet it is*, provides us with further details about the way in which Mercury itself can behave. (A well-placed Neptune can make a first-class ruler of house 3!)

When Mercury is strong in the chart, and without difficult aspects, yet is forced to cooperate with a poorly placed ruler of the 3rd, the verbal skills of the native and his or her ability to communicate are more impaired than would be supposed from the favorable position of Mercury. On the other hand, if a Mercury with a difficult placement is supported by a strong ruler of the 3rd house, mercurial matters and capacities will flourish more than we would otherwise have a right to expect. Therefore, we can make a judgment on someone's learning abilities, on verbal and communicative skills, and so on, only if we analyze the house ruler concerned in addition to analyzing the proper planet.

Perhaps readers will ask if planets in the 3rd house should be included in the above analysis. The answer is yes, but the part played by the house ruler is decisive. A golden rule in interpretation runs like this: *Planets in a house carry a potential and may make things hard or easy, but the house ruler decides the way in which the potential is realized.*

For instance, Jupiter in the 2nd house generally augurs well for the obtaining of a firm foothold and financial and material security. This is why wealth is attributed to this planetary position. But if the ruler of the 2nd house receives difficult or undermining aspects and/or is not well placed in some other respect, then the promise of security will be made good only through hard work, and by overcoming opposition and reverses. Indeed, there is a question as to whether the promise will ever be wholly fulfilled.

The Difference between a House Ruler and a Planet

As has already been said, a house ruler must not be treated simply as a planet. In itself, a planet always represents an archetypal reaction pattern, a universal psychic factor that has become more and more differentiated during the course of the centuries. A house ruler, on the other hand, is absolutely individual and indicates psychic reactions that result from various experiences. Incidentally, such experiences need not have been registered consciously, but may have happened in early infancy, or even when we were in the womb, for example. However, they include the incidents occurring at all ages of our lives. All these experiences are represented by the houses, and the house rulers introduce the archetypal patterns of the planets as individual characteristics. I have a strong impression that house rulers are concerned with inherited family traits. So often we see that children inherit either some of the planetary placements of their parents or grandparents, or house connections that are analogous to certain planetary positions. Thus a Cancer father can very well have an Aquarian son, but the son's Sun may be in aspect to the ruler of the 4th, the Cancerian house, so that the son has something of the Cancerian about him and expresses this in response to his experiences. Research into astrological family relationships frequently reveal this sort of thing.

Both a planet as such and a planet as a house ruler can be interpreted psychologically. We can illustrate this by comparing Mercury and the ruler of the 3rd house. Mercury represents the general need to communicate and to relate to others mentally. It expresses itself in a personal manner through the sign and house it occupies and through the aspects it forms. The 3rd house also represents communication and mental exchange, but contains some additional features because of its psychic formative factors. Among other things, it has to do with brothers, sisters, and neighbors.

If, for example, there is a hard aspect between the ruler of the 3rd house and Saturn, it is likely that the native has no brothers or sisters or that, due to circumstances, he or she has had little or no contact with brothers and sisters, or has suffered some other form of deprivation in this sphere. Numerous expressions of the aspect are possible in everyday life. To name but a few — children split between parents after a divorce, an illegitimate child in the family (the native or one of the other children), chronic illness preventing much contact with a brother or sister. Often, with this aspect, I have seen rather inapproachable children who refused to share in the cheerful rough-and-tumble of normal youngsters, preferring to keep their own counsel and to play by themselves.

In any event, something must have happened in childhood to prevent quick and easy-going contacts, with the result that later in life, the native finds it hard to handle informal negotiations with tact. Certain experiences, or the lack of them, will color a person's mode of thinking and communicating.

So we see that the role of a planet, as representative of human needs in general, is enacted differently by each individual according to experiences. And these experiences are more or less determined by the house that corresponds to the planet. It really makes no difference whether these experiences are the consequence of circumstances that seem to come from outside — such as being separated from one's brothers and sisters after parents divorce — or are the consequence of one's own behavior — such as becoming withdrawn and unfriendly. Clearly, these individual experiences may be ascribed both to the house and to its ruler, and that is the reason why, in interpreting some specific area of life, we have to look both at the planet concerned and at the ruler of the house that is similar in nature to this planet.

A further illustration of the different functions of a planet is the following: Sagittarius is ruled by Jupiter. Jupiter is its day ruler, and its functioning as ruler of this sign has an effect therefore on any planets placed in Sagittarius. As house ruler, its functioning has an effect on any planets placed in the house with Sagittarius on its cusp, even if the planets are actually in Capricorn. Thus Jupiter exercises a double influence. First, a difficult placement of Jupiter will cause it to be a troublesome factor in itself. Second, it will have an adverse effect on any planets that happen to be in Sagittarius. The sign of Sagittarius is much more likely to be a source of problems than it would have been. A sign always functions in keeping with the way in which its ruler works. This means that, merely on the grounds of differently placed rulers, there will be dissimilarities between individuals with the same Sun sign.

Then again, Jupiter is also a house ruler and, as such, determines the manner in which the promise of the house is realized. What is more, Jupiter as a planet has a strong affinity with the 9th house (in fact, we call it the collective or mundane ruler of that house). The 9th house is the house of journeys, both literal ("with bags all packed and ready to go") and mental (study, the development of philosophical beliefs, etc.) and it guides our judgments and opinions. Similarly, Jupiter has to do with travel, study, and the formation of judgments and opinions. It is closely allied to the 9th house, even when it is not the real ruler of the 9th, which, with Taurus on the cusp, say, would be Venus. (The position of Venus in the chart would give us information on the ups and downs of matters germane to the 9th house).

How ought we to view the relationship between sign, planet, house, and house ruler? The sign is always the background indicator of the way in which planets in that sign will function and express themselves. Further information on their effectiveness in this regard is provided by the position of the sign ruler. In our example, the placement of Jupiter particularizes the functioning of Sagittarius. A planet *per se* may be said to represent an archetypal reaction pattern in human beings—the need for a certain element of human nature to express itself. In the case of Jupiter, this is the religious sentiment and the need to travel in the broadest possible sense—to form one's own opinion, to arrive at a place where one has one's own vision, and to make a synthesis of all one's perceptions. Jupiter (or any other planet for that matter) may be regarded as an instrument, a basic internal reaction pattern that helps us to give shape to certain things. At the same time, it is a drive impelling us from within to behave along certain lines, each in our own way.

The 9th house, which has so much affinity with Jupiter, is its field of operations and source of materials. It indicates the extremely individualistic mode we shall use to try to perform the Jupiter function. Any planets in the 9th house are employed as raw materials for realizing Jupiter's aims. The ruler of the 9th reveals, by its placement and aspects, how we are going to handle these raw materials, and what the possibilities and problems are. The situation of the ruler of the 9th in the horoscope shows how, and by what route, the archetypal drive represented by the planet (Jupiter in our example) can manifest itself.

Therefore house rulers are of the utmost importance in interpretation. They provide information on:

• The individual experiences belonging to the area covered by the given house, and in particular;

• On the way in which the promise of the house may be realized, and;

• On individual experiences that are character-forming and that supplement the activities of the planet that is analogous to the given house.

2

House Connections

General Rules

Several rules need to be remembered when we are judging house rulers and house connections. Because everything depends on the house in which a planet is placed, we require a firm grasp of the following:

• When a planet is within *four* degrees of the cusp (the starting point) of an angle, it is deemed to develop its potential in the following house (the angle). Angles are the 1st, 4th, 7th and 10th houses.

• When a planet is within *three* degrees of the cusp of one of the other houses, it takes effect in this following house.

• These rules are applied with a significantly smaller orb when a planet is retrograde. Only if a retrograde planet is right on the cusp of the following house, is it counted as coming within the ambit of that house, otherwise not. It is hard to give a precise orb rule for retrograde planets. A retrograde Mercury, for example, when used in secondary directions, will normally turn direct during the native's lifetime and will enter the following house; but a retrograde Neptune or Pluto are much less likely to do so. There is more room to maneuver with a retrograde fast-moving planet than with a retrograde slow planet. Fast-moving planets can be allowed an orb of $1^1/_2$ degrees maximum.

Before these rules can be applied, the time of birth needs to be known with great accuracy. Correction of the time of birth can help us in doubtful cases. With a slight difference in time, a planet may well shed its influence in a house quite unlike the one we had supposed, and this affects interpretation considerably. So although the rules are inherently very useful, we must be careful with them.

If we have determined which signs are on the house cusps, and thus in which houses the planets stand, we shall automatically know in which houses the house rulers stand; each planet rules one or more houses. On looking at Chart 1 (page 9), we see that Pluto is in the 1st house. Pluto belongs to Scorpio, and that sign is on the cusp of the 5th house. Accordingly, Pluto is lord of the 5th and provides information on the matters of the native's 5th house. We say that the ruler of the 5th is in the 1st. This is a circumstance that connects the two houses, and I call it a *house connection*. We need to be aware of which ruler is standing in which house. That is to say, it makes a difference to the interpretation whether the ruler of the 5th is in the 1st, or the ruler of the 1st is in the 5th. For house connections the following rule always applies:

The house over which a planet rules serves the purposes of
the house in which that planet stands.

A simple example can clarify this point. If the ruler of the 1st house stands in the 7th, then we look to our opposite number, or partner, and manifest ourselves (1st house) through him or her (7th house). But if the ruler of the 7th house is in the 1st, the reverse is true, and it is our partner or companion who has to look to us. With the ruler of the 1st in the 7th, we could well find ourselves at the beck and call of our partner; but, with the ruler of the 7th in the 1st, the partner is more likely to be answerable to us. In both cases, there is a close connection between houses 1 and 7, and a strong involvement between the parties concerned. (See Part II for a more detailed explanation of the house connections.)

Sometimes two house rulers occupy each other's houses. For example, the ruler of the 7th can be in the 1st at the same time as the ruler of the 1st is in the 7th. This is known as *house reception*. The involvement of the houses with each other is then much stronger. In fact they go together. In other words, wherever the 7th house plays a role, the 1st house joins in. The houses cannot be seen apart from one another; the activities they represent flow together.

When interpreting the house rulers, we must always forget about their ordinary significance as planets for the time being. It makes absolutely no difference which planet acts as ruler of a given house; as house ruler it simply informs us about the ups and downs of that specific house. What matters is whether the planet is well or poorly placed, and in which house it stands.

For instance, if Scorpio is on the cusp of the 3rd, then Pluto is the ruler of the 3rd. It is quite erroneous to say the native will have a compelling way of talking, and will be very secretive and unwilling to pass on information, etc. When functioning as house ruler, Pluto loses its Plutonian characteristics and just conveys the qualities of the 3rd house. Everything to do with Pluto now has a direct reference to the 3rd house. A somewhat inaccurate yet effective way of looking at this is to treat Pluto as if it were Mercury, the planet that has an affinity with the 3rd house—always provided we do not confuse the instrument, Mercury, with the sphere of action and the raw materials! In other words: Pluto in its capacity as ruler of the 3rd in our example will display Mercurial traits. But note well that Pluto is certainly not a second Mercury here (it merely consists of one archetypal factor that is symbolized by Mercury). It does have something to say about how we gather information, talk, think, analyze, make brief contacts, and deal with other 3rd house concerns. This role is exclusively involved with the way Pluto functions as an archetypal factor, and not with the archetypal factor, itself. So we must not combine the planetary characteristics and the house rulership.

The aspects made by Pluto have to be interpreted not only as aspects of Pluto to the planets concerned, but also (in our example) as aspects of the ruler of the 3rd to these planets. The two things—Pluto as such, and Pluto as ruler of the 3rd—have to be considered completely separately in interpretation.

Rather paradoxical results can arise from the above, results that seem often to create misunderstanding. The significance of a planet is not always in agreement with the significance of the house (or houses) over which it rules (or is the secondary ruler). At one time the role of the planet as a planet *per se* appears to predominate, at others its role as house ruler appears to do so; while, in still other cases, the two roles seem to be played together. Let us see what happens when Pluto as lord of the 3rd is placed in the 1st.

Pluto in the 1st

This placement gives great physical strength and a desire to do well in the outside world; it makes the native inwardly tense and alert, and it combines a great need for power and recognition with an obvious combative streak. The native makes excessive demands of the people with whom he or she comes in contact, but gives them hardly anything in return. He or she makes a close study of the people around, tries to fathom them so as to get to the bottom of their drives and motives, and searches for background influences and undercurrents. The knowledge of human nature acquired like this can be used in a positive way, but can also be misused in order to gain power. The native's will-power is very great.

The Ruler of 3 in the 1st

This gives a great need for a multiplicity of contacts; and usually these are made in a bright and friendly fashion. The native is mad about facts of all kinds, likes to keep lines of communication open, and is curious about whatever is going on around him or her. Talking usually comes easily, and quick connections are made between persons and things. In any case, the native soon gets the hang of things, sometimes jumping from one topic to another, and wants to do most of the talking. Contacts of all kinds are extremely important in his or her attitude to the outside world.

As will have been observed, the two descriptions differ considerably, and even conflict with one another on some points. When we meet with this sort of discrepancy, we must never say that the factors cancel one another out! On the contrary, *each factor strives to express itself, and will express itself, come what may*. That is to say, conflicting factors do not neutralize each other, they actually impart certain tensions to the character.

Pluto, as ruler of the 3rd in the 1st, leads to the conflicting desires just described. With Pluto in 1, we hardly ever commit ourselves, but hold our cards close to our chest. With the ruler of 3 in 1, we speak frankly—perhaps sometimes naïvely so. Pluto in the 1st is looking for depth, and makes excessive demands in contacts and relationships, whereas the ruler of 3 in 1 is looking for large numbers of contacts and plenty of information without being too exacting. With this placement we shall notice the following effects:

• Sometimes we are very reserved, at other times more open and talkative. These two attitudes manifest themselves in turn;

• We are inquisitive about everything and have no trouble in making contacts (ruler of the 3rd), but are not so eager to part with our own news in exchange. So we tend to have a say in any information gathering in which we are involved, or even take the reins into our own hands as independent investigators in order to gain permanent control of a situation. Here, the horoscope factors do not alternate but combine.

• Also, the purely Plutonian influence can predominate in such a way that outwardly the native is very uncommunicative, but satisfies his or her curiosity by checking things out quietly, by reading a lot, and by keeping abreast of current affairs.

A great deal depends of course on the background of the signs, but the important point here is that the normal functioning of one and the same planet can come into conflict with its functioning as a house ruler.

The Placement of the House Rulers in the Houses

As we have seen in the previous section, a house ruler exerts its influence in the house in which it stands. However, because it also has a big say in the house it rules, we may safely assume that this house, together with any planets in it, also exerts its influence in and serves the purposes of the house occupied by the ruling planet. When we have had a little practice in combining, we shall quickly notice that it is not a particularly difficult problem in interpretation, although one combination is rather more tricky than another. A good way of interpreting a house connection is as follows:

• Consider the meaning of the house ruled by the planet in question;

• Consider the meaning of the house in which this house ruler stands;

• Try to derive a sensible judgment from the idea that the house ruled, which we call our starting point exerts its influence in the house in which the house ruler stands. In doing so, we need to have a flexible approach. The idea "exerts its influence in" can also be expressed as "has as its goal" or "leads to," and so on. We must simply remember that *the house in which the house ruler stands is the terminal point or final purpose*. Often the house ruler (and the house it represents) is an instrument of the house in which it stands—in the widest possible sense.

Perhaps an example will clarify this. Let us suppose that we have the ruler of the 3rd in the 9th. How do we deduce the meaning of this house connection? In the first place, we look at the significance of the 3rd house. It is the house of communication, contacts, exchange, information, thinking and arranging, to name but a few of the many key words.

Then we go to the 9th house; the house governing the formation of our opinions and the way in which we expand our horizons. This is the house that represents our studies and our travels, the formation of our opinions, the publication of our views and discoveries. It is also the house standing for the synthesis of our ideas and for our philosophy of life.

What we require now is a formulation showing how the sphere of the 3rd house expresses its influence in the 9th (the ruler of the 3rd is in the 9th in our example). One possibility is the gathering of knowledge and information (3rd house) is carried out for the purpose of forming a judgment, a synthesis, or a vision. In other words, with the ruler of the 3rd in the 9th, we gather information and make (brief) contacts in order to gain an overview.

When the ruler of the 9th is in the 3rd (a connection which is the reverse of the one we have just considered), the two houses still act together but their rules are reversed. The 9th house is now subordinate to the 3rd in the sense that our opinion, or judgment, or some idea or vision that we have, involves us in the search for further information to refine, support or substantiate it; or perhaps we feel impelled to keep talking about this opinion or idea. The significant feature here is that we have a jumping-off point, an incentive, for the acquisition of more knowledge, whereas with the ruler of the 3rd in the 9th, we set to work more or less without any preconceived ideas, but in the hope of arranging in a coherent pattern any facts we may discover.

In each case, information gathering and opinion forming go hand-in-hand, but in each case the picture is completely different. Naturally, more could be said about this particular house connection;

the above is intended simply as an example of the difference in working.

Among those houses in which house rulers stand, the house containing the ruler of the Ascendant is prominent. In one way or another, it plays an important part in the life of the native. When making our judgment, we ought to lay more weight on that house and to attach more importance to such things as planets in the house, the role of its ruler, and so on.

There is one more case in which a house receives greater emphasis, and that is when the ruler of a house is in its own house. The influence of the house is increased because its ruler is occupying its own domain, and is expressing its influence there. The interpretation of this situation is simple: consider the meaning of that house as such and note its great importance for the native. At the same time, do not lose sight of the fact that, by their placement, the house rulers express a need, but the rest of the chart must show how far the meeting of this need encounters resistance or support. Emphasis on a house does not invariably mean that the needs of that house will be satisfied.

For example, consider the case where the ruler of the 1st house is in the 1st. The influence of the ruler is then concentrated on the terrain it actually rules. This strengthens the native's preoccupation with himself or herself and increases the desire to be noticed in the outside world. Regardless of what may be found in the rest of the chart, the individual can impress others as a forceful personality, but also as someone who is too self-centered. The need to draw attention to himself or herself is powerful, but other horoscope factors may hinder or even obstruct this.

Let us suppose that someone has a Taurus Ascendant, which is generally an indication of a very reserved nature, and that Venus is placed in the 1st house. The ruler of the 1st is then found in the 1st. If Venus, as lady of 1, is also square Saturn, the reserve will be increased, and so the need shown by the ruler of 1 being in 1—the need for powerful self-manifestation—is opposed by other factors. Now we know that we must never think of two such factors as cancelling one another out; therefore, in the present case, we must assume that the native experiences an internal struggle between the inclination to be reserved and to stay in the background, and the need to come to the fore. He or she will tend to take a prominent position, but will prefer to do so unobserved as much as possible.

Generally speaking, however, we can say that a house ruler in its own house does add extra weight to that house. This will play a big part in the life of the native, either directly or indirectly. In judging the horoscope, it is important to take note of the house in which the ruler of the Ascendant is placed, and also those houses that contain their own rulers.

If we look at one or two house connections in Fred's chart (Chart 2), we shall be able to see how all this works out in practice. Fred has Scorpio on the Ascendant. Pluto is the ruler, and it stands in the 9th house. So Fred has the ruler of the 1st in the 9th. This means that Fred involves himself in the outside world for the sake of 9th house matters: literal journeys (abroad) or mental journeys (study, philosophical speculation, etc.). With the lord of the 1st in the 9th, he is certainly going

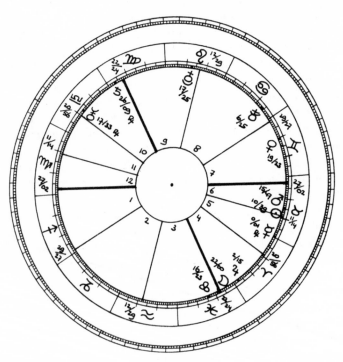

Chart 2. Fred's chart. Placidus houses. Registered time of birth: May 1, 1951, 21.30 hrs. Groningen, Holland.

to interest himself in one or more of the areas covered by the 9th house, but it is not easy, just by inspecting a chart, to say exactly what is going to occur when. As it happens, Fred is fascinated by foreign lands. He loves to travel and hike and wants to see all the countries in the world. Study has little attraction for him. He is more a man of action who likes to use his hands. (See the Sun and Mars in Taurus in the 6th house for this!)

With the ruler of 1 in 9, he feels the need to broaden his horizons; he forms opinions based on personal experience — what he has seen with his own eyes (the 9th house always involves making a judgment or forming an opinion).

If, for the purpose of making a more detailed analysis, we examine what the ruler of the 9th house is doing, we discover that Leo is on the cusp of the 9th and therefore the Sun is the ruler of that house. Now the Sun stands on the cusp of the 6th house, which means that the ruler of the 9th is in the 6th. Fred's 9th house activities concentrate themselves on the 6th house. Or, to be more specific, Fred's need to travel physically or mentally, to broaden his horizons, and to form his own opinion, will make itself felt in the field of self-criticism and analysis, of work and working conditions, of sickness and health, and of social adjustment. Fred's spiritual development resulting from the expansion of his horizon can be of special use to him in his work, and it will also affect the way he sees himself (self-criticism is always a factor in the 6th house). He will be inclined to take practical advantage of whatever he learns from experience (the 6th house is geared to usefulness and serviceability). It is also not impossible that someone with this connection has foreign contacts in his work, or works abroad. The old saying that a person with this connection will fall ill in a foreign land has never come true in the cases that have come under my observation; although in one instance there was a link between a foreign country and disease: the native was a volunteer who helped with medical projects in developing countries. In Fred's case, the connection between his 9th and 6th houses expressed itself in the fact that he took temporary employment abroad in order to cover part of the cost of his world tour. What is more, his experiences overseas gave him a totally new understanding of his work, of society, and of himself.

Fred's 6th house also contains Mars, which rules his 5th house. So the ruler of the 5th is in the 6th. This means that everything involving hobbies, self-assurance, self-expression, play, and pleasure (5th house) is channeled into the house of work, analysis, service, and sickness and health. In practice, this means that work for Fred is, or must be, a sort of fad; and, at the same time, that he gains the feeling from his work and/ or charitable activities that he is appreciated or regarded as an authority. Hobbies can lead to work or can be utilized in his work. Also there is a need of independence and of opportunities for development (5th house) in order for him to give shape to his work (service), or he gets a great deal of pleasure (5th house) in being useful (6th house).

Fred's friends have often found this. Fred takes pleasure in helping them, and doing so builds his self-confidence. The help he offers borders on work—odd jobs and minor house repairs. Although Fred likes pleasure and relaxation, there is something about him that says work comes first (the ruler of the 5th in the 6th makes the 6th the end point). If he had had the ruler of the 6th in the 5th, work and recreation would still have gone hand in hand, yet he would not have given it priority, but would always have consulted his own convenience before engaging in any task. However, Fred's ruler of the 5th is in the 6th, and his self-expression is channeled into work and service. He is extremely helpful; he also likes encouragement along the way. To some extent the presence of the Sun in the 6th contributes to this, because any house occupied by the Sun will figure prominently in a chart.

The sign on Fred's 6th house is Taurus, which makes Venus the ruler of the 6th, so work and service are controlled by the partner or by a close friend or friends. Before his travels, Fred worked in an office. He had no special friends but did have a regular workmate with whom he got on well. With the ruler of the 6th in the 7th, Fred's life partner will tend to supervise Fred's work, health, and service. And, in fact, Fred has become an able assistant to his partner. He likes working with her and values her input and advice. He will work well with her if the rest of his chart points in the same direction. Fred's critical attention (the 6th) is turned on his partner's way of life; something that she may find annoying if he takes notice of every little detail in the relationship. He does show signs of this.

Flexibility is essential in combining the houses in house connections. Try to avoid abstract formulations and use everyday terms and concepts. With practice, this will not be difficult.

Finally, it cannot be stressed enough that we must never rely blindly on only one indication in the chart. Confirmation of it needs to be found elsewhere. One indication is a possibility; two are a probability; three or more may be treated as a near certainty. House connections are no exception to this rule.

3

Important Houses

The Strongest House

As we have just seen, certain houses are given more weight in interpretation. But, in addition to this, there is another line of inquiry that will identify important houses. The significance of these houses has nothing to do with that of the house containing the ruler of the 1st or with the house occupied by its own ruler. What I mean is the following.

All of us behave and, indeed, run our lives, in accordance with set patterns, which are for the most part unconscious. As soon as something happens, we tend to react in a given way. Now the type of reaction may be deduced partly from the planets in the signs and in the houses, but the house connections afford us the opportunity to trace patterns and sequences. What we have to do is to work out a chain of house rulers. To start with, we find the house where the ruler of the 1st is placed. Then we find the ruler of the house in which the ruler of the 1st is placed, and then the house in which that ruler is placed, and so on. For example, we could discover the following chain: the ruler of 1 is in 7, the ruler of 7 is in 9, the ruler of 9 is in 2, the ruler of 2 is in 11, the ruler of 11 is in 7. This series provides us with an insight into a reaction pattern that, for this person, is related to the 1st house (we always begin with the 1st house). We can begin with the ruler of each house, and the sequences obtained will tell us something about the behavior stereotypes of the individual concerned in the area of life governed by the said house. Quite often, the patterns are so rigid that we can even recognize familiar paths taken by the psyche in certain situations.

The following features are displayed by the above example. In approaching the outside world, the native (1st house) takes his cue from his partner (ruler of 1 in 7), apparently without being prompted. He may not seem to be particularly submissive; but, subconsciously, he takes note of what she likes and does in certain cases, and fits in with her plans where possible. Because the ruler of 1 is in 7, he is in her field of influence.

With the ruler of 7 in 9, the native finds it useful to have a partner with the same interest in philosophical matters and, preferably, with the same outlook on life; someone who loves studying or, at least, is eager to broaden her horizons—perhaps through travel. But, in any event, the partner (house 7) is required to share or appreciate the native's personal vision. It is important to him that his partner adopts his view of existence; he is not inclined to be guided by the partner in this (as he would be if his ruler of 9 were in 7). On taking things a step further, we see that the ruler of 9 is in 2: the formation of philosophical views and the sharing of these with another, i.e., with the partner (since the ruler of 7 is in 9) can give the native a sense of security.

The reader need hardly be reminded that the 2nd house is not always interpreted in terms of possessions and finances. The primary ideas conveyed by this house are security and feelings of satisfaction and dissatisfaction. Money and goods are simply means to obtaining these things. The native feels impelled to share his vision and to broaden his horizons in order to gain a sense of security. With this house connection, we quite often see strongly held opinions, which help the native to feel confident.

When the ruler of the 2nd is in the 11th, the native's certainties govern his attitude to his circle of friends and to those with views similar to his own. He turns to them for confirmation, and his sense of security is largely dependent on the extent to which they give that confirmation. Nevertheless, their reactions, if they are to be at all influential, must enrich his relationship with his partner and must not impair it. This is clear from the fact that the ruler of 11 is in 7. What the partner thinks has a great deal of sway over the freedom of development in 11th house.

In short, we see here the following pattern of behavior. In his outer behavior, the native is very much involved with his partner, either directly or indirectly. He needs a partner who will share his opinions and outlook, so that he can build up a sense of security and can feel that he is standing on solid ground. He turns to friends and coworkers to reinforce this sense of security, but the opinion and attitude of his partner are decisive in every respect. All this is true of him whether or not he is aware of it. The pattern is one into which he falls whenever the 1st house has a part to play in what he is doing.

It is important to note that, in a chain like this, each of the preceding links has a role; we do not use just one link when working out the pattern. In the above example, it is not simply the need for certainty (2) that affects the 11th house: the native's personal vision is important, too, as is the way in which, and the extent to which, his partner can share that vision.

In this manner we can analyze every one of the houses, and put under the magnifying glass what the native does in regard to each house. And we shall find that certain extremely important connections recur again and again. The needs and attitudes that these connections represent will then be characteristic of the native. Several rules should be borne in mind:

• The orb rule, namely that a planet within 3° of the cusp of the following house (or 4° if that house is an angle), must be treated as if it were in that house. However, if the planet is retrograde, the orb allowed is much smaller.

• What matters, in determining the connections, is the day ruler of the sign on the cusp. The rulers of intercepted signs have no say.

• A chain ends with the last house before the chain starts repeating itself.

• A chain also ends when the ruler of a house is in its own house.

We can illustrate how the chain ends by going back to the example given earlier. We had this series: ruler of 1 in 7, ruler of 7 in 9, ruler of 9 in 2, ruler of 2 in 11, ruler of 11 in 7. Thus the 7th house crops up as an endpoint twice — ruler of 1 in 7 and ruler of 11 in 7. If we were to continue, the series ruler of 7 in 9, ruler of 9 in 2, etc. would repeat itself. We should start circling round and round endlessly, so we stop at the house which forms an endpoint for the second time in our series. In this case, it is the 7th house. This series can be written more succinctly as:

$$1 \ 7 \ 9 \ 2 \ 11 \ 7$$

the 7th house being the endpoint here. And now, if we write the series of house connections for each house individually, not only will the recurrence of certain connections catch our eye, but we shall also probably observe one or two houses in which some series keep cropping up. There may be only one house of this sort; sometimes there are two or three, but seldom more. Such houses will play a commensurately important role for the native: they form a hub on which the various house connections turn.

The identification of these one or two important houses is known as finding the strongest house. The strongest house should be given more weight when the horoscope is judged. The strongest house need not contain many planets, although it may do so. And it is not always the house we might have expected. Observe: there is definitely no rule that the house should be propitious. What the word "strong" implies is that the needs and desires represented by the house are pivotal, and that the fulfillment of these needs and desires has a major influence on what is done or not done in other areas of life.

Horoscope II: Fred

We can now proceed to draw some inferences from Chart 2 (page 24). Fred has several borderline planets. The Moon is on the cusp of the 4th and, according to the orb rule, is in the 4th house. Fred's Sun is 10° 39′ Taurus and the cusp of the 6th is 11° 14′ Taurus. Here, too, we must apply the orb rule and assign the Sun to the 6th house. What does this give us in the way of house connections?

The ruler of 1 is in 9, the ruler of 9 is in 6, the ruler of 6 is in 7, and the ruler of 7 is in 7. In the 7th house we have our first repetition, so the series stops there. In condensed form we write this as:

$$1 \ 9 \ 6 \ 7 \ 7$$

The other houses can be treated in the same way so as to obtain the following series:

1st house) 9, 6, 7, 7.

2nd house) 4, 10, 5, 6, 7, 7.

3rd house) 8, 5, 6, 7, 7.

4th house) 10, 5, 6, 7, 7.

5th house) 6, 7, 7.

6th house) 7, 7.

7th house) 7.

8th house) 5, 6, 7, 7.

9th house) 6, 7, 7.

10th house) 5, 6, 7, 7.

11th house) 7, 7.

12th house) 9, 6, 7, 7.

The example of Fred's chart is very straightforward, because only one house stands out as the strongest—the 7th. It is the endpoint of all twelve series. Fred cannot get on without his partner. His satisfaction with the various areas of his life ultimately depends on her. No matter what he is concerned in, he needs her stimulus, and a great deal depends on her participation. Obviously, we shall have to make a closer study of the 7th house and the situation of its ruler, in order to see how Fred handles this.

At first sight, we might not have anticipated that the 7th would be the strongest house. Two important personal factors stand in the 6th house (the Sun and Mars) and, in the 4th house, we find both Jupiter and the Moon, making this house also quite significant. However, the house connections do emphasize the 7th house and, in practice, Fred cannot escape from it. Of course, considerable importance is also attached to the 4th and 6th houses because of the powerful planets placed in them; and to the 9th house, because it is occupied by the ruler of the 1st. But irrespective of the energy and application given to the matters represented by the other houses, these are all to some extent subservient to one and the same house—house 7—which must justify (or complete, as the case may be) the efforts put into and the satisfaction obtained from the others.

In another example, we can look at Paul's chart (Chart 3) and find the following house connections.

1st house) 9, 3, 10, 9.

2nd house) 3, 10, 9, 3.

3rd house) 10, 9, 3.

4th house) 8, 8.

5th house) 8, 8.

6th house) 8, 8.

7th house) 9, 3, 10, 9.

8th house) 8.

9th house) 3, 10, 9.

10th house) 9, 3, 10.

11th house) 9, 3, 10, 9.

12th house) 9, 3, 10, 9.

In Paul's chart, we end up five times with the 9th house, four times with the 8th house, twice with the 3rd house, and once with the 10th house. So houses 9 and 8 come strongly to the fore. This is hardly surprising since each contains three planets, including very personal ones such as the Sun and Mercury. Here the results are much more in line with expectations than in the case of Fred's chart.

Paul's keen philosophical and psychological interests led him to study religion. Obviously, the 8th and 9th houses are directly involved in his choice. Emphasis is laid in several respects on these houses in his chart:

• The ruler of 1 (Pluto) is posited in the 9th house, which is already a strong house within the series of house connections;

• The 8th house contains its own ruler, and is also a strong house in the house connections;

• What is more, three planets stand in each of the two houses, and several of these planets are personal ones (it is important to take this

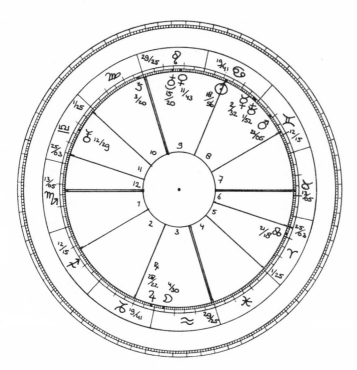

Chart 3. Paul's natal chart. Placidus house. Registered time of birth: July 11, 1949, 15.30 hrs. Oosterhout NB, Holland.

into consideration when making a judgment); therefore the houses are significant from this point of view, too.

Since these houses are so prominent, it is no wonder that they play such a leading role in Paul's study, interests, and work. That work and interests and the strongest house are often connected, is illustrated in the following example, the chart of a leading Dutch politician (Chart 4, page 34), whose houses are linked together as follows:

    1st house) 9, 3, 10, 10.

    2nd house) 10, 10.

    3rd house) 10, 10.

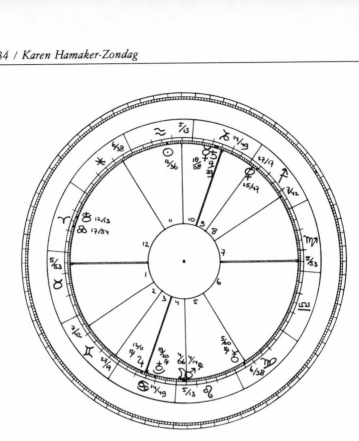

Chart 4. A Dutch politician. February 2, 1931, 10.15 hrs. Geldrop, Holland. Source: Jan Kampherbeek. *Cirkels,* p. 186.

4th house) 5, 11, 12, 5.

5th house) 11, 12, 5.

6th house) 10, 10.

7th house) 4, 5, 11, 12, 5.

8th house) 3, 10, 10.

9th house) 3, 10, 10.

10th house) 10.

11th house) 12, 5, 11.

12th house) 5, 11, 12.

We find here, seven times the 10th house, three times the 5th, once the 11th, and once the 12th. The 10th house is very appropriate to someone who has always held public office in government. This house represents the making of decisions, laws and rules, and the organization of the community.

Once again, we must remember to apply the orb rule. The Moon and Mars both stand on the cusp of the 5th house. The Moon can be assigned without difficulty to the 5th house. Mars is retrograde and, in theory, ought to belong to the 4th, but it is a borderline case (there is no hard-and-fast rule for deciding when a retrograde planet should be assigned to the following house). However, in this instance, Mars does not matter; it is co-ruler of the 12th, and co-rulers play no part in this application.

Venus stands on the cusp of the 9th and is assigned to the 9th. Jupiter stands on the cusp of the 4th, but is retrograde. Because it is more than two degrees from the cusp of the 4th, its effect is felt in the 3rd. Neptune is also a borderline case: it stands on the cusp of the 6th but is retrograde. It is more than $1^{1}/2$ degrees from the cusp of the 6th, so is considered to still be in the 5th house, all the more so since it is moving so slowly that, although (in secondary progression) it *should* turn direct during the lifetime of this politician, it will be active in the 5th for most of that period.

By no means does the example of this politician imply that everyone with a strong 10th house is bound to enter politics in exactly the same way! Often we find people of this type in positions where they can tell others what to do. But this could be in a small way, the scale does not matter, perhaps authority is exercised only in the family. Even people with very unassuming charts who have a strong 10th house can be seen to develop in the direction of guiding and leading. They may exert their influence behind the scenes, but the impulse to do so is irresistible.

The strongest house will not tell us what the native is going to do with that house. As I have already said, we must also look at the position of planets in that house, and above all at the part played by the house ruler in the remainder of the chart. What is more, for each house, there exists an immense range of possibilities between its destructive and constructive extremes. Both extremes show up in each of the areas of life covered in the horoscope, but also we see an emphasis on one extreme.

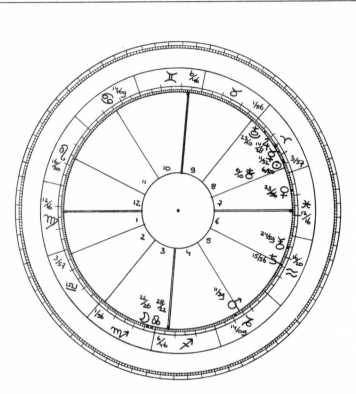

Chart 5. The natal chart for Wilhelm C. Röntgen. March 27, 1945, 16.00 hrs. Lennep, Holland. Source: Jan Kampherbeek. *Cirkels,* p. 186.

A good illustration of this is the chart of Wilhelm Röntgen, the discoverer of the electromagnetic radiation known as X-rays. (See Chart 5.) On looking at his houses, we observe the following picture.

1st house) 8, 5, 6, 8.

2nd house) 7, 6, 8, 5, 6.

3rd house) 8, 5, 6, 8.

4th house) 8, 5, 6, 8.

5th house) 6, 8, 5.

6th house) 8, 5, 6.

7th house) 6, 8, 5, 6.

8th house) 5, 6, 8.

9th house) 7, 6, 8, 5, 6.

10th house) 8, 5, 6, 8.

11th house) 3, 8, 5, 6, 8.

12th house) 8, 5, 6, 8.

Altogether, we finish at the 8th house seven times, at the 6th house four times, and at the 5th house once. The 8th is therefore clearly the strongest house, followed by the 6th. No one will deny that Röntgen's research into the forces latent in matter, and into what lies hidden in the material world, fits in very well with the 8th house, which is much emphasized in his chart. The idea of life and death associated with the 8th has been given shape by his discovery of the X-rays: the correct dose can be life-saving, an overdose can result in death.

Murder and homicide, which used to be ascribed to a strong 8th house, are not a foregone conclusion, although they can of course be linked with it. It is impossible, from the bare horoscope, to say which factor will prove to be destructive or not. Let us be cautious when judging a strong house that (in our eyes anyway) is "difficult." Even on this point alone, Röntgen's chart is very instructive. Because, what is more, Mars, the ruler of his 8th house, is square as many as four out of the five planets that Röntgen has in the 8th. The old style of astrology, which saw everything in black and white, would have drawn further negative conclusions from this. Fortunately, our more psychological modern astrology judges matters from a humanistic rather than from a moralistic angle, and says something like this: yes, there is an element of danger in this horoscope situation, because it gives the native a need to live on a knife-edge rather than to play safe. On the other hand, this 8th house with all its squares, represents a powerful creative potential, which the native can carry to great heights, either socially or in his personal development, or in both.

The orb rule still has to be applied in Röntgen's chart. Mars stands on the cusp of the 5th at 11° 39', while the cusp of the 5th is 14° 09' in the same sign. The difference of 2° 30' is less than 3° for an intermediate cusp, so that Mars is assigned to the 5th house. Saturn stands at 15° 56′ Aquarius, while the cusp of the 6th begins in 16° 20′ Aquarius, so Saturn is assigned to the 6th house.

If we disregard this rule, the emphasis on the 8th house is greater still. Mars will then be in the 4th, and, through house reception between the 4th and 8th houses (Jupiter Lord of the 4th in the 8th and Mars, Lord of the 8th in the 4th) nearly all the house connections will end in the 8th. This might seem to suit the bill very well indeed, but it would be at the cost of the analytical 6th house — which also played an unmistakable role in Röntgen's life.

The Interpretation of the Strongest House

So how do we treat the strongest house in our interpretation? In every case, we consider the significance of the house as such and interpret it as an important need and/or character trait. Briefly, we then have the following possibilities in interpreting the houses, which are offered to the reader not as a complete list, but more by way of illustration.

1st House

When it is strongest, the 1st house gives a person a powerful desire to stand out in the crowd. Such a person will usually seem to "be some-one" and will not (knowingly or otherwise) hide his or her light under a bushel. Anyway, generally speaking, this person will not go unnoticed. The wish to hold his or her own is well developed, and there is a lively reaction to outside stimuli. In addition, this person likes coming to terms with new experiences and situations, and seeks adventures, or wants to occupy him- or herself with new (or, at least, personal) things. This individual has a nose for what is recent, and for action — which is sometimes precipitated by this person's very presence. With the accent on the 1st house, this person likes to have his or her own way and tends to be self-centered and wayward.

2nd House

When the 2nd is the strongest house, there is a need to play safe and to stay standing on firm ground. The native needs some form of safety net before venturing into a new situation. The 2nd house is deep-rooted in the material and the tangible, and in the security represented by these things: from which there follows a pronounced desire for financial security in particular, often enough. The attitude of the native can be, "How much can I make out of this?" And yet, the attitude toward matter can be not one of enslavement to it, but of control, so that it is used to express personal sentiments and feelings. Artistry and craftsmanship, too, belong to the 2nd house.

3rd House

When the 3rd is the strongest house, there is an obvious need for exchange, conversation, gathering information (including reading), arranging and passing on information, mulling over facts and ideas, either with others or on one's own, and for performing mental analyses. Even if someone has a very "reserved" horoscope, a strong 3rd house will make the person talkative, clever with words, and a skilled communicator. The native's lively mind sorts and arranges a host of facts and things worth knowing. Often there is calculating ability and the commercial instinct.

4th House

When the 4th is the strongest house, domestic life and the feelings and emotions of others become important. There is a great need for emotional security, and we find attachment to the trusted circle of those with whom there are emotional ties.

The individual with this as the strongest house enjoys settling down in a snug little group, and sometimes has a reserved attitude toward outsiders. Such an individual is continually studying his or her environment and arranging it so as to make others, and himself or herself, feel at home. There is a great fondness for the past and for objects having a sentimental value. The native's home can become a hoard of heirlooms and mementos with which he or she is reluctant to part. In general, he or she craves for firm family ties, or finds in friendships the opportunity to care for others.

5th House

When the 5th is the strongest house, there is a clear desire to make the most of one's own individuality and to hold the center of the stage. Often this desire bestows a natural gift of leadership. The native is inclined to do what pleases him or her and gives self-satisfaction. Professional hobbyism is one tendency. For preference, relationships with others must be calculated to boost the self-image. The native sometimes wants to run the show, while giving others the privilege of doing things for him or her, and is not one to worry over details. Yet he or she is not afraid to tackle ambitious projects personally, if there's a mind to do it. The desire to be the center of attention may lead to egocentricity—the placement of the ruler of the 5th will shed further light on this.

6th House

When the 6th is the strongest house, the native has a down-to-earth, practical disposition. He or she likes doing things and working with the hands. Usually he (or she) is happy to help and serve others, and is not a shirker. For some, work is a form of self-expression. Being useful is important, and the motto is often "duty before pleasure." The strong sense of what is fitting associated with this house expresses itself not only in a willingness to abide by the wishes of the majority, but also in an analytical and critical attitude, and the need for objectivity. Sometimes we find an interest in health matters, and even activity in this field.

7th House

When the 7th is the strongest house, the partner and/or companion plays a very important and sometimes decisive role in the life of the native, who expects much of the relationship, and of the partner or the companion, and invests a great deal of psychic energy in the relationship. The stimulus of someone close is badly needed, and so a partner may well be sought early in life. Nevertheless, the fact that the 7th is the strongest house does not guarantee a successful relationship; it just means that the other person will be put first in everything. Therefore the native has a great capacity for getting on with a partner, and will no doubt always be prepared to compromise with them. A disadvantage sometimes is overdependence.

8th House

When the 8th is the strongest house, the native is constantly aware of his or her vulnerability. The 8th house represents both repressions and hidden gifts and talents. The individual with this emphasis on the 8th house feels the full weight of personal, usually unconscious, problems; this gives him or her the inclination to adopt an attitude calculated to disguise the vulnerability from the outside world. Not being able to show feelings openly means that most of the strife is internal. The native has a great desire to delve into what is secret, both in himself or herself and in others, and may, for example, find arcane knowledge attractive. The ability to investigate and to uncover matters is usually well developed and intense. When these faculties are developed positively, we see high creativity and a strong regenerating capacity. When the development is not so positive, crises easily occur. These may be a need to defy dangers and to "dice with death" literally or figuratively.

9th House

When the 9th is the strongest house, the need to expand and to widen one's horizons runs, like a red thread, through everything done by the native. The main motive is to travel, either physically or mentally. The native makes up, and speaks, his or her mind. What is said has the character of a message, and the style in which it is delivered is teaching or moralizing. Usually the need is felt to place facts and figures in a fairly broad context and to make a synthesis of them. In this way, it generally happens that a definite philosophy of life is formed, sometimes on the basis of religion. Personal ideas and opinions are important, and so is their propagation. The native may follow a course of higher education provided other pointers in the same direction are found in the chart.

10th House

When the 10th is the strongest house, there is an inner compulsion to become responsible for or to take control of part of the community, and to issue rules and regulations for it. Because the native is so aware of his or her responsibilities, he or she is not easily influenced, and might prefer to resign rather than give in to outside pressure. He or she is therefore likely to be a good organizer and leader. The native generally attaches great importance to everything concerning the outside world and to having a duly recognized role in running it.

Quite often, the native places so much value on the part he or she plays in society that the result may even be an identification with it to some extent. The native hopes to produce clearly defined structures, not only in a material sense but also in society, and needs to have a well-expressed ego. He or she generally likes to feel officially confirmed in a position of authority. Needless to say, this can lead to egocentricity.

11th House

When the 11th is the strongest house, there is a great need to associate with people having the same views and interests. Generally speaking, these are friends, members of the same club or political party, etc. In order to keep in with these folk, the native makes an effort to be adaptable, and to find his or her level in their society. He or she learns to treat them as individuals with their own needs and sense of values. It is characteristic of the 11th house to see others as equals and to make contact with them on terms of equality. The native avoids over-familiarity, as this might hinder the development of the individual development of self and others.

12th House

When the 12th is the strongest house, the native has a great desire for quietness, privacy, and the experience of unity. However, it certainly does not follow from this that there will be a dissolution of the personality or any sort of loss or bereavement. But there is a definite need to reflect and to get things straight inwardly. The purifying and refining process can be sought through religion, yoga, meditation, communing with nature, listening undisturbed to music and becoming absorbed in it, and so on. With the 12th house, emphasis is also often laid on service to the community in a selfless way, and on coming to the aid of the infirm and the oppressed. The native may be inclined to retreat into a dreamworld, and to chase after shadowy and fleeting thoughts; but, with this house, he or she can just as easily use this capacity to feel and imagine what it would be like to be someone or somewhere else, and to use it (probably completely unconsciously) in such a way as to "tune in" to social developments in the making, which are still below the surface, or to feel the emotional undercurrents running through the local community.

● ● ●

When a house, as the strongest house, is exercising a pivotal function, the need it represents cannot be ignored. But it is by its function that the house makes itself felt, not by its properties *per se*. We must not assume that this need is bound to be satisfied. How the native fares with the house depends on the nature of the planets in it, the placement of its ruler, and so on. What is more, the significance of the house must not be judged in terms of good or bad. The need it represents is merely the main element in a pattern of personal desires. The main need has to be satisfied if the most is to be made of the other needs in the chain; also, it will supply the motivation to clear away obstructions from the other needs.

From what has been said so far, it appears that the houses can receive an emphasis in very different ways. Sometimes the various types of emphasis are widely scattered among the houses; but, more frequently, a limited number of houses will be emphasized from varying points of view, thus gaining in importance. Houses that play an especially significant role include:

1) The house in which the ruler of I stands;

2) A house containing its own ruler;

3) The house in which the Sun is placed;

4) A house containing many planets, particularly personal ones;

5) A house functioning as the strongest house.

The Individual and the Collective House Rulers

As we saw in chapter 1, we can work with sign rulers as well as with house rulers. The sign rulers apply to us all, because each sign has its own special planet or planetary pair. The house rulers differ from one person to another, since the exact way in which the houses are laid out varies a great deal, and depends on the individual birth moment. These house rulers are called individual house rulers.

We can also distinguish house rulers of another type on the basis of the connection between signs and houses. The meaning of each house is analogous to that of a zodiac sign, and the order of the signs corresponds to that of the houses. Thus the meaning of the 1st house is analogous to that of Aries, the meaning of the 2nd house to that of Taurus, and so on in order through all the twelve signs and houses.

Figure 3 shows this connection schematically. As already mentioned, each house has its own day ruler. The day rulers are included in the figure. To name just two examples, Aries, Mars and the 1st house come together in the same segment, and so do Capricorn, Saturn, and the 10th house. The planets associated with given houses in this way are known as the collective rulers of the houses. Some astrologers term them

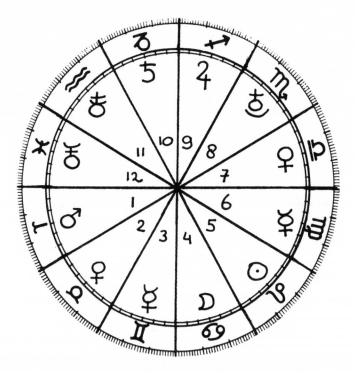

Figure 3. The house rulerships based on the natural zodiac.

the mundane rulers. Anyway, they are always the day rulers of those signs that correspond in meaning to the houses in question. So, in principle, everyone has Mars as the collective ruler of the 1st house, Mercury as the collective ruler of the 3rd house, Uranus as the collective ruler of the 11th house, and so on.

Accidentally of course, these collective rulers can coincide with our individual rulers; but usually they do not. Thus we have the much more important individual rulers that are special to ourselves, and also the collective rulers that are the same for everyone.

The point I wish to make is that the collective ruler of a house comes into play when it makes an aspect with the individual ruler of the same house. Let us suppose that the Ascendant is Leo. The individual ruler of the 1st house will then be the Sun. But the collective ruler is always Mars. We should look to see if there is any aspect between the Sun and Mars and, if so, what kind of aspect it is. An aspect shows the degree to which our individual expression of the house is in step with a more collective course of events, or is in agreement with a more collective quality of the age we live in. The sort of thing we are likely to observe is this:

• In hard aspects, we continually suffer from small setbacks and irritations, because what we want in a certain area of life is, so to speak, in conflict with what is possible at the time or with what others are obviously expecting of us;

• In easy aspects, it is comparatively easy to have what we want in a certain area of life, and people fall into line fairly readily with what we wish to do;

• In the conjunction, collective and individual expression go hand in hand. This means that, generally speaking, the effect of the mode of expression is more pronounced;

• If the collective and the individual house ruler are one and the same, the result is similar to that of the conjunction;

• If there is no aspect, the situation is neutral and there is no particular pattern.

The links between the collective and the individual house rulers form small supplementary factors in interpretation. We can never hang weighty matters on them! What they do is to supply helpful information on the many things in daily life, things for which it is not always too easy to find an explanation although they keep cropping up in our personal affairs.

To give an example: when the collective ruler of the 11th (Uranus) conflicts with our individual ruler of the 11th, we often find that friends of ours are going to be away on a day we were hoping to visit them, or they do not hear the telephone when we ring them, or something else happens to get in the way. In short, considerable effort is needed for success in 11th house matters. On the other hand our friends can turn up on the doorstep unexpectedly at the most inconvenient moments.

What can be gathered from the relationship between a collective and an individual house ruler is the extent to which we have to struggle against small obstructions and miscalculations; or the extent to which we find it easy to take up some activity in the area of life concerned. It is generally a question of timing, and may be known by the (spontaneous) choice of the moment. However, the relationship between the two house rulers tells us absolutely nothing about the quality of the activities in the said area of life, or about how they will work out for us.

The best way to handle the interpretation is to consider the meaning of the house and the type of activity it involves, and to see it in terms of lucky breaks or disappointments, possibly taking into account the situation at a given moment. Once again, I would impress on the reader that nothing can be inferred here about important or far-reaching matters, but only about minor encouragements or inconveniences.

When Mars is in conflict with the individual ruler of the 1st, we speak of a 1st house conflict. Venus square to, in opposition to, or inconjunct the individual ruler of the 2nd, we treat as a 2nd house conflict, and so on. If Mars is sextile or trine the individual ruler of the 1st, we speak of a 1st house harmony.

Here is an actual example. A married man has Jupiter (collective ruler of the 9th) in opposition to the individual ruler of the 9th, and thus has a 9th house conflict. His wife has a trine of Jupiter to the individual ruler of the 9th, which gives her a 9th house harmony. Both partners are, in different ways, interested in the philosophy of life. But whenever the man presents his ideas, either to her or to his friends or acquaintances, he encounters resistance. This can take an active form; for instance, when he ventilates a perfectly sound idea in the wrong company: or it can take a passive form; for instance, when people let him speak but take no further notice of his ideas — perhaps because of his presentation, or because he will keep introducing them at an inappropriate moment. His wife encounters less external resistance to her ideas and more approval, because she has no 9th house conflict. However, this does not mean that her ideas are right and her husband's are wrong. She may have a much easier time getting people to pay attention to her, yet in fact her vision is not always as reasoned and detailed as his in some respects.

The man finds it a nuisance to have to keep on overcoming resistance, but, at the same time, this very resistance is a help to him because his minor setbacks motivate him to make sure that his ideas are well researched and set on a firm basis. He formulates them better than his wife does hers, arranges them better, and pays more attention to digging out facts that could lend support to these ideas. Through the resistance he has had to overcome, he has been obliged to organize 9th house matters very efficiently. His wife has never, or hardly ever, felt the need to emulate him in this. Since she rarely meets with opposition, there is nothing to check her when she goes off at a tangent, and she can wander away from the main point for quite a while.

Turning now to the 12th house, we should note that it seldom refers to prisons and institutions! Twelfth-house conflicts of the sort we are considering often entail something that thwarts the wish to be alone and to experience the unity of things. The hindering factor can be either internal or external. Thus you decide to spend a quiet weekend in order to regain your equilibrium and, believe it or not, this is the very weekend your neighbors decide to throw a noisy party. Or you are just settling down to meditate when the telephone rings, or someone presses the front door bell.

So the question is, "What can we do about it?" The answer is "Something, but not as much as we would like," for opposition and the crucial moment are never entirely in our power. With a house conflict, we know that we are going to encounter difficulties and make miscalculations in a certain area of life, but the form they take and the precise time when they will occur is quite unpredictable. This means that we are unable to anticipate effectively. Of course, we can eliminate certain factors (in the meditation example, by removing the receiver from the hook, and disconnecting the doorbell before we commence), but it is impossible to guard against everything that might happen, and the nature of the conflict means that we sometimes simply overlook things.

4

House Rulers in Aspect

Aspects in General

Psychologically speaking, an aspect connects two or more psychic contents with one another, and reveals the manner in which these contents work with or against each other. Astronomically, the planets form certain angles with one another as viewed from the Earth. We learn which angles are aspects from tradition and by experience. Aspects are classified as major and minor. The major are the conjunction, sextile, square, trine and opposition, and according to many (in line with new psychological insights), the inconjunct as well. All other aspects are minor (see analysis of the aspects, for a synopsis).

In general we use the major aspects, although the minor aspects ought not to be entirely ignored. The effect of the major aspects is more obvious and therefore less debatable. In the following examples, we shall confine ourselves to the major aspects, but the rules and methods that are given are equally applicable to the minor aspects.

From planet to planet, each aspect offers a fresh spectrum of possibilities. If we bring in the rulerships, an aspect can help us to extract further information from the chart. As we have already seen, a planet represents not only a psychic factor, but also one or more houses in the horoscope. We can deepen our understanding of the meaning and effect of a house by studying the aspects made by the planet that rules it. And so, a single aspect can be looked at and analyzed in various ways.

Let us return to our example of Fred's horoscope (see page 24). Fred has a conjunction of the Sun and Mars in Taurus. The Sun-Mars conjunction can usually be analyzed according to the rules (see analysis of aspects). But the Sun and Mars are house rulers: the Sun is ruler of the 9th and Mars is ruler of the 5th. So we must also consider that the conjunction is one between the ruler of the 9th and the ruler of the 5th. But, at the same time, the lord of the 9th is conjunct Mars and the lord of the 5th is conjunct the Sun. This gives the following picture:

The Sun conjunct Mars;
The Sun conjunct the ruler of the 5th;
The ruler of the 9th conjunct Mars;
The ruler of the 9th conjunct the ruler of the 5th.

The rules for the interpretation of the aspects between house rulers and between house rulers and planets are the same. Nor is there any difference between the orbs allowed in the two cases. What is more, whenever we treat a planet as a house ruler, it loses its significance as a planet. Therefore, an aspect is regarded as being formed *either* by a house ruler *or* by a planet, but not by a house ruler with the properties of a planet. Thus, in essence, it is immaterial that the Sun is the lord of the 9th. Any other planet with the same placement and the self-same aspects would have had an identical meaning as the house ruler of that house. As far as Fred is concerned, his ruler of the 9th in its capacity as a ruler of the 9th refers only to the area of life represented by the 9th house, that is to say, to the forming of his opinions, his need to widen his horizons, etc.

As already mentioned, everyone born on the same day is likely to have the same planets in the same signs in nearly the same aspects (with the exception of the Moon). Therefore, someone born on the same day as Fred will have a Sun-Mars conjunction, but by no means everyone who came into the world on the same day as he did has a conjunction between the ruler of the 9th and the ruler of the 5th house. In other charts, the Sun and Mars will rule over other houses; so, in three out of four of the ways in which this conjunction can be regarded, its meaning will vary. Only the conjunction of the Sun and Mars as planets remains the same; the rulerships differ. For this reason, the study of the rulerships is very enlightening; there is nothing so personal as factors depending on the time of birth!

Aspects between Planets and House Rulers

We saw in the previous paragraph, that a single aspect between two planets can be approached in four different ways in making an interpretation. Two of these involve the aspect between a planet and a house ruler. The interpretation itself is not too hard. As a rough guide, we can apply the same keywords to the ruler of a house as we apply to the collective ruler of that house, provided we bear in mind the main differences between them.

Let us return once more to Fred's chart. His Sun-Mars conjunction is also a Mars-ruler-of-the-9th conjunction, among other things. A conjunction combines two factors. The effect of the one cannot be seen apart from the effect of the other. Thus, in Fred, we see the need to widen his horizons, to form opinions, and to travel mentally or physically, going hand-in-hand with the need to say "I" with emphasis, to look after himself aggressively, and to be energetic and ambitious (Mars).

Many readers will observe, no doubt, that this formulation looks very similar to what we might say about a Jupiter-Mars conjunction. But appearances can be deceptive. To obtain a more accurate picture, we need to ignore static properties and characteristics, and place things in a dynamic perspective.

Jupiter as an archetypal factor, provides the lifelong motivation and energy for making sense of and synthesizing things within as wide a framework as possible. The manner and the sphere of life in which it seeks to develop its power is determined by the sign and the house in which it stands. Aspects say something about the extent to which it manages to develop this power effectively, and about the psychic factors and areas of life involved. It is important to understand that Jupiter represents the impulse to seek a synthesis and inner truth without telling us whether or not this synthesis has been found. The synthesis itself is an affair involving the whole horoscope, because it necessarily rests on the integration of all factors. And this is where we must look for it.

We know that there is an area of life, the 9th house, that provides us with information on how we can achieve a certain synthesis, however imperfect or one-sided it may be. For example, this house indicates the sort of metaphysical thinking or philosophy of life we find attractive, and whether we would do better with other philosophies. It also indicates the degree to which travel or study plays a part in our life, and says something about the nature of the travel or study. Thus the house gives the circumstances in which and the material with which we realize a synthesis.

The fact that Jupiter, as a general human drive, is active in each one of us, means that we shall automatically interest ourselves in the area of life that supplies and determines the material that suits the drive. It offers an opportunity for self-expression. But if a house — in this case the 9th — is empty of planets, it is difficult to see how its active function is going to develop. An answer to this problem is found in the house ruler. The dynamics of the house are derived from the (particular) way the house ruler functions; representing, as this does, the varied and fluctuating activities taking place in the given sphere of life. Now, here we are looking at Jupiter with the motivation it supplies, and when we have a Jupiter and Mars conjunction or a ruler-of-the-9th and Mars conjunction, there is a disparity between the two factors that makes it hard for them to express themselves jointly.

Another way in which a collective house ruler and an individual house ruler are dissimilar is that, although the house ruler represents the characteristics of the house, it loses in its capacity as house ruler certain planetary qualities it would otherwise possess. Thus Jupiter in its own right may lead to stoutness; a ruler of the 9th does not. Obviously, this affects the interpretation. A Jupiter-Mars conjunction can highlight problems with doctors, because Jupiter has to do with the healing profession. With a ruler-of-the-9th-Mars conjunction nothing of that sort is found.

Bearing all this in mind, we can try to work out the various ways in which his ruler-of-the-9th-Mars conjunction will affect Fred. For example:

• Enthusiastically, and perhaps in an undisciplined manner (Mars), he can take up some form of study, in order to learn about things and to be able to see them in a wide context (ruler of the 9th). Or he can devote himself to some foreign interest, to the administration of justice, to education, to profound reflections on life, or to any other 9th house matter.

• Owing to the conjunction with Mars, he will put over his opinions quite sharply. It appears that he makes up his mind quickly, which is typical of Mars aspects. Mars is very much inclined to act first and think later! Under the Martian influence, what is said about 9th house matters can be clever and witty; the danger is that it may not be as well-considered as it should be. What is more, because Mars is unable to express itself smoothly here, the presentation of what is said can be so lacking in tact that it is liable to cause quarrels and differences of opinion.

• Very often, with a Mars-9th-house combination, the native believes that a foreign land (9th) will offer better opportunities for development and achievement (Mars) than is offered at home. The Mars-9th-house combination helps to get emigration plans off the drawing board.

Of all the possible interpretations only a few will materialize. Not all the facets, by any means, will be seen in one individual. The particular facets that are in fact seen will depend on the rest of the horoscope. Even so, it is not easy to identify them. Also, it frequently happens that one form of expression manifests itself at one time of life, and another form of expression puts in an appearance later on.

Anyone who get to know Fred will soon observe how quickly he reaches a decision. His opinions are generally very sharp, and sometimes provocative. Also, he is an inveterate traveler, and has always believed that he has more possibilities abroad to do what he wants than he has in his own land. These are the most obvious results of Mars conjunct the ruler-of-the-9th in Fred's chart.

As we said before, it is the house rulers that make such a difference between people born just a few hours apart. And someone who was born several hours later than Fred will no longer have the Sun as Lord of the 9th, and will simply not have his attitude or experiences as far as 9th house matters are concerned.

Let us examine another example. In chapter 3, we saw in Paul's horoscope (Chart 3, page 33) the 8th and 9th houses were the strongest houses. I made a point of saying that it would be wrong to interpret this fact as positive or negative without more ado—not only because each house has both positive and negative potential, but also because we need to know whether the native feels at home with the strongest house or houses or not. Planets in these houses and the condition of the rulers of the houses are necessary to know if we are going to make any headway with our interpretation.

On looking at the ruler of the 9th in Paul's chart, we see that although his 9th house is so strong, it is beset with a number of difficulties. The ruler of the 9th, the Moon, is in Aquarius in the 3rd, and makes the following aspects: inconjunct Saturn, opposition Venus, inconjunct Mercury, and inconjunct Uranus. In fact, the Moon forms the apex of a Yod-aspect with the sextile between Saturn and Mercury-Uranus as its base. (For further information on the Yod-aspect see *Aspects and Personality*.)

We can put the situation of the 9th house in a clearer light by studying the position of its ruler the Moon. That the Moon is involved in a Yod-aspect shows that Paul does not find study plain sailing. The Yod-aspect gives puzzling confrontations, and the feeling that one has one's back against the wall; and eventually, this produces a crisis. Usually, however, the crisis gives access to a certain amount of creativity, although, as likely as not, this will be hampered by a sense of insecurity. In the case of Paul's 9th house, it seems clear that he may make several false starts with studies for which he has no aptitude, or which he is liable to outgrow. His views on life and on the interrelationships of things could well change quite radically more than once. Finally, when he has passed through a crisis such as this, and every Yod-aspect conceals one within itself, he may have a more wary attitude to philosophical or scientific truth, and conclude that much of it is individual rather than absolute.

For the person who is a seeker, the ruler of the 9th in a Yod-aspect makes the finding of answers to questions about the meaning of life, about the why of things and about truth and justice, more pressing. It expresses itself in a nagging feeling that there must be more to life (and everything) than has so far emerged.

A ruler of the 9th with this sort of hard aspect is most likely to make studying a problem, but I want to draw attention to the fact that I have seen individuals with the worst 9th house conflicts going on to graduate. If the conflicts are handled positively, the result can be accurate, well-ordered thinking.

The ruler of the 9th inconjunct Saturn usually reduces the confidence in one's ability to study (the proverbial inferiority complex). Sometimes there is not even the wish to begin, "because it just wouldn't work." On the other hand, feelings of inferiority may act as an incentive to become a success by sheer dogged perseverance with one's studies — this is the other side of Saturn.

When the ruler of the 9th is inconjunct Uranus, there is a need, even though it may be devoid of inner tension, to build up, in a humanistic and original way, a completely individual view of life. This view may not be realistic in every instance however; in conflicts between Uranus or Neptune and the ruler of the 9th, there is always a danger of utopianism. A restless mind is given by Uranus inconjunct the ruler of the 9th, and the same is true of Uranus conjunct Mercury, and Mercury inconjunct the ruler of the 9th. When a certain detail is so strongly emphasized, it is bound to show itself.

Paul has felt all this very strongly. Even when he was young, his brain was running in top gear. He was idealistic and religious, and attended a Catholic school. His teachers had differing opinions of him. One thought that Paul would never amount to much because he did not have a proper grasp of what he was being taught; another thought that there was much more to him than met the eye, and that Paul possessed above average intelligence, but made such incredibly hard work of everything that it was difficult to see that he was so bright.

Paul is definitely a seeker, and he likes it that way. Being a seeker fits in with his life and his personality, and feeds his longing to immerse himself in all sorts of philosophical, psychological, and religious questions. He turned his back on what the priests taught him, but did not leave their terrain because he was still interested in the study of religion. During his studies, he fell under the spell of a certain philosopher, and perused every available piece of writing by this individual. And he decided to write a thesis on the philosopher. But the Yod-aspect struck again. As soon as he had made some progress, his interest in the man faded. Paul had developed in another direction, had come to see things completely differently, and found it very hard to go on working on his thesis. To have switched to another topic would have taken too much time and, anyway, he now knew a great deal about the philosopher. But what is so intriguing as far as we are concerned, is that once again Paul had got on a new tack.

In the area of study and ideology, we see Paul chopping and changing, and going from one thing to another following the changes in his point of view. But one can hold a good conversation with a seeker like Paul, for his search has taught him to be open to opinions other than his own.

We have just been looking at a very brief piece of interpretation using Paul's Yod-aspect with the ruler of the 9th at its apex. In actual fact, pages could be filled on each of the aspects mentioned. It is impossible to write a book dealing exhaustively with all the possible interpretations of all the possible aspects of house rulers with planets, or of house rulers with house rulers. Anyway, it is a question of applying known principles. But, to assist the reader, I shall work out in more detail one or two aspects taken from Paul's chart, and shall show how we can interpret the aspects between planets and house rulers.

First of all, we must try to form a picture of the house before concentrating on its ruler. The house ruler carries the meaning of the house. That is to see, the house is developed by the activity of the ruler. The manner in which the latter behaves can reveal how we give shape to the characteristics of its house.

We should attempt to have a clearly defined idea of each house. Let us consider as an example a house that is usually regarded as "difficult" to interpret — the 8th house. The 8th house reflects an urge to challenge life under the shadow of death and to live on a knife-edge; it reflects an urge to plumb the deepest secrets of life outside us and the deepest hidden psychic contents in ourselves. Therefore, the house also reveals our complexes and neuroses and how we come to terms with them. The house shows our unconscious attitude toward a partner, and also inner struggles. Fear of death and fear of the challenge of life, paradoxical as it may seem, both emerge from the deathwish and love of life found in this house. The 8th house contains a powerful hold on life and, at the same time, our most important, if still hidden, gifts and talents.

The ruler of the 8th gives form to its house, and therefore supplies information about the way in which the native deals with problems and tackles his or her complexes and neuroses. It says something about the internal struggle that goes on in the native and about the willpower that supports him or her. It shows how he or she will stand up to the pressures and anxieties of life. And, of course, we must never forget that, if there are planets in the 8th, the ruler of the 8th will indicate how these planets express themselves.

Paul has Mercury as Lord of the 8th. And, as we have already seen, Mercury forms part of the Yod-aspect. It is conjunct Uranus, sextile Saturn, and inconjunct the Moon. In the light of the foregoing, what is the significance of the ruler of the 8th conjunct Uranus? After we have gained some idea of the nature of the ruler of the 8th, the next step is to discover the meaning of Uranus. Uranus is our desire for originality and individuality, and our need to break free from constricting limitations. Uranus gives us the longing to develop a clear personal identity and to put ourselves in a position to go our own way. It also gives the urge — and with it a certain capability — to change, to renew, to sever, and to transcend. It can be capricious and impulsive, startlingly unpredictable, and unique.

These characteristics of Uranus now have to be combined with the significance of the ruler of the 8th, with which Uranus is in aspect. In the first instance, the type of aspect does not matter too much: what matters is that there *is* in fact an aspect, and that the two factors are mingled. The type of aspect comes in for consideration at the end of the interpretation, as we shall see.

The ruler of the 8th in aspect with Uranus gives, for example, the following possibilities for Paul: he will feel the desire to live his life in a surprising and highly individual way. Hidden deep inside him there is a challenging, even provocative, attitude to life; and he wants to make progress by looking for new forms of expression. Insights regarding himself, his problems, and his possibilities will strike him suddenly; and he will do best to tackle them unconventionally. Since the ruler of the 8th reveals his approach to his problems, an aspect of the ruler to Uranus lets us know further that, after a sudden breakthrough, Paul's life can take another (inner, but sometimes outer) turn, and that, as far as Paul's problems and their solution are concerned, he needs to pursue an extremely individual course. Now, Uranus is also the planet of equality and comradeship, so a therapist, if he needs one, should treat this patient as his or her equal, and should be open to new ideas.

Uranus is very allergic to patterns that have rusted solid and, with an aspect between the ruler of the 8th and Uranus, Paul will keep on maneuvering himself into situations in which he suddenly confronts himself. However, the same aspect gives him the power and the possibility to cope with such situations, even within a Yod-aspect. But the planets or house rulers in this chart will more or less carry things to extremes.

That the aspect is a conjunction signifies an indissoluble association of the two factors, but does not signify whether this association will be helpful or unhelpful. If the aspect were a square or opposition between the ruler of the 8th and Uranus, the confrontations of Uranus would be more problematical, sudden, and violent than if it were a sextile or trine; yet even with a conjunction we often see an almost explosive intensity. But, regardless of the nature of the aspect, the main consideration is that there *is* a connection of some sort. All that a knowledge of the type of aspect does for us is to let us know whether its effect will be relatively good or bad.

Paul also has the ruler of the 8th sextile Saturn. This means that whatever Saturn stands for is connected with the 8th house. In many respects, Saturn is the polar opposite of Uranus; and, of course, a connection between a house ruler and its polar opposite always spells tension—but it can also spell a sometimes successful struggle to achieve a balance. Let us take a look at this.

Saturn represents borders and limitations and, in particular, the impulse to carve out a clearly defined ego by means of circumstances that are often painful. It is our weak spot, part of ourselves that we would prefer not to feel or experience. Nevertheless, once we have learned how to cope with disappointment and have braved failure, and have learned to recognize our limits in the process, the selfsame Saturn bestows on us restfulness and calm, depth and purposefulness, soberness and tenacity. But, if we hide our heads in the sand, we shall merely end up running away from problems we ought to face, or may overcompensate by shouting down what Saturn is trying to tell us. In other words, we shall indulge in evasive action, in closing our eyes and ears to things, and in frantically clinging to the past out of dread of the new. In general, our outlook will be pessimistic.

Saturn in aspect to the ruler of the 8th makes an already vulnerable 8th house (the reservoir of our complexes and neuroses) still more vulnerable. People with a connection between Saturn and the 8th house (irrespective of whether the aspect is easy or hard!) usually have the inclination to shut their eyes to difficulties and to behave as if nothing had happened. "Tomorrow is another day!" they exclaim airily, but not from any inner conviction. The fear of confrontation hides deep inside them, and the aspect of Saturn to the ruler of the 8th can make this hidden fear clearly felt. I quite often observe that those with a connection between a ruler of the 8th and Saturn have trouble with their attitude to authority (Saturn is the law!) and also with deciding how to shape their lives. Yes, and I have frequently seen this with harmonious aspects too! Sometimes the problems seem to arise from a difficult relationship with the father in childhood.

The other side of Saturn also puts in an appearance in many cases. In those who have spotted the game of hide-and-speak they have been playing and, with the courage born of despair, so peculiar to Saturn and to the 8th house, have made up their minds to confront the real world; we often see, after a generally quiet and sometimes prolonged struggle, the achievement of success. They get a grip on their problems, put their lives in order, and set to work very systematically to deal with their frustrations and fears. Then Saturn can cause these natives to persist until there is clarity on the main issues. Clarity does not mean that all problems are solved, however. Saturn is matter-of-fact, and will give the sense to know that there are limits to the solution of problems: we cannot be human without having problems. On the basis of this realism, a connection between Saturn and the 8th house can signify acceptance of limitations and the attempt to channel the things mentioned in such a way as to prevent Saturn from using unconscious actions (also a property of the 8th house) to confront them externally with their weaknesses.

As we have seen, Paul has a fight on his hands with conflicting aspects. On the one hand, the reforming and defiant Uranus, and, on the other hand, the restrictive and often apprehensive Saturn, are found to be in aspect to the ruler of the 8th. If we wish to know which is the more powerful, then we must look to see which of the two is more dignified astrologically. This will usually express itself more strongly. With Paul, Saturn is in Virgo, in the 9th house, which makes it strong both by sign and by house. Uranus in Cancer in the 8th cannot match this. But this will not prevent Uranus from making itself felt quite substantially. It simply means that the motivation provided by Saturn is greater. As far as the 8th house is concerned, this represents a tendency to cling to the old to wait to see what happens with the new. In a negative sense, we may expect Paul to keep on avoiding issues raised by confrontations with the less powerful Uranus. But there are also positive effects. With this combination, he can make a calm and thoughtful approach to the problems of the 8th house, using the originality and flashes of brilliance from Uranus without taking his eye off the goal. And his composure can become a source of creativity that gives him greater depth.

A combination of a conflicting planet with a house ruler can be used very creatively and fruitfully, although we cannot deny that problems will occur from time to time.

With an aspect between the ruler of the 8th and Saturn, Paul may feel attracted to the traditional forms of psychology and psychotherapy (by which we do not imply that he will find himself on the psychiatrist's couch!). But also, as will be realized, Uranus could make him favor a modern approach. However this, in Paul's case, has worked out very harmoniously. He could quite happily immerse himself in the teachings of classical psychologists like Freud, while thinking for himself, discussing his own ideas, and forming his own opinions. In other words, he casts a critical eye on the older theories and, where they do not fit in with his personal ideas (Uranus), he discards them. And so Paul is able to work with both individuality (Uranus) and tradition (Saturn). Nevertheless, his critical attitude in the field of psychology can land him in difficulties. His teachers may not always feel an urgent desire for dissentient views on the accepted dogmas of the day.

Another thing to note is that Paul's ruler of the 8th is inconjunct his Moon. Very often, a connection between the Moon and the 8th house gives very intense feelings and emotions, which the native is not always able to control. Hard aspects between the ruler of the 8th and the Moon, or a placement of the Moon in the 8th, are quite likely to be found in association with hysteria according to some astrologers. However, speaking for myself, I would say that this is painting the picture too much in black and white. Naturally, hysteria has a good breeding ground in intense feelings and emotions that have no safety valve, but other results are equally possible.

The Moon is the attitude we tend to adopt when we feel insecure, and it represents our need to satisfy others emotionally and to take care of them. The sign, house, and aspects of the Moon provide us with a picture of this. In Paul, the Moon is in Aquarius in the 3rd house. As soon as Paul is unsure of himself or wishes to feel more at ease, he will withdraw into himself (the Moon in a fixed sign) and will brood over his problems mentally in order to reach some conclusion that will give him a feeling of repose and relief. The mental facet is emphasized again by the 3rd house, and it is possible that he will use reading, writing, and contacts with others as a means of getting back on his feet. This feature is in conflict with the influence of the Sun in Cancer, a water sign that looks at the surrounding world mainly through the feelings, and judges people, objects, and situations on the basis of the feelings they evoke. So, the Moon in an air sign and in an air house forms a big tension field with the Sun in Cancer. Once more we see that there can be tensions in the horoscope without "red lines," just as there can be harmony without "green lines!"

I have mentioned this background information because we must look at planets in their total situation before combining them with some other interpretive part of the horoscope. In the foregoing, I have restricted myself to house rulers and planets. Now let's take a further step and look at the more broad-based situation of a planet before linking it with the house ruler being studied. We have just seen that the Moon is in conflict with Paul's nature, for example, causing him to experience a strong internal struggle between feeling (Cancer/water) and thinking (Aquarius/air). (See my book *Elements and Crosses* for a detailed analysis of Paul's water/air duality).

What is more, the Moon forms the apex of the Yod-aspect, making Paul inevitably unsettled. He constantly falls prey to tension, insecurity and the questing spirit that belongs to the Yod-aspect. As soon as we feel insecure, we relapse into Moon-behavior. With Paul, this carries with it the disadvantage that he once more experiences the Yod-tension at full stretch, but strengthened by the duality between being (the Sun) and the search for emotional security (the Moon). To make matters worse, the Moon is inconjunct the ruler of the 8th, a connection with the 8th house which puts it in touch with things one would rather avoid, such as problems, neuroses and conflicts. Paul's 8th house shows what he will do about these things; and, accordingly, the inconjunct to the Moon gives us good reason to think that, initially, he will be at a loss to know what to do; also that he can tackle his 8th house problems only through his feelings and via conflict (the inconjunct) with the feminine principle or with a female partner (the Moon). In men, an aspect between the ruler of the 8th and the Moon indicates that they are hoping to meet a fascinating woman with whom they can enjoy an intense and deep relationship. They exhibit an all-or-nothing attitude to this, and also they need their partner to play an important role in bringing to the surface their unconscious and repressed psychic contents. Therefore, in general, ruler-of-8th-Moon connections produce initial difficulties in relationships, because such powerful emotions and knotty problems are involved. In any case, not every partner is able to take the impact of a projection of this sort. Nor is a power struggle with the partner out of the question, not by any means: the 8th house also has to do with the need for power to deal with everything that might upset us.

In fact, what the aspect is saying is neither more nor less than that Paul's inner feminine component, his anima, is crying out to him for attention; an that, because of the inconjunct, he does not know what to do about it. Now, psychologically speaking, the integration of the anima or animus in ourselves is no easy matter, and many of us wrestle with it. But with Paul the emphasis is elsewhere. Because of the confrontation and the threat of nonstop crises by the inconjunct, he cannot afford to hide his problems. In everything he thinks and does he is unable to avoid intense confrontations. For him, the problem is more intractable than it is for many other people.

Paul has experienced all sorts of problems with relatives: intense involvement, incomprehension, and struggles to be "king of the castle" have all cropped up in turn. On each occasion, he has tried sweet reasonableness, but has come to the conclusion that that approach is not sufficient in itself. Also, his Sun in Cancer seeks for realization!

In the light of the above, we shall appreciate that the aspect between the Moon and the ruler of the 8th is very dominant in Paul's life; and all the more so as the ruler of Cancer is the dispositor of his Sun. Paul's life expresses this aspect most distinctly, but in a decidedly positive sense, too. He is prepared to examine his feelings, to look at them objectively, to subject them to criticism, and to ask himself what is really going on inside him. Of course he can draw the wrong conclusions from time to time; but we all do that—after all, we are only human! In any case, the inconjunct does not exactly smooth his path for him; but the probing, analyzing and feeling-in-depth of emotions can help him to make progress—because there is a very positive side to the reputedly difficult connection between the ruler of the 8th and the Moon. Paul has that enormous conflict between feeling and thinking which almost compels him to bring his thinking side to the fore. The inconjunct of the ruler of the 8th to the Moon keeps impressing on him, however, that he is not emotional enough, and that he needs to use his feelings, too, even if he has little idea of how to do so. It confronts him, day in and day out, with a side of him that he tends to neglect—his feelings. In fact, this conflict takes him back to his being—represented by the Sun in a water sign. That the path is not easy, that it passes through relationship problems, and that Paul travels it as a seeker, is perhaps the price he has to pay for the peace of mind given by a steady balance between his superior and his inferior function, between his Sun and his Moon.

We one and all pay a price in life for genuine individuation. And we ought never to forget that the aspects that bring us difficulties offer us, at the same time, a means of solving those difficulties. What is more they provide the incentive to tackle all the psychic factors and contents that together make up our psyche and, in a uniquely individual manner to fuse them into the unique individual each of us is. This is true of the ruler of the 8th inconjunct the Moon. Intensity plus uncertainty in the feelings give tensions and problems. But through experiencing our emotions, and through coming to terms with our confrontations and reading and talking about them, we can enjoy later in life an emotional calm that rewards us for dealing with this aspect positively. The gradual process of integration will bring with it a certain restfulness, reduced tension in the 8th house, and a better understanding and acceptance of ourselves.

Mutual Aspects between House Rulers

Because each planet rules a house, we can also look at the aspects between the ruler of a house and the rulers of other houses. In the case of Paul, we know that his ruler of the 9th (the Moon) is inconjunct Saturn, Mercury, and Uranus. If we treat these planets as house rulers, we have the ruler of the 9th inconjunct the ruler of the 3rd, the ruler of the 8th and co-ruler of the 10th, and the ruler of the 4th.

In judging aspects between house rulers, we set to work as follows. We start with the meanings of the house rulers concerned, as we have learned them from the previous sections, and then we combine these house meanings two by two with one another. Aspects between house rulers imply that their houses influence one another. Thus, the ruler of the 9th inconjunct the 3rd signifies that whenever we enter the terrain of 9th house, the 3rd house is automatically involved, and *vice versa*. The aspect shows the way in which the interplay will occur, and so the type of aspect adds the finishing touch to our interpretation. But what matters in the first place is that there is, in fact, a connection between the two houses (exactly as in the case of aspects between house rulers and planets).

Let us continue to use Paul's chart as our specimen. In this chart, the Sun is the ruler of the 10th and Neptune is the co-ruler of the 4th. We may safely give a co-ruler full weight when interpreting aspects between house rulers. The Sun and Neptune are square one another, which means that there is a square between the ruler of the 10th and the co-ruler of the 4th. So, to begin with, we must study the significance of both house rulers, and then we can connect the houses with one another.

The 4th house represents our need of emotional security, and our attitude to domestic circumstances, which is based partly on experience. It is our need to care for others, and our feeling for family and tradition, and our sense of history. The ruler of the 4th indicates how we are going to express the need to be caring, how we manage home and hearth, and what we think of our families and loved ones.

Psychologically, the 10th house expresses our need to carve out an identity, and to form a clear-cut picture of ourselves, so that we can aspire to a recognized social position. The house shows how we exercise authority and how we respond to authority, and how we react to the external world in the light of our self-image. Generally speaking, the 10th house relates to our concrete position in the world and to the made-to-measure mask we wear in order to impress others and hold our own. The ruler of the 10th, therefore, shows how we deal with and how we react to all these things.

Now, if the ruler of the 10th is square the co-ruler of the 4th, then (either internally or externally) we shall experience a struggle between our social activities on the one hand (10th house) and our domestic life on the other (4th house). This struggle can take place in a number of ways. For example: professional commitments may interfere with domestic life, or working at home can make it hard to separate private life from public life, so that the family suffers; or, conversely, domestic circumstances can regularly stand in the way of our social development—at least without special adjustments being made.

However, inner effects are also possible, and these are much more important, by and large. Our desire to care for others and to make them feel at home (4th house) is something we like to express in the public domain when there is a connection between the rulers of the 4th and the 10th. In other words we want to bring a caring spirit into our social and professional activities. There is a wide range of possibilities here. For example, it may be that we choose a profession (from which we invariably derive social standing) in the sphere of caring for the elderly or for children, or in child nursing, or in supporting certain underprivileged groups, or in some other work in which we can help people. If there is a conflict between the ruler of the 10th and the ruler of the 4th then either we do not know how to go about achieving this aim, or, sometimes, we lay too much emphasis on what we are trying to do in the field of welfare while at other times we seem to have lost much of our interest in it (a hard aspect usually makes it difficult to hold a balance). With patience, time, and trouble (typical of a hard aspect), we can succeed in uniting the two houses harmoniously. Then, having learned to direct our energies more efficiently, we can set to work in an active and effective way in order to put a public face on our caring spirit.

Yet another possible result of this square is that our social or professional activities create emotional problems for us; we are not comfortable with them. In that case we may well go looking for a different situation, for instance in another line of work; and yet, we will find that we experience the same emotional insecurity. Therefore conflicts between the ruler or co-ruler of the 4th and the ruler of the 10th are liable to go hand in hand with (big) changes in work or social status. However, if we are able to see that the source of this unrest and emotional insecurity is to be found in ourselves, then the conflicting aspect can finally produce a creative solution.

Individuals with hard aspects between the ruler of the 4th and the ruler of the 10th are more inclined than others to let off steam at home over their dissatisfaction with their jobs; or, *vice versa*, domestic problems interfere with the professional life more often than is normally the case. Society and the home are always closely linked by a hard aspect of this type.

Since the 4th-house-10th-house axis also shows how we have got on with our parents in early life, tensions between the ruler of the 4th and the ruler of the 10th indicate trying situations when we are young. There is no need to start thinking in terms of parental separation or divorce here. Generally the situation is one for which nobody is to blame. For example, I regularly encounter this aspect in children whose parents wanted to have them but were working hard to better themselves socially at the time of the birth. It could be that the father was away a good deal, or brought a lot of work home from the office, while the mother took his place as much as she was able. Or perhaps the father was out of work, and the whole family lived under the shadow of this; which is another form of tension between the 4th and 10th house. These are situations which cannot be predicted with certainty, yet they are quite likely to occur as influences on children growing up with an aspect of the type in question.

Let us consider another example. In Fred's chart, Mars is square Pluto. Mars is ruler of the 5th and Pluto rules two houses—the 12th and the 1st. Therefore, this aspect with Pluto as house ruler has to be given two interpretations. We have the ruler of the 1st square the ruler of the 5th and the ruler of the 12th is square the ruler of the 5th. Often situations like this show conflicting or, at least, very divergent character traits and desires. Nevertheless, every latent possibility will seek to express itself, and this means that although the ruler of the 5th square the ruler of the 1st and ruler of the 12th is but a single aspect, two completely contradictory needs can arise out of it.

The 1st house represents our direct, undifferentiated approach to the outside world. It is the way in which we respond, mentally, emotionally, and physically to stimuli from without, the way in which we go to meet the outside world and allow it to have access to us—a way uninfluenced either by the outside world or by the nature of the stimuli it has to offer. The ruler of the 1st will tell us how we give shape to this activity.

The 5th house has been called the house of pleasure: it shows how we express the things that give us enjoyment, such as sport, fun, amusements, romance, etc. It represents our need to be creative and to occupy the center. It also indicates our desire for leadership and exclusiveness, as well as indicating the things we like doing—sometimes at the expense of the things we ought to be doing. A somewhat egotistical attitude is not foreign to the 5th house.

The ruler of the 5th house will express the desire to play an important role and, above all, to follow personal preferences. Because Fred's 1st and 5th houses are linked, others will always observe this in his attitude. The square between the ruler of the 1st and the ruler of the 5th may mean that Fred considers himself important and that he squares up to the world. He craves attention and wants to be noticed. This does not do away with the opposing significance of the Sun in Taurus in the 6th, on the contrary, it sharpens the inner struggle between modesty and the desire to be important—which also comes to the fore elsewhere in the horoscope.

Because the ruler of the 5th is in conflicting aspect with the ruler of the 1st, there is a danger that Fred's behavior will be erratic at times. At one moment he could be clearly dominant doing precisely what he fancies and, the following moment, he could feel so uncertain that he resigns himself to doing what others tell him to do; and yet, in the process of obeying them, he would probably forget his instructions and start doing things his own way again. Also, although he likes to have a pat on the back and a compliment every now and then (the 5th house corresponds to Leo, of course), the hard aspect prevents him from knowing how to accept these graciously. Either he puts the person down, or he cracks a cynical joke, with the result that, if the individual who made the compliment does not know Fred very well, he or she will think twice before praising him again. And then Fred must angle even harder for the desired pat on the back. The link between the 1st and the 5th house makes this sort of stimulus necessary every so often but, with a square, Fred—by his own attitude—is liable to thwart his own chances of getting what he wants. This hard aspect can also indicate insecurity, an insecurity for which he tries to overcompensate by putting on an air that suggests the opposite is true.

Nevertheless, with this conflict, Fred will feel good in an environment where he can be himself in the knowledge that he is valued, even if he is not praised to his face. Also he can very much appreciate half-humorous compliments, because these offer him a chance to cover his confusion when praised. When Fred comes to terms with this problem in himself, he will be able to use the energy that is now being absorbed by his insecurity and overcompensation, and will be able to work very creatively while winning a central function. Creatively, although not necessarily artistically. Fred is extremely clever with his hands, and can make anything he sees. Complete confidence to take his place in the outside world (the ruler of the 5th square the ruler of the 1st) will also bring release for his Sun in Taurus in the 7th, which loves to work.

However, the conflict between the ruler of the 5th and the ruler of the 12th is an even bigger problem for Fred. Now, the 12th house is not always easy to interpret; so let us dwell on it for a moment or two. The old-fashioned view that "one loses everything connected with the 12th house" is as sweeping as it is incorrect. The 12th house represents our need to retire and pull out of things in order to seek the unity behind diversity, the unity that binds everything together. We find in the 12th a hankering after mystical union and the concept of the universal in life; but this means setting on one side our personality and our limited social and mercenary aims, or at least according them less importance; otherwise we shall never penetrate to the essential nature of this house.

In the light of research I have been carrying out in the past few years, it seems to me that the (hard to overestimate) role of the 12th house as an area of life is chiefly determined by our experiences during infancy (and perhaps even when we were in the womb) and by how they affected us. In many respects, these experiences have a big influence on our later attitude to life. Frequently I have seen 12th house conflicts linked either with conflicts between the parents of the child, or with social tensions that had repercussions on it. Therefore the 12th house also has to do with secret fears, fears we are unable to trace back to specific events. They are, in fact, due to actual happenings, and these took place at a time when our consciousness was not formed; so nothing could be repressed.

Seen in this light, the ruler of the 12th shows how we handle our need to experience unity, either positively in the form of social awareness, willingness to make sacrifices, meditation, and the like, or negatively in the form of addiction or depersonalization. Both extremes lead to an intoxication in which unity is experienced.

This house reveals our capacity for relativizing and depersonalizing, and for dealing with unreasoned fears. The 12th house also reveals the degree of empathy we possess. For the 12th house enables us to get in contact with our fellows along unconscious ways, and to intuit what makes them tick, where their needs lie, and even perhaps what is going to happen to them, etc. Clairvoyance, telesthesia, prophetic dreams and so on, all flow from the 12th house. A ruler of the 12th shows what we make of this. A horoscope does not inform us to what extent a person is clairvoyant or telepathic. Such abilities are latent in us all — in some more than in others. Therefore, the ruler of the 12th does not say whether or not we are clairvoyant; what it does say is what we are inclined to do with our latent powers.

Conflicts in the 12th house, or involving the ruler of the 12th, often point to problems in infancy, and generally in the entire mythic phase of childhood (which lasts to around the 7th year on average).

Fred's ruler of the 12th is square the ruler of the 5th, which can have the following possible results. Hidden fears and uncertainty (12) exert an influence on the self-confidence Fred seeks (5), so that he can feel very insecure where his self-expression, hobbies, and leadership are concerned. Owing to the conflict of the ruler of the 12th, he struggles either with the tendency to undermine himself, or with the problem of really not knowing what he wants to do and of always searching for some self-reliance and identity without quite achieving them. I have observed more than once that such problems involving the 12th house and the 5th or 10th house go hand in hand with a situation in which the child was not properly understood by one or both of its parents, was not encouraged to be itself and therefore was unable to build up a feeling of self-confidence. But even here we must not pass judgment. The child born with this configuration quite often does not give its parents enough to go on for a decision as to how it should be encouraged.

Whatever the case may be, the child with this aspect will initially have little self-trust and is not likely to know what it wants. Often the consequence is questing behavior with the attendant possibilities of overcompensation and of withdrawal into a dream world. Thus the very same square aspect offers the child the chance to develop activities within the 12th-house domain — namely dreaming and fantasizing — which could blossom later into a talent for writing fairy stories or film scenarios for example. Other modes of expression are also possible — music, or those forms of creative expression in which the native sits alone for hours studying, drawing, painting, writing, etc. Likely hobbies are such things as hypnotism, meditation, yoga, religious retreats, prayer, the occult, social work, and so forth.

Underwater sport is one of Fred's longtime hobbies. He has also traveled widely (among other things, this is represented by the ruler of 1 in 9); but, in all this traveling, an important objective has been to experience the stillness in himself in the solitude of unspoiled nature. Thus he has remained for months at a time in the woods and wastes of Australia in order to recharge his spiritual batteries. Therefore, even conflicting aspects between the ruler of the 12th and the ruler of the 5th can express themselves creatively and acceptably — although this is not to say that Fred does not wrestle with inferiority feelings, vulnerability and insecurity, too.

We have now obtained two different aspects between house rulers from the one aspect of Mars square Pluto. One of them, the ruler of the 5th square the ruler of the 1st, gives a strong desire to do what you feel like doing, while the other, the ruler of the 5th square the ruler of the 12th, brings with it the problem of not knowing what you feel like doing, and an initial lack of self-confidence when you do know it. The aspects can exert their influence separately or in combination. Thus the insecurity caused by the aspect with the ruler of the 12th can lead to powerful overcompensation when the ruler of 5 decides (as it were) to make its square with the ruler of 1 felt; but, at the same time, it leads to greater vulnerability.

The above examples illustrate how we can extend and refine the interpretation of a chart with the help of the house rulers; which also informs us why the native does certain things or makes certain statements or overcompensations. Nevertheless, we must always look for confirmatory factors in the horoscope. In dealing with examples, it is very difficult not to wander off too much to other parts of the horoscope, because everything in the psyche is so connected. For instance, Fred's ruler-of-5 aspects, at which we have just been looking, must also be seen in the light of planets in 5 and of other aspects to the ruler of 5. The part played by the Sun is important, too. Failing this, we shall not be able to make a balanced judgment, because our preliminary findings may need modification. But, before we attempt these refinements, we have to master the basics of the subject with uncomplicated examples.

Aspects between house rulers will often corroborate other things in the horoscope, and in this sense may seem superfluous. For instance, we could ascribe Fred's desire to do what he likes to the Sun conjunct Mars in the obstinate sign Taurus, strengthened by the square of both planets to Pluto. We could also say that this is the source of his need to stand up to others in order to preserve his own individuality. But the background of this combination, and therefore the "why" of this attitude, differs considerably from the background of a house connection! This has been already mentioned, of course.

The fact that Fred's house rulers fall in line with the basic pattern of his planets confirms the view that Fred really wrestles with this problem. When we spoke just now of house connections seeming superfluous, that was something of an exaggeration. In Fred's (and in many other cases), they confirm or strengthen the other factors. If we do not take into account the aspects between house rulers, we shall miss some highly individual impressions. Fred's conjunction of the Sun and Mars will obviously apply to everyone born on the same day (and even to those born on neighboring days!) but by no means everyone will have the effect of this conjunction confirmed and strengthened by a conflict between the ruler of the 1st and the ruler of the 5th and between the ruler of the 12th and the ruler of the 5th.

It is impossible to deal with all the aspects between house rulers. However, I will give one more example — one that often proves difficult for beginners. This is the connection between the 8th and the

12th houses. Aspects between the two house rulers are found hard to interpret as often as not. But if we keep to the guidelines, we shall manage better than we might expect. Let us just take a look at what an aspect between the ruler of the 8th and the ruler of the 12th can contain.

In the first place, the two houses join together and influence one another. How this happens is shown by the aspect formed. We have already examined the meanings of the 8th and 12th houses. From a psychological point of view, the following possibilities exist. The ruler of the 8th has to do with the manner in which we face our problems and deal with our complexes and neurotic tendencies. The 12th house is deeply immersed in the unconscious, and has the power to express itself through dreams and fantasies by means of picture language and symbolism. If the two house rulers are in harmony, the native can get to the root of personal problems in various ways, and may even be able to solve them, through fantasizing, dream analysis, word association, (self-)hypnosis, creative imagination, and the like. The process can take place by the operation of an inborn mechanism as much as by therapeutic help.

On the other hand, a conflicting aspect warns of initial difficulties. Among other things, the 12th-house fantasies and dreams will probably be misleading and will keep us skirting round our problems instead of targeting them. Even if the dreams, fantasies, and symbols contain potentially useful information for the psychotherapist, the native may conceal a part of them, or may produce a distorted version (usually without being conscious of the fact). He or she is liable to go around in circles and to interpret the imagery incorrectly. With a hard aspect between the ruler of the 8th and the ruler of the 12th, I have often seen the therapeutic process move very slowly while being constantly sidetracked. Also the number of anorexia patients I have met who have hard aspects between the 8th and 12th houses is above the statistical average. And here again, we are speaking of people who are hard to cure.

There are other possibilities for aspects between the ruler of 8th and the ruler of the 12th. For example, our psychological insights and knowledge of human nature can be very useful in social work (a 12th house feature). Generally speaking, a connection between the 8th and the 12th gives the welfare worker a desire to probe and pry. Naturally, with easy aspects this can be done more smoothly than with hard aspects, but the latter tend to give an enormous involvement in that work. Energy is always generated by the hard aspects.

Here is another possibility: it may very well result from the solving of problems in ourselves (8th house) that we acquire a more broad understanding of humanity in general, and a greater sense of proportion (12th house). Conversely, our involvement in 12th house matters, from prayer to working in a jail, to name but two, can confront us to such an extent with ourselves and our conflicts that we are forced to become preoccupied with them.

All these forms of expression depend, in the first place, on the fact that a connection exists. And here I would remark that, in the hard aspects of this particular house connection, I have seen extreme effects, from crises (e.g., in anorexia nervosa) to very creative activities in defense of the underdog. Once again, it may be as well to remind ourselves not to be afraid of the hard aspects. One cannot make omelets without breaking eggs, as the saying is. And 12th house aspects can take us only so deep and no further.

The connection between the 8th and the 12th has something to offer on the occult front, too. Profundity and the experience of unity go hand in hand. The search for the core (8) and the source (12) of things can yield unsuspected insights into ourselves and into the unseen world. Harmonious aspects make it easier to conduct this search, but the disadvantage is that the energy to persist has to be drawn from elsewhere, for these aspects are usually rather inert. On the other hand, disharmonious aspects tend to produce conflicts and error. But they do give the energy to take the necessary steps to acquire and extend our experience. We may fall down and pick ourselves up, metaphorically speaking, a number of times, but eventually we shall arrive where we want to be.

Unaspected House Rulers

Just like any other planet, a house ruler can be unaspected. In my book on the analysis of the aspects (*Aspects and Personality*), I devote a chapter to the question of how unaspected planets work. In principle we can apply the same guidelines to the house rulers. Unaspected planets are liable to express themselves in an all-or-nothing kind of way. The same is true of house rulers.

Let us quickly remind ourselves what being unaspected signifies. We say that a planet is unaspected when it makes no major aspect with any planet. The major aspects are the conjunction, sextile, square, trine, and opposition. The inconjunct is being increasingly accepted as major, but is not part of the traditional set of aspects. What we must ask ourselves, therefore, is whether or not a planet with no other aspects than one or more inconjuncts should be treated as unaspected. An unaspected planet usually creates tensions and uncertainty (as we shall see); and, interestingly enough, an inconjunct also gives uncertainty and latent tension. So it is very difficult to tell if a planet with no aspects but inconjuncts is behaving as if it were unaspected or not. I will say this, however: my own experience suggests that the inconjunct is a major aspect. My opinion is based mainly on the various cases where I have seen an inconjunct produce stability after a crisis (it can always become a steadying influence). Through planets carrying only the inconjunct aspect, the natives had, on average, become more sensible and mature, often at an earlier age, than one would see with completely unaspected planets.

With unaspected planets the tendency is to bring the factors they represent well to the fore, but in an unpredictable manner and generally — as I have already said — in an all-or-nothing way. An unaspected house ruler behaves similarly. In other words, it will emphasize in our personality the house over which it rules, but without giving us the ability to handle the matters represented by that house or to take a firm hold on them.

Sometimes unaspected planets can have a very powerful effect, and then, at other times, they can do absolutely nothing; but, usually, unbridled action predominates. It is as if we are constantly trying to obtain something substantial from the house with an unaspected ruler, without knowing what we are doing or how to tackle this strange and seemingly alien area of our lives. The resulting impact made·by this house on personal development gives it an almost unlimited potential. There are opportunities for big achievements here, and a number of people have made history thanks to their unaspected planets and house rulers.

The native experiences the contents of an unaspected planet as difficult, and the same is true of a house with an unaspected ruler. The problems felt give a sense of insecurity in the area concerned, and the individual's confidence requires boosting with small compliments and other encouragement. More often than not, those around see no need to keep patting the native on the back and encouraging him or her to carry on the good work; they are fully aware of the power of that house and of what the native is doing with it. And so misunderstandings can arise.

Aspects are one of the main means for integrating psychic factors (planets) in the psyche. And the same is true of other sorts of psychic needs and desire patterns (house rulers). However, the Ascendant and the Midheaven do not represent dynamic needs; so aspects of planets to the Ascendant and MC, no matter how major they may be, do not prevent a planet or house ruler from being unaspected. Nevertheless, the link with an exit point gives the opportunity of experiencing reactions of the outside world to the factor more quickly. This is even more noticeable in house rulers.

There are unaspected planets in both Fred's and Paul's horoscope. For Fred, this is Mercury, as ruler of the 8th and ruler of the 10th. For Paul, it is Mars as ruler of the 5th and ruler of the 6th, and Jupiter as ruler of the 2nd. How should we set about making the interpretation of house rulers like these? First of all we make a note of the meaning of the house ruled. We emphasize the role of that house in the chart, with particular reference to the extreme manifestations of the house; for the fact of being unaspected introduces the all-or-nothing principle. Then we take into consideration that everything connected with the house involves the native in uncertainty; and for a long time, apparently, is neither recognized nor understood. This provides the main outline of the interpretation.

Let us consider an example. Paul's ruler of the 6th is unaspected. The 6th house stands for our awareness of, and our analysis and understanding of, facts; and especially our need to apply the results of our analysis in a concrete and useful way. We find expressed in the 6th house our critical sense and our attitude toward work or service and toward working conditions. Also expressed there is our attitude toward our body, and toward hygiene, illness, and health. The house says something about the degree to which we can fit into society and function there, and also exercise self-criticism.

Now, if the ruler of the 6th is unaspected, we see a number of extremes put in an appearance. We can work all out month after month, and even year after year, without realizing that the main reason we are toiling away is that we are never satisfied that we have done everything we could. Then, all at once, it no longer seems to matter, and we put down the tools, often just in some critical situation. It is as if there is a blockage somewhere inside us, and we have to rest before we can continue.

For quite a while, we can be over-critical at work (often to the annoyance of colleagues, for they are included in the criticism); and then, suddenly, we can be paralyzed by an overdose of self-criticism and not know which way to turn. We can neglect ourselves for some years through bad eating habits, or through not sparing our body; and then, without warning, we can turn into a health fanatic. Or, against our better judgment, we can persist in bad habits for years, and then, one day, we can simply give them up.

Our ability to give form to things is first class, because we have an eye for detail and are very analytical. But we must be given the chance to think matters through without being pushed. For if society makes immediate demands on someone with an unaspected planet or an unaspected house ruler, the person may "clam up" permanently, however gifted he or she may be.

With an unaspected ruler of the 6th, it is not always easy to function within the existing social framework. We have our own ideas and often fail to see where we go wrong. Not that we are unwilling to see it, but we simply do not grasp what our own position is. This makes an unaspected ruler of the 6th, in spite of all its penchant for service and work, more of a loner than might have been expected. Good advice seldom makes any impression, there seems to be nothing in it. Nevertheless, we will analyze our experiences meticulously and store them away somewhere; and so with the passing of the years we can carve out our own place in society, which may be more individual than originally seemed possible.

Someone with an unaspected ruler of the 6th frequently turns out to be a hard worker, with a sense of form, and a person with a feeling for details and practicalities. but, through his or her uncertainty, the opposite can be true, such as slovenliness.

5

The Role of the House Ruler
in Complex Interpretation

House Ruler and Planets in the Houses

There is a small, but fundamental and not unimportant, difference
between the role of planets in a house and the role of the house ruler.
As has already been pointed out at the beginning of this book, *planets
in a house hold a certain promise (in one way or another), but it is the
house ruler that decides how the promise is realized.* Therefore, the
house ruler is the key element in our interpretation. It always indicates
the direction taken by the things promised by a planet, although it
cannot cancel them. The worst it can do is to weaken or hamper them.

The difference can best be illustrated by a few examples. For our
present purposes, I shall neglect the other horoscope factors; but, of
course, they must always be considered when making a full interpretation. Let us suppose that we have to judge the following two horoscope
situations:

Chart A: Leo Ascendant, Saturn in 1, and ruler of the 1st
conjunct Jupiter;

Chart B: Leo Ascendant, Jupiter in 1, and ruler of the 1st
conjunct Saturn.

The two situations are quite similar, and a very rough assessment would read something like this: someone who needs a great deal of attention paid to him or her (Leo Ascendant) and likes to appear jolly (Jupiter in 1 or the ruler of 1 conjunct Jupiter), yet feels somewhat anxious or inhibited (Saturn in 1 or the ruler of 1 conjunct Saturn). There is nothing wrong with this superficial interpretation, but we can go much deeper.

A Leo Ascendant means that we want to come to the fore in our contacts with the outside world, and to "show off" as a means of gaining recognition. We need to play a central role and to exercise authority and we radiate self-confidence and pride. Not that we really feel this degree of self-confidence with a Leo Ascendant, but we seek a means of gaining self-confidence through our functioning in the outside world. At the same time, there is a certain amount of reserve: the individual with a Leo Ascendant does not readily show their hand. They can brood over problems without speaking up. At best, the native with a Leo Ascendant radiates warmth and sympathy and is a friendly, paternal figure in the community. At worst, we see the egotistical potentate with a desire for self-affirmation and flattery.

The sign on the Ascendant tells us a great deal, but what it tells us is colored by planets in the 1st house. If we picture a horoscope as a closed castle, then the Ascendant is the drawbridge. The impression made on the outside world by this drawbridge (inviting, defensive, cheerful, or weak) is determined by the sign on the Ascendant, by planets in 1, by aspects to the Ascendant, and by the placement and aspecting of the ruler of the 1st. Thus there are all sorts of factors that have to be brought together to form a whole when an interpretation is made. In what follows we shall give extensive examples of interpretation; and we will begin by looking at Saturn in the 1st house.

With Saturn in 1 we are vulnerable in our approach to the outside world. The form in which we manifest ourselves needs to be clearly defined, we feel; and so we make the impression of being serious, reserved, and perhaps inhibited or fearful, unwilling to be forthcoming, and modest. Often, with Saturn in 1, we treat the world very seriously and expect a serious response. Quite often we see the world as vaguely menacing. With Saturn in the 1st there is a lack of spontaneity. We like to act responsibly, and may not creep out of our shell unless we are sure of our facts (and it may well take us some time to make sure of them), or have had long enough to grow accustomed to a situation.

The ruler of the 1st conjunct Jupiter as the shaper of this fairly restricted "promise," gives a rather more genial and optimistic tint to the picture however. Yet Jupiter conjunct the ruler of the 1st gives an urge to expand, and the ruler of the 1st conjunct Jupiter sallies forth to meet the world with optimism and conviction, with a vision or philosophy, and Jupiter conjunct the ruler of the 1st is very much set on finding ways and means of expressing itself freely. Also, Jupiter is ready to assist others in word and deed, and the cheerfulness it bestows makes the native a source of comfort to the community. The reverse side is that Jupiter conjunct the ruler of the 1st gives an attitude to others of "I know best," so that the native appears arrogant and pedantic.

There seems to be little intrinsic difference between a planet in a house and a planet in aspect with a house ruler. What we have already said of Saturn in the 1st can be used in interpreting Saturn conjunct the ruler of the 1st, and our description of Jupiter conjunct the ruler of the 1st can be used, without more ado, in interpreting Jupiter in the 1st. Before we examine the differences between them, it will be helpful to sum up the main distinctions. A planet in a house expresses its nature in the area of life covered by the house and even colors what goes on there, but has nothing to do with the way in which the house as a whole expresses itself. That is dependent on the house ruler. If the house ruler is linked with a planet, then the nature and properties of this planet will also color the manner in which the house can reveal itself. But now let us return to the difference in our example.

With Saturn in the 1st house we approach the outside world with reserve (see above). This, in combination with a Leo Ascendant, modifies the need to thrust ourselves forward (Leo Ascendant), because with Saturn in the 1st house there is something hesitant about the way we seek to make an impression, or else we may overcompensate by being more obtrusive than necessary. Saturn always has the tendency to exaggerate certain attitudes owing to feelings of inferiority and vulnerability while acting as if everything were quite normal. The reserve of the Leo Ascendant is increased through having Saturn in the 1st house. In a certain sense a Leo Ascendant is insecure, because it looks for self-confirmation. Therefore, having Saturn in the 1st house simply makes matters worse, because it intensifies the sense of insecurity and the need for reassurance.

And so, people with a Leo Ascendant and Saturn in the 1st, will approach the world in a rather reserved and aloof fashion, even suspiciously at times, or at any rate cautiously; but, underneath it all (because they are so interested in themselves) they are asking for attention. Now, if Jupiter is conjunct the ruler of the 1st, this rather inhibited outlook becomes less bleak. In other words, although we may still exhibit a cautious reserve and perhaps feel nervous about meeting people in an outgoing, spontaneous way, yet, with Jupiter conjunct the ruler of the 1st, our heart tells us that everything will come out better than expected. This planetary combination gives self-confidence, it can help us rationalize cautious behavior, and it provides a cheerful outlook in general. Another thing it does is to make us want to gain a reputation as a benefactor of the local community, as someone who improves the environment, who is full of charitable projects and good works. We may seem somewhat vulnerable in doing these things, but comfort ourselves with a deep-down feeling of our own worth. In a positive sense, Jupiter's enthusiasm and tendency to rush matters can be canalized by Saturn in the 1st, with the net result of a placid and balanced outlook. However, we must not forget that this is a case of equilibrium reached between anxiety, inhibition, and reserve on the one hand (Saturn in 1) and a hidden feeling of inner confidence (Jupiter conjunct the ruler of 1) on the other.

With Jupiter in 1, we approach the outside world full of spontaneity and verve, for we feel ourselves simply bubbling over with enthusiasm. We want to let everybody share what we have to offer, we lend them a helping hand regardless of whether our interference is welcome or not, and are very free with a lot of well-meaning advice. Nothing irritates us more than frugality and austerity. With Jupiter in 1, we often display an open, paternal attitude, which is even more evident in combination with a Leo Ascendant. This stands in complete contrast to what we saw with Saturn in 1. Jupiter in 1 can produce the childlike enthusiast, but also someone who is moralizing and boastful. Its combination with a Leo Ascendant frequently gives us the charmer who captivates others with his free, spontaneous and open behavior but also makes use of them.

Now if Saturn is conjunct the ruler of 1, we shall certainly retain this spontaneous attitude to the outside world, but with a touch of reserve about it. We no longer talk quite so freely and, in spite of our jovial appearance, we feel insecure at times and may be subject to insecurity feelings. On occasion, we shall be constrained to ask ourselves, "What on earth am I doing here?" even when we are joining in enthusiastically in the middle of the action. This conjunction also colors the way in which things from outside affect us and the way in which we experience them. So we see that the cheerful and genial promise of Jupiter in 1 is hampered by the conjunction of the ruler of 1 and Saturn.

Here, too, a balanced attitude is a very possible result, but now *via* a very different process. Through the vulnerability of Saturn conjunct the ruler of 1, we may learn that there is another side to our contacts with the world around than just the exuberant side, and that seriousness and depth are valuable, too. Plagued as we are by inner uncertainty, we shall gradually learn to accept that our interaction with the outside world can be much smoother if we let others have their say now and then — something that is not always easy to do for Jupiter in 1 or a Leo Ascendant. The exuberance of Jupiter can be usefully controlled here by Saturn conjunct the ruler of 1 and, in that case, what we have is Saturn holding back and restricting the natural spontaneity of Jupiter. By way of contrast, with Saturn in 1 and Jupiter conjunct the ruler of 1, our insecurity is kept within bounds by an inner sense of confidence.

As we see from this example, two horoscope situations can seem very much alike on the surface without being as similar as we might think. Great differences in the psychic mechanisms are observable when we put the chart factors concerned under the magnifying glass. Anyway, by this time, the role of the house ruler should be much clearer to us. To some extent it has the decisive say in what happens, but it cannot nullify anything contained in a house.

A further question that may arise is what is the nature of the difference between an aspect to the Ascendant and an aspect to the ruler of 1. For example: what is the difference between Saturn square the Ascendant and Saturn square the ruler of the 1st? In the light of the foregoing, we can state that Saturn square the ruler of the 1st has to do with the realization of the promise, whereas the contents of the promise are determined, as we know, by planets in the house concerned. But, with the Ascendant or Midheaven, aspects to these house cusps form part of the promise contained in the 1st or 10th house respectively. In other words, Saturn square the Ascendant is subordinate to the effect of the ruler of 1, while Saturn square the ruler of 1 has a partial influence on the role of the ruler of 1 and thus on the working of the whole house. As a factor in our interpretation, Saturn square the Ascendant certainly displays some similarity to Saturn in 1 or Saturn square the ruler of 1, but we must remain careful not to confuse them. One very important way in which Saturn square the Ascendant differs in its effect from Saturn in 1, is that Saturn square the Ascendant sheds its influence from another house and from the background provided by another sign, and so on. And this can make a substantial difference to the interpretation as a whole.

I am going to deal in the following section of this chapter with how the same or very similar looking horoscope factors can have distinguishable results. But, to conclude this paragraph, here is what may be a superfluous remark. When we examine the house rulers, the ruler of the 3rd in the 1st seems to have a different effect from the ruler of the 1st conjunct the ruler of the 3rd. And, here again, the aspect to the ruler of the 1st is much like a dash of sauce on top of the interpretation, and the action of a house ruler in a house is dependent on the role of the actual ruler of that house for the realization of what it (as the ruler of another house) has imported into the house, and also on the aspect of this house ruler to other house rulers.

How Should We Interpret a House?

When we are beginners, working with house rulers and house connections can give us the feeling that we have to wade through a morass of factors before we can make some sort of interpretation. But, after a certain amount of practice, we begin to feel more at home with them. However, even from the very beginning, we must get into the habit of approaching our analysis systematically. One should never start in a wild way interpreting all kinds of aspects and house connections, for then we shall be sure to lose the thread of what we are doing. Instead one should start by writing down what has to be looked at in interpreting a certain area of the horoscope. After doing this, one needs to examine which factors point in the same direction. To give an example: in a Scorpio Ascendant with an aspect from the ruler of the 8th to the Ascendant, we can rest assured that the effect of the Ascendant is reinforced by an aspect pointing in the same direction. Naturally the various factors must all be separately interpreted; but, in making a final judgment of some theme or house, we can gather together everything that points in the same direction and can weave them into a single account. And then, not only have we tackled the interpretation systematically, but we have also established what is more important and what is less important, this enables us to keep our interpretation within reasonable bounds and to concentrate on essentials. It is easier for us to apply the rule of thumb that one indication in a given direction represents a possibility, two indications a probability, and three indications or more a probability bordering on certainty. But, when considering the various factors, do remember the difference between planets in a house and the house ruler!

Let us suppose that we want to analyze someone's Ascendant (1st house) in order to see what is his or her attitude toward, and behavior in, the outside world. The following factors have to be observed:

a) The sign on the Ascendant;

b) Planets in that house;

c) House rulers in that house;

d) Aspects of planets to the Ascendant;

e) Aspects of house rulers to the Ascendant;

f) The house in which the house ruler is posited (the sign in which it is posited appears to be less important);

g) Aspects of the house ruler to planets;

h) Aspects of the house ruler to other house rulers.

It will be obvious that the sign applies only to the Ascendant. The sign standing on any other cusp is unimportant, except in determining which planet is the ruler of the house concerned. So far, at any rate, I have seen little evidence of any effect of signs on house cusps apart from the sign on the Ascendant. The effect of the sign on the Midheaven is still under discussion. Some astrologers attach great value to it, whereas others regard it as unimportant. My own experience inclines me to agree with the latter.

Let us take another look at Fred and Paul to see what factors in their charts have a bearing on the interpretation of the 1st house:

Fred

a) Scorpio Ascendant;

b) No planets in 1;

c) Therefore no house rulers in 1;

d) The Moon trine Ascendant, and Saturn sextile the Ascendant;

e) The Moon is co-ruler of the 8th, which means that the co-ruler of 8 is trine the Ascendant. Saturn, as co-ruler of the 2nd sextile Ascendant;

f) The ruler of 1 (Pluto) is in the 9th;

g) The ruler of 1 is square the Sun, sextile Venus, square Mars and sextile Neptune;

h) The ruler of 1 is square the ruler of 9 (the Sun), sextile the ruler of 6, 7 and 11 (Venus), square the ruler of 5 (Mars), and sextile the ruler of 4 (Neptune).

Paul

a) Scorpio Ascendant;

b) No planets in 1;

c) Therefore no house rulers in 1;

d) The Sun trine the Ascendant, Venus square the Ascendant and Pluto square the Ascendant;

e) The ruler of 10 (the Sun) trine the Ascendant, the ruler of 7, 11, and 12 (Venus) square the Ascendant, and the ruler of 1 (Pluto) square the Ascendant;

f) The ruler of 1 (Pluto) is posited in the 9th;

g) The ruler of 1 is conjunct Venus and sextile Neptune;

h) The ruler of 1 is conjunct the ruler of 7, 11, and 12 (Venus) and sextile the co-ruler of 4 (Neptune).

On comparing the two sets of factors, we notice that they have much in common, e.g., Scorpio Ascendant, no planets in 1, the ruler of 1 in 9, Venus aspects, Neptune aspects, and so on. However, the differences in those factors having a bearing on the attitude to the outside world are very great. Why that is so will be analyzed in the following paragraphs, in which we shall examine, as briefly as we can, the contents of our two lists.

Fred's 1st House

With a Scorpio Ascendant, the approach to the outside world is cautious and reserved. We often find that people with this Ascendant take the emotional temperature of their environment very carefully without being in a hurry to expose their own feelings. The native with a Scorpio Ascendant feels a certain personal vulnerability when putting in an appearance on life's stage, and tries to conceal this either by a show of confidence or by neatly side-stepping issues and avoiding confrontations. The native often has a good nose for the weak points of others, not least because of knowing his or her own weak points so well. He or she seems to have a gift for digging into the hidden problems of other people, and can readily see a sore spot. Not that this person is always deliberately trying to find some sore spot in others; and this is often discovered when (usually quite unconsciously) satisfying a wish to fathom the motives and undeclared desires in the people he or she meets. The intuitive side of a Scorpio Ascendant is well-developed, and the native can sense whether a thing is on the level or not.

Some astrologers say that a Scorpio Ascendant makes one distrustful and suspicious; but to take this statement just as it stands is misleading unless we look into the thinking behind it. An internal struggle is always going on, owing to the very nature of Scorpio, over the question of the extent to which the native rules his or her own life and the extent that life is consciously or unconsciously influenced by others. The question is not one that makes the native miserable, generally speaking, but Scorpio is the sign that lets us experience our own vulnerability and confronts us with our own problems (it is a fixed sign), and the native naturally wants to know the reason for these things. The individual with a Scorpio Ascendant is constantly aware of this vulnerability when contacting the outside world. This is why he or she can be so cautious and reserved; and yet, under cover of this caution and reserve, can be in a ferment, and can be eagerly trying to reach the core of everything going on in self and others. The outside world is assessed and weighed in the balances and, if it is found to be too light, it is irrevocably set aside (quite possibly in a friendly manner). The Scorpio Ascendant usually has an all-or-nothing attitude.

Because of this sensitivity (which will not be admitted on any account), the native is very much involved in his or her environment. This native will go through fire for the person he or she cares for. Once forming a definite opinion, this individual will not change it for anybody (fixed sign!) and will defend it with dogged determination. There is another trait associated with a Scorpio Ascendant, too, one that is not so easy to understand or accept. What we mean is that the sign of Scorpio has to do with the process of transformation. Now, one of the fundamental things about transformation is that the old has to die before the new can come into being. The phoenix rising from the ashes is a fitting symbol of Scorpio. People with planets in Scorpio, a Scorpio Ascendant, a strongly placed Pluto or a powerful 8th house, usually like to demolish the old fabric of their lives in order to build something more viable. However, if they belong to a lower type of humanity, there is no progress beyond the destructive stage.

People with a Scorpio Ascendant are able to gain the interest of others and to stir them up. But, only if they, themselves, are prepared to engage in self-criticism and to seek a balance on the human plane, are they able and willing to perform constructive work. Then we see them helping to solve the problems of friends and neighbors, and finding ways and means of stimulating themselves and others to persevere with hard tasks in spite of hindrances and liabilities. Psychologically, this can involve dealing with repressions in oneself and others; while, in the business world, it can mean replacing the antiquated machinery that is holding up production, it can mean reorganizing the chain of command, and so on.

People with a Scorpio Ascendant like to keep control of the environment to avoid the emotional upset of being constantly confronted by a sense of personal insecurity. In those who are less refined, this develops into an avid thirst for power; but, in those who are more mature, the attitude is one of trying to influence the course of events from behind the scenes.

Fred is very open and cordial in greeting people, which does not bear out what has just been said. But the attentive observer will soon see that this friendliness and openness is only a mask, and that the real individual is very reluctant to remove it and show himself. Wherever he is, Fred indulges in a certain style of humor (appealing to many and irritating to some) and in wry banter; hoping that, by raising a laugh, he can influence the atmosphere in such a way that no situation can become serious enough to make him feel threatened. As a matter of fact, there are occasions when Fred is perfectly serious, but then only one or two people are present. In large gatherings, he puts on an act without being aware of it. As we have said, this is his way of controlling the situation. We should never forget that joking and light-hearted chatter are not necessarily the marks of an empty-headed buffoon. Often they are just a disguise. Horoscope readings that fail to make allowance for this fact of human nature can go badly astray. Thus, we should fall into a trap if, because Fred has a Scorpio Ascendant, we were to suppose that he clams up in company. He talks a great deal, and very effectively, too. And if we should say that a Scorpio Ascendant makes a person grim and humorless to the extent that others find him crabby, we should be wrong again; for Fred is often in high spirits and he loves a good laugh. Not that we would be *entirely* wrong — Fred does keep quiet on the topics of himself and his feelings; and, although he appears happy, he is melancholy underneath. So we have to be careful how we phrase our conclusions. On its own, a chart will never tell us precisely how the native will give expression to a Scorpio Ascendant: the background influences are always the same, but how they are either revealed or concealed varies from individual to individual. All we can say of Fred in this connection is that he finds it hard to commit himself; and, as a mechanism for avoiding confrontations, he either talks breezily in a way that makes him seem more superficial than he is, or else makes himself unapproachable to keep well clear of any unpleasantness. A pronouncement such as, "he is very taciturn," is so simplistic that it stands a good chance of being wrong; also it fails to throw light on the whys and wherefores in the background.

The person with a Scorpio Ascendant is often more involved in the environment than might appear. Intensity is the keynote of Scorpio, and a Scorpio will feel intensely everything that is going on around. Some experiences that others would treat as trivial can assume such an exaggerated importance that the Scorpio Ascendant smoulders over them for years.

Regarding planets and house rulers in the 1st house Fred has no planets, and therefore no house rulers, here. If he did have any, we should have to interpret the significance of planets in Scorpio or Sagittarius in the 1st house.

Aspects to the Ascendant

Fred has two aspects to the Ascendant: a trine from the Moon and a sextile from Saturn. The Moon's trine to the Ascendant gives Fred considerable emotional involvement with the environment. Quite often, we see that someone with harmonious aspects between the Moon and the Ascendant can present themselves well, and therefore can easily be wearing a mask. The good side of these aspects is that the environment is not felt to be emotionally threatening. This, of course, is in contrast to the Scorpio Ascendant, which is all too apt to feel threatened in this way. The trine of the Moon to Fred's Ascendant will reduce his sense of vulnerability, and will help him to function more easily in his surroundings. And this is what he does, as we have already seen. However, he retains his cautiousness.

The second aspect to the Ascendant, the sextile from Saturn promotes a wait and see attitude; and so we have two conflicting aspects to the Ascendant: one representing openness (Moon) and the other representing reserve (Saturn). That we have to do with a sextile here takes nothing away from the attitude of caution; because, in any aspect, the fact of there being a connection between two or more factors is what matters — the nature of the aspect is always of lesser importance. And Saturn remains the same old reticent Saturn, however smoothly he is joined to the Ascendant. All the sextile does is to make the connection more harmonious and the integration easier. The native still approaches the world in a serious and conscientious fashion, and is rather reserved. This may not seem to be in keeping with what was said earlier about Fred's mask of jollity when in company, but that mask has something of the proverbial sadness we associate with the smile on the face of a clown; and Fred's friends know very well how serious and punctilious he can be in spite of all his jokiness and bluster. We must never dismiss conflicting factors as if they cancelled one another out, for nothing could be further from the truth. Both factors make themselves felt; so that, in this case, Fred's need for free and friendly contact with others (Moon trine the Ascendant) will come into play alongside his cautious, serious approach (Saturn sextile the Ascendant), as we have already seen, and this fits in well with the Scorpio Ascendant. However, it is entirely possible that other forms of expression will manifest themselves during his life, while the underlying feelings and needs remain the same.

The Moon's trine to the Ascendant gives Fred the desire to do something of a sympathetic nature for the community — to care for others to be warm-hearted toward them, and the like. But this does not mean that he will make himself out to be some sort of Florence Nightingale, or even that he will display his feelings: much of what he feels can remain bottled up inside him. Nevertheless, the added input from serious Saturn's sextile to the Ascendant can indicate that, although Fred seldom puts his emotional commitment to others into words, he lets it be known by his trustworthiness that they can always rely on him.

Aspects of House Rulers to the Ascendant

The Moon is co-ruler of the 8th in Fred's chart, and so we have to interpret a trine between the co-ruler of the 8th and the Ascendant. The difference between a chief ruler (the planet ruling the sign on the cusp of the house) and a co-ruler (the planet ruling over an intercepted sign in a house) is not very great. The chief or true ruler is the deciding factor, as might be guessed, but the co-ruler makes an important contribution.

When the co-ruler of the 8th is trine the Ascendant, we apply to matters belonging to the Ascendant our need to dig deep, to look for the core of things, to tackle our complexes, to uncover hidden gifts, and to acquire influence, and do so in a harmonious manner. Of course, this strengthens the attitude given by Fred's Ascendant in Scorpio, which works in the same sphere. So here is a repetition of the scanning and weighing of the environment, because often (quite unaware) he is engaged in a secret power struggle with it and he wants to calculate how far he can go. Here, too, we see a cautious reserve once more (possibly masked by a show of openness).

I have often observed that people like Fred give those in their vicinity a great number of tests (thus they are very demanding), and if those tested fail in some small point, contact will be kept on a very casual basis. Only those who pass these tests with flying colors (and sometimes this is just one person!) will be admitted into these people's confidence. The exactingness is the result of the same sensitivity that we saw in the Scorpio Ascendant. Therefore, as the people with this aspect begin to feel more secure internally and more able to accept themselves, their testing of others becomes more easy-going. I have been unable to discover much difference between the effects of trines and squares of the ruler of the 8th (Pluto) to the Ascendant; except perhaps that with a trine the natives can persist somewhat longer in a line of conduct because they have a knack of getting others to accept it, or because it fits in with what others are doing anyway, and that with a square they are more likely to provoke opposition but, at the same time, nip problems in the bud quite quickly.

A further consequence of a connection between the 8th house and the Ascendant is that our problems, or whatever we are wrestling hard with, tend to show themselves in our outward behavior before we are properly aware of it, and whether we wish it or not. This specifically applies to a connection between the 8th house and the 1st; it does not apply to an aspect between Pluto and the Ascendant. Pluto does not represent our personal problems and complexes; it has to do with the general human drive to get to the bottom of things and to undergo transformation through confrontation. Therefore it differs from the ruler of the 8th in some points of interpretation.

Fred's ruler of the 8th is trine the Ascendant. Because of this, as I have already said, he knows how to take advantage of things. Without realizing how he does it, he can approach others in such a way that they respond to him sympathetically, and possibly help him. Nevertheless, it is hard for him to abandon his problems and secret intentions. In my own circle of acquaintances, I have more than once observed that those who are good mimics or comedians often have important factors (such as the Ascendant) in Scorpio, or an emphasized 8th house or dignified ruler of the 8th. Perhaps it is because they so unerringly put their finger on small emotional nuances, and can use them? Anyway, Fred, with his Scorpio Ascendant and co-ruler of the 8th trine the Ascendant, easily plays the clown when the fancy takes him.

Saturn is co-ruler of the 2nd and is sextile the Ascendant. The ruler (or co-ruler) of the 2nd sextile the Ascendant harmoniously links a need to create and acquire solid security with our approach to the outside world and our reactions to external stimuli. Often this means that we are security-minded. Not that we are particularly secure, but because we are looking for security in our environment and are also trying to introduce it there. We need to keep in touch with the outside world in order to have a handhold and a settled place in it. What is more, we rely on the outside world for some of our motivation. The 2nd house always has to do with our feelings of satisfaction and dissatisfaction, and with our motivation. The ruler of the 2nd aspecting a Scorpio Ascendant can lend obstinacy and tenacity to our behavior toward the outside world, and, since there is a Scorpio Ascendant in the present case, this side of things is strengthened — as is the inscrutability of the native.

Now, if we stand back and survey the total "promise" of Fred's Ascendant, with Scorpio on the cusp, the Moon trine and Saturn sextile the Ascendant, and the co-ruler of the 8th and the co-ruler of the 2nd sextile the Ascendant, then we see uncommunicativeness as the leading characteristic, but that it is softened by the trine between the Moon and the Ascendant, which also alleviates the standoffish attitude due to other factors in the chart (whether or not this standoffishness is disguised by a show of good humor). We shall take a look further on at the way in which Fred is inclined to give shape to this "promise."

The House Where the Ruler of 1 is Posited

Pluto rules Fred's 1st house, and Pluto stands in the 9th. So now we have the task of interpreting the ruler of the 1st in the 9th. With this placement, we are taken with the idea of travel in the broadest possible sense—either literally by going abroad, or metaphorically by studying, philosophizing, and so on. Which of the two general options will be chosen is impossible to say without further information. Possibly we shall engage in literal travel during one period of our lives and in metaphorical travel during another part. One thing is certain, however: we shall want to look beyond the narrow horizon of our everyday surroundings. The 9th house also has to do with the formation of our opinions and judgments, and we shall endeavor to take everything we meet in the outside world and place it within some framework, maybe religious, maybe philosophical, or maybe some other scheme of things. We have independent theories and ideas and we try to live by them. Also our freedom, a typical 9th house matter, will be dear to us, and we shall prefer to lead a life in which we suffer as little interference as possible from outside rules and regulations. Rules from within, agreeing with our own notions and ideals, are the only rules to which we happily submit.

Fred held down a steady job for a long time. His work took him out and about, it is true, but he was subject to all sorts of stipulations and conditions of service. At the first return of his Moon/Saturn, he made a break and began to travel. Before finally tying himself to work, wife, and children, he wanted to see something of the world, and this is what he did. It led to emigration plans, and Fred has emigrated.

Here the 9th house has expressed itself in the form of travel; it has never really caused the native to study. However, Fred is attaching more and more value to his own opinions—which are part and parcel of the 9th house, of course—and this is a tendency that is strongly suggested by the ruler of the 1st in the 9th (see also Part II for the meaning of the ruler of the 1st in the 9th). The ruler of the 1st in the 9th is one of the factors showing the way in which he tries to give shape to the things indicated earlier. However, we must not become confused and treat these new data as a "promise." How, then, should they be treated? As we have seen, Fred has a certain reticence about him, and yet is very emotionally involved in his surroundings, although this is something he does not find easy to express. Also, he has a serious side to him and is really over-sensitive—a fact he tries to disguise in some way. And, as we have seen, he weighs up the outside world.

The realization of some of this promise is found in the 9th house. With the ruler of the 1st in the 9th, Fred will attempt to place all these things in a wider perspective, so as to arrive at a philosophy of life, a view of society, or something along these lines. Then, so he hopes, he will have a peg on which to hang his often dualistic feelings regarding the outer world. There is another way in which his interest in foreign parts can be connected with his attitude to his surroundings. If one is very sensitive but finds it hard to show it, it may well be difficult to stay in a sphere where so much has happened that is never mentioned. The act of going to a foreign land can then give temporary or permanent relief, because it creates the impression of starting again with a clean slate.

What is more, visiting another country, or engaging in study, or taking an interest in various philosophies, can make one feel liberated; it provides room to grow and to come to terms with oneself and others. Thus, with the ruler of the 1st in the 9th, we can use all sorts of 9th house factors to make sense of our attitude to the outside world, to understand and integrate it; alternatively, we can use the selfsame factors as a means of evading important issues in our lives. But whatever we do, we do it in a 9th house manner!

Aspects of the House Ruler to Planets

In Fred's chart, the ruler of the 1st, Pluto, is square the Sun, sextile Venus, square Mars, and sextile Neptune. We must now make an effort to forget that the ruler of the 1st is Pluto. The content of a planet adds nothing to its function as a house ruler. So it is a ruler of the 1st, with its 1st house properties, that we are connecting with the Sun, Venus, Mars and Neptune.

The fact that the ruler of the 1st is square the Sun indicates that Fred experiences difficulty in approaching the outside world. He has a great need to be himself, to attract attention, to prove himself, to be recognized, and to feel important in and for his community. (This is indicated by the connection between the Sun and the ruler of the 1st). But the square means that he does not know how to bring these things about smoothly. Firstly, his courage fails him and he pulls back prematurely; secondly, he starts shouting people down; thirdly, all goes well; and fourthly, he starts trying too hard again, and so on. Inside, Fred feels that something is holding him back from being himself and from being accepted in his neighborhood. Of course the best thing to do is to get over these feelings as far as possible; but, as always with squares, disruptions keep occurring until the native realizes where the problems lie. Then they can be tackled intelligently.

In a positive sense, with the Sun square the ruler of the 1st, Fred might be expected to choose an active form of manifestation and play an important role in it, full of fire and enthusiasm (sometimes overdoing it perhaps), were it not that this rather conflicts with what is promised elsewhere in the chart. The uncertainty of the square reacts with the vulnerability Fred already feels. The square between the ruler of the 1st and the Sun reinforces his feeling of insecurity whenever he looks for security. But he is inevitably confronted with his need for security whenever he makes those contacts with his environment that are so necessary for his self-esteem. We have already seen this when studying the promise in the chart, but the ruler of the 1st square the Sun also gives a desire for small compliments and pats on the back. So the problem is increased.

The ruler of the 1st square Mars is a further aggravation of the problem created by the ruler of the 1st square the Sun. Mars, too, likes to be seen and to be cock of the rock, and takes a great deal of pleasure in activating self and others. The native needs outside stimuli in order to have something to react to, but his or her response is often rather too sharp or quick-tempered, too thoughtless or too hasty (the square), it can be tactless as well. Mars also goes with a degree of ambition; not with the idea of shining at the center of things, but from the love of a good contest. So Fred sees himself in competition with the outside world in which he feels so vulnerable. However, his vulnerability is a leading characteristic; being self-assertive is one of the ways he handles it. It gives Fred the impulse to fight his way out of difficult situations, sometimes in an unthinking and tactless manner, but always energetically.

Nevertheless, whatever action he takes, it does not release him from his insecurity; not only because the aspect is a square, but also because he has a 1st house conflict. His individual ruler of the 1st conflicts with the collective ruler of the 1st (Mars). And that produces tensions in the approach to the outside world; either through an inner feeling of uncertainty, or else through external confrontations because he fails to do things at the right moment. Fred experiences that likewise.

In addition to these two hard aspects, Fred also has two easy aspects to the ruler of the 1st, namely a sextile from Venus and a sextile from Neptune. With Venus sextile the ruler of the 1st, we are very fond of social contacts, are good at personal relationships, and strike others as sensible and friendly. We like our dealings with our fellows to run smoothly, and have no wish to dig too deeply into their backgrounds, because this could so easily disturb the harmony between us. Venus sextile the ruler of the 1st encourages the native to major on the pleasant side of life and to keep cheerful; it can do much for the preservation of social contacts in the broadest sense.

When we think about the sextile between Neptune and the ruler of the 1st, remember that many people of Fred's generation, and even those born some time before or after he was, have a sextile between Neptune and Pluto. But by no means all of them have a sextile between the ruler of the 1st and Neptune; so that, through the use of the house rulers, this generation aspect is immediately transformed into a personal aspect.

The friendliness characterizing the sextile from Neptune to the ruler of the 1st has something indefinable about it, so that we sometimes appear to be a little vague or dreamy or somehow difficult to pin down. Neptune's aspects often introduce an element of indistinctness, as if a veil must first be removed before the underlying reality can be unraveled. In spite of the fact that a sextile makes for friendliness, Neptune's hypersensitivity — whatever the aspect, means that Fred is more than usually sensitive in his functioning in the community. The ruler of the 1st sextile Neptune either gives him a great deal of empathy or makes him very sensitive to atmospheres and undercurrents. It can also mean that he is easily influenced. Neptune makes the native idealistic, and the native can express emotions beautifully in music and art. Fred is mad about music, and a number of his contacts are concentrated on sharing a love of music. In combination with Venus sextile the ruler of the 1st, artistry, musicianship, or something of that sort, active or passive, can play an important part in contacts with the outside world. As already said, music is Fred's interest. (In actuality, Neptune has many more possibilities than the above; such as love of the sea, mysticism, religion, photography, films, and so on. Any of these could have come to the fore — and may yet do so, for that matter).

Well, how are we to combine this with what has gone before? Where we kept finding caution, reserve, a need of contacts in order to feel reassured and, at the same time the ill-effects of personal insecurity and ambition (Sun and Mars square the ruler of the 1st) in his attitude to the outside world? On the whole, the aspects of Venus and Neptune favor friendliness. Fred can count on a great deal of understanding from some of his friends, not only because they like him, but also because they realize and sympathize with his insecurity. Therefore they see his sometimes very tactless remarks in a different light from the one in which they are seen by another group of friends to whom this other side of Fred is quite common. The latter know him as the Fred of quick repartee — always larking about — or the Fred who, in spite of his clowning, can settle down seriously to hard work. In the circle of his intimate friends, Fred has always found protection, even though his insecurity can make him rather abrasive. In other circles, for instance in his employment, he has often caused annoyance with his standoffish and opinionated behavior; but, because the quality of his work has been so good, people have found it difficult to take him to task. And, in any case, he has always known how to save the day with a friendly joke. Eventually, however, at the time of the first Moon-Saturn crisis, he could no longer put up with the idea of spending his life on the treadmill (because of the combination of his vulnerability with the freedom-loving placement of his ruler of the 1st in the 9th).

Thus we see that Fred definitely displays the sharp edges of the Sun and Mars square the ruler of the 1st, and yet he radiates a certain friendliness that does much to repair the damage caused (although not always, of course). Both sides of his character influence the way in which the promise in his chart is realized. In addition, Neptune's sextile to the ruler of the 1st, which increases his vulnerability and sensitivity in the environment even though it *is* a sextile, is not always easy to live with for someone who likes to keep both feet on the ground — Fred is a Taurus.

Aspects of the Ruler of 1 to House Rulers

As we have just seen, the ruler of the 1st makes a square to the Sun and to Mars. The Sun is ruler of the 9th and Mars is ruler of the 5th, so that we have to interpret the ruler of the 1st square the ruler of the 9th, and the ruler of the 1st square the ruler of the 5th. What is more, the ruler of the 1st makes a sextile to Venus as ruler of the 6th, ruler of the 7th and ruler of the 11th (giving us three separate sextiles to interpret), and to Neptune as lord of the 4th. All in all, we have to examine the following: the ruler of the 1st sextile the ruler of the 4th, square the ruler of the 5th, sextile the ruler of the 6th, sextile the ruler of the 7th, square the ruler of the 9th and sextile the ruler of the 11th.

The ruler of the 1st sextile the ruler of the 4th gives Fred the desire for emotional ties with his environment, and the need for domestic security and an atmosphere of mutual caring. Emotional response is important to him; and, because the ruler of the 1st is in harmonious aspect with the ruler of the 4th, he comes over as someone who is sympathetic, warm-hearted, adaptable, and interested in others. The aspect strengthens the promise of Fred's Moon trine Ascendant, and will certainly help to provide the desired warmth and emotional security. It can help to gradually open up the feelings given by the Moon's trine to the Ascendant, so that they are not so hidden away and, as it were, hermetically sealed. Placement and aspect always show how a promise can be realized, and here there is obvious support for the Moon.

The ruler of the 1st square the ruler of the 5th saddles Fred with the problem that he wants to play a central role in his community, craves attention and likes to be praised, but is not sure how to set about satisfying these desires. Therefore, at one moment he gives the impression of being egotistical, and at another he appears to be quite the opposite. The 5th house is analogous to Leo, and so the square between the ruler of the 1st and the ruler of the 5th aggravates the effect of the square between Fred's Sun and the ruler of the 1st. Because, in both cases, we have to do with realizers of the promise, we are forced to conclude that Fred has to battle against doubts, uncertainties, and overcompensations before he feels he has made any headway.

Possibly, through the impulsiveness and activity that squares always imply, he has already gained recognition in his community, and yet has not noticed this because he is plagued by doubts and because his need for recognition is never satisfied. With these aspects, we are not so likely to consider the actual situation in which we find ourselves, as to be governed by what we feel. And, for Fred, a square from the Sun *and* a square from the ruler of the 5th to the ruler of the 1st indicates a strong desire for self-manifestation, for self-pleasing, and for occupying a prominent and central position. But, owing to other horoscope factors and to the circumstance that the aspect in question is a square, this desire is not easy to fulfil.

The 5th house also shows our attitude toward children. Fred has always said that he does not want children, and that if he did have them, he would keep them in their place because he could not bear his partner's attention to be diverted from him to them, or for the children to get in the way of his activities. Yet his attitude is not purely one of selfish ignorance. He once confided, "I just know I couldn't stand having them, and then I sit down and eat my heart out over what I am missing."

The ruler of the 1st sextile the ruler of the 6th means that Fred will, to some extent, be prepared to assist and serve others. Here we have what appears to be a flat contradiction of the above, in which we saw Fred as self-serving. However, in spite of his self-centeredness, Fred will do anything for those he likes—for people who have shown their esteem for him and to whom he feels beholden. He helps them eagerly—perhaps a trifle too eagerly at times. Sometimes he runs himself into difficulties by making ill-considered promises he feels bound to honor. But, under the influence of the ruler of the 5th house, he has for a long time indulged a passion for music, cookery (a hobby of his) and other pastimes. Helping people alternates with enjoying himself, but not always smoothly. The two activities are in conflict; and we must not forget this when making our judgment.

The sextiles to the ruler of the 7th and to the ruler of the 11th give Fred a number of opportunities to move easily in society—in keeping with what we have seen elsewhere. And so, in spite of his hard aspects, he has enough going for him to be able to solve any conflicts that might arise between himself and his partner or friends. What is more, the sextile between the ruler of the 1st and the ruler of the 7th gives a need for a partner. With this connection, Fred is ready to be candid, agreeable, and friendly toward his opposite number (with hard aspects, and openness would still be there, but it might not seem to be so rewarding). And Fred not only needs a partner with whom he can have a candid relationship, he needs friends of a similar sort, too — as we see from the fact of the sextile to his ruler of the 11th. No significance attaches to the two sextiles being formed by one and the same planet. Fred looks for free-and-easy friendliness (both in himself and others) in his contacts with the outside world. On the one hand this can increase his openness, also the love of liberty indicated by the ruler of the 1st in the 9th. On the other hand, it runs counter to his caution and suspicion. Somehow or other, Fred has to find a middle way to prevent his need of freedom and candor being side-tracked by his reticence and reserve. Now the "promise" of reserve and caution is realized through the need of openness. Therefore we may expect that what he experiences and feels in the course of his life will give Fred the chance to abandon some of his reserve and to meet difficulties in a calmer and freer frame of mind.

The last aspect of the ruler of the 1st is a square to the ruler of the 9th. This is an important aspect, because the ruler of the 1st is placed in the 9th as well as being square the ruler of that house. A square to the ruler of the house occupied is always a burdensome thing, for it stirs up very conflicting feelings regarding the area of life concerned, and often raises doubts as well. Fred's wanderlust was — and is — exceptionally strong; but his uncertainty as to whether it would be a good thing to give up his job was equally as strong for a long time. When he had overcome his doubts and had made up his mind that travel was right for him, the question of emigrating arose in earnest. Once again he was thrown into confusion, but he suppressed his doubts only to have them affecting him physically in the form of a rash! Here we see two realizers of the promise in conflict with one another, with all the attendant uncertainty that implies.

Fred's need to be free and to widen his horizon is actually increased by this conflict, which always has a creative potential, even though — in my experience — the difficult features are the first to show themselves. Active involvement in study or in foreign travel, the continual adoption of new interests, a lack of rigidity and the courage and willingness to modify one's opinions all make from a ruler of the 1st in the 9th and a ruler of the 1st square the ruler of the 9th a dynamic person with a restless, resourceful mind. The disadvantage is the ever-lurking doubt, and Fred has to learn that this doubt must not be suppressed but must be accepted as a challenge, if he is going to make progress and not stagnate. And progress is very much in Fred's line, because he dreads an existence that is dull and tedious. He is ready enough to avoid becoming dull, but pays the price of inner doubt for this.

Now that we have taken a look at all the factors surrounding Fred's Ascendant, a number of things seem to point in the same direction. Certain factors can be taken together, while others can be used to fill in the details and to bring out shades of meaning, until, finally, a picture emerges of Fred's everyday world and how he presents himself in it. Of course, it is a picture that has to be improved by, and fitted into, the rest of the horoscope. But we now have a better idea of Fred's attitude to the outside world, and we can see his activities and opinions in broader perspective, than would have been the case if we had ignored the house rulers. For then our interpretation would have been confined to the Scorpio Ascendant and the trine between the Ascendant and the Moon and the sextile between the Ascendant and Saturn!

Paul's 1st House

Scorpio Ascendant

As we noted earlier, the 1st house for Fred and Paul have much in common. The great differences in their approaches to the outside world will be deduced in the following section. In order to point out these differences, it will be necessary to return to Fred from time to time.

We have already dwelt on the Scorpio Ascendant in Fred's chart. Paul gives a different form to his Scorpio Ascendant. He is thoughtful and likes to discuss abstruse topics, preferably those to do with philosophy or psychology (he also has the ruler of the 1st in the 9th!). He keeps his own personality out of sight of the crowd, but is prepared to reveal himself to a small circle of friends. Unlike Fred, Paul has no need to laugh and joke in order to come to grips with others. On the contrary, placid Paul sets himself up as a sort of father figure, to whom others can bring their troubles and have a good cry, while he usually keeps himself out of range of their sympathy for him. Essentially, this is a form of behavior by which he can control his environment without having to commit himself.

As we mentioned when looking at Fred's chart, it is very difficult to state unequivocally that Fred will travel and that Paul will prefer to study. Both possibilities are always present in the 9th house. It is quite likely that, later on, Fred will begin to study and that Paul will get itchy feet. We can never draw such concrete conclusions with absolute certainty from the horoscope. So we need to be careful; to state that there is a *possibility* of this or that is the best plan when making an interpretation.

When we look at its ruler to discover the effect of the 9th house, we see that Paul, like Fred, has an embattled ruler. His ruler of the 9th forms the top of a Yod-figure, which is hard to interpret because a Yod-figure tends to go with extremes of behavior—from great doubt, unrest, and wondering what to do next, to setting out on a highly motivated, even fanatical, quest. Also this throws no light on the question of whether Paul's travels will be physical or mental (studying and the like). What we do see is that both Fred and Paul are very reluctant to reveal what is going on inside them and that both of them have devised a plan to exercise control at long range, so to speak, which is exactly what a Scorpio Ascendant aims at.

Planets and Rulers in the 1st House

Like Fred, Paul has no planets, and therefore no house rulers, in the 1st house.

Aspects to the Ascendant

Paul has three aspects to the Ascendant, namely a trine from the Sun, a square from Venus, and a square from Pluto. Paul's trine from the Sun to the Ascendant is an indication that he wants to establish himself in the center of his environment and to *feel* established there— something that the trine makes very easy to achieve. He needs to feel important in some way or other wherever he is, and this fits in really well with his Scorpio Ascendant. For instance, if Paul acts in a fatherly manner from a veiled authoritarian position and offers someone a shoulder to cry on, this is a form of behavior that can give him a sense of self-importance, and it is also a form of behavior that is perfectly acceptable to this Sun trine the Ascendant. What is more, the Scorpio

Ascendant easily adopts it in order to keep its distance from the prying of others.

Fred had the Moon trine the Ascendant, and this gave him a need to become involved in his community, not to be told what a fine fellow he was (which is something that would be given by an aspect between the Sun and the Ascendant), but for the sake of emotional support. We cannot rule out a certain fatherliness with Fred's Moon trine the Ascendant, but it would not be anything like as authoritarian as that given by the Sun trine the Ascendant. (In any case, Fred, as we know, had problems with the expression of authority; among other things because of his ruler of the 1st square the Sun and square the ruler of the 5th). So the ways in which the two men give shape to their external behavior give us our first difference between them.

Paul's Pluto square the Ascendant increases his tendency to keep a keen eye on his surroundings and to analyze what is going on. But the fact that the aspect is a square means that he can easily come into conflict with those around him, through expressing his observations tactlessly or at the wrong moment, or through stupidly touching a raw nerve in someone who then strikes back defensively. Nevertheless, Paul's need to examine his surroundings is genuine enough, and he sets about doing so just as Fred did with his co-ruler of the 8th trine the Ascendant. While carrying out this examination, Paul can ask such unexpected and penetrating questions that the other person is scared. However, he himself does not realize this, and it is certainly not his intention to sow panic.

As an aspect, the square bestows energy; and Paul can keep on burrowing away into everything and anything. This square enables him to gain a good knowledge of human nature and, although he sometimes has to learn by his mistakes in this field, he eventually acquires a fine insight into the hidden motives of those he meets. Paul does not have quite the same advantage with his square from Pluto to the Ascendant as Fred did with his trine from the ruler of the 8th, which made it easier for him to approach others and to hold his own with them. Paul seems fated to provoke power struggles and the like with those around him, quite unintentionally, and this does force him to weigh his words and actions more carefully. What is more, Pluto's aspects also often give the need to take up a position that is unassailable. Pluto is frequently strong in the charts of people who have some position of authority (either small or great), in which they create a certain distance between themselves and others. Paul's square from

Pluto can therefore strengthen his need to adopt a paternal attitude which, in spite of all his good intentions and the warmth he can display, is motivated by his desire to stand aloof. And, because the aspect is a square, this desire to stand aloof is bound to provoke confrontations with those around.

Venus square the Ascendant often gives the desire to be thought attractive, as does every aspect between Venus and the Ascendant, and this can make the individual rather charming. As it happens, in this instance squares are not always detrimental; sometimes they even impart that little extra personal magnetism that arouses interest. And yet, with Venus square the Ascendant, we have a certain amount of difficulty in expressing affection. A square always makes it difficult for the native to handle things smoothly; and so, at one moment, Paul can be very pleasant and friendly, but, at another, he is withdrawn and hard to fathom.

What is more, with this aspect, Paul needs balance and harmony in his environment, and he likes to act as a peacemaker. But the danger with the square is that what he sees as being a peacemaker sometimes strikes others as being a busybody.

It will be obvious that Venus square the Ascendant does not sit comfortably with Pluto square the Ascendant (quite apart from the fact that Venus and Pluto are conjunct) because Pluto likes to dig deep and this often disturbs the Venusian desire to have everything working smoothly on the surface. Although, in theory, Venus could mitigate the activities of Pluto, I have seen no convincing examples of this in practice. On the contrary, it seems to me that Venus (conjunct Pluto!) shows traces of Pluto's influence. In any case, with these two conflicting aspects to his Ascendant, Paul can experience an emotional upheaval in regard to the outside world, and he sometimes displays inconsistent behavior; at one moment acting like a sleuth, and at another just being sociable and friendly. However, his Scorpio Ascendant will always bring the Pluto aspect to the fore.

Where the combination of the squares to the Ascendant of Pluto and Venus can play him false is in situations where he tries too hastily to mend matters (Venus in a square) after he has put a good relationship at risk by prying into someone else's soul. He can overdo things and misread the state of affairs entirely, and only make things worse. Problems with relationships can also play a (sometimes great) part in determining the way in which he approaches the outside world; therefore, if he wished, he could become an outstanding relationship therapist. In fact, in his own small circle, he is already acting as such, for most people turn to him for sympathy and advice when their relationships run into trouble.

Aspects of the House Rulers to the Ascendant

Paul has the ruler of the 10th (the Sun) trine the Ascendant, and also the ruler of the 1st (Pluto) and the ruler of the 7th, 11th, and 12th (Venus) square the Ascendant. The ruler of the 10th tells us what we do to carve out an identity for ourselves, and supplies information on the way in which we form a picture of ourselves as a basis for functioning in the outer world. The ruler of the 10th also has to do with the degree of authority we possess and with how we respond to authority. From the point of view of our own authority, a trine between the ruler of the 10th and the Ascendant can give a self-assured bearing, a bearing that exudes authority. This fits in well with the same need as represented by the Sun trine the Ascendant. It is fortuitous that we are talking about one and the same aspect, there is no significance in it. It is fortunate for Paul that planet and house ruler do not work against one another.

With the ruler of the 10th aspecting the Ascendant or with the ruler of the 10th in the 1st, we often see someone's social position (10th house) having an effect on daily intercourse with people "out of office hours." This need not mean that the native continually stands on his or her dignity, although that may be so. Quite possibly he or she is surrounded in private by people who are directly or indirectly involved in public, and so the idea of authority subtly intrudes itself in general contacts.

As we have already seen, Pluto is ruler of the 1st and, in Paul's case, the ruler of the 1st is square the Ascendant. This means that in his approach to the outside world he is not sure how to behave. He is timid and forceful by turns. With a square, he needs to ease up. Those around him often fail to see even half of the intensity of the conflict that is going on inside him, although they cannot help noticing some inconsistency in his behavior—something we encountered in a different way with the conflict between the squares of Venus and Pluto to the Ascendant. The uncertainty produced by this latter conflict is supplemented and increased by the square of the ruler of the 1st to the Ascendant.

With the Sun trine the Ascendant, Paul is able to tackle the above-mentioned uncertainty to some extent, although it will not melt away like snow beneath the sun. And his feeling of doubt and uncertainty can bring Paul the renewed temptation to hide behind the solicitously friendly mask of the Scorpio Ascendant, and behind his fatherly attitude. However, the square of Pluto to the Ascendant does not let Paul off the hook, because it confronts him with the fact that he has cast himself in a role of his own creation, although he still needs to maintain a certain reserve. All these facets will show themselves in Paul's behavior, although it is hard to predict when.

Paul's ruler of the 7th and 11th square the Ascendant gives him a great need of human contacts — which is typical of any connection of an air house with the Ascendant. But, because the aspects are squares, Paul is not very good at handling these contacts. Sometimes he is too ready to compromise (ruler of the 7th) and at others he absolutely refuses to consider it, sometimes his manner is very chummy (ruler of the 11th) and then again it can be very authoritarian (in accordance with the first-named aspects). It is essential for him to find a middle way in his contacts. He is greatly in need of a partner (Venus and the ruler of the 7th square the Ascendant) but the squares show that he will have to learn by hard experience how to make a relationship work, and how to give and receive affection. With the ruler of the 11th, converse with kindred spirits is also of great importance to him; but, here, too, the square points to conflicts between his own needs (1st house) and the wishes of his circle of friends (11th house).

Because both the 7th and the 11th house require him to display openness as a person, the squares of their rulers can — for a time at least — incline him, consciously or unconsciously, to persist in his paternal role, as this keeps him out of range. Of course, there are other roles that would do to save him from baring his soul, but the paternal role suits the situation around his Ascendant so well, as we have seen. Thus, as soon as personal contacts come into play, the squares (certainly in combination with Pluto square the Ascendant) inevitably bring his more unsettled side to light.

The ruler of the 12th square the Ascendant gives Paul a certain gentleness. I have very often noticed, in aspects of the ruler of the 12th to the Ascendant, something friendly yet shy, something hard to pin down, as if this person doesn't have much idea of how he ought to manifest himself, and therefore makes a vague impression, and is seen in a very different light by different people. Naturally others may find him rather incomprehensible, even though the impression he makes is so amicable. Usually, people do not know how to take this type, nor does he know how to take himself! This aspect can also make the native over-sensitive, frequently very intuitive, and full of empathy (sometimes strongly so), and that is something Paul can use in his investigation of the psyche. His intuition and empathy can put him on the track of the nature and solution of problems, but can also make him unsure and vulnerable, because he can pick up energy from his environment without being able to identify it, or even to distinguish it from processes going on in himself. With aspects to the ruler of the 12th especially with hard aspects and the conjunction, he does need to learn to distinguish the two. All this can sometimes give escapist tendencies, or persuade him to defend things that are completely unimportant, or things that are none of his business anyway. Sensitivity and vulnerability are great with this aspect, as Paul has discovered.

Now that we have looked at what is promised in Paul's chart, we observe that in addition to the points of agreement with Fred's chart, there are a number of striking differences. The need to have a central role, or to exercise authority hardly figures in Fred's chart (certainly not in the realization of the promise), but in Paul it strikes the eye immediately. Possibly, as I have already hinted, this is one of the reasons why we find a more fatherly attitude here. In a number of respects Fred and Paul are similar due to the Scorpio Ascendant, and yet they are completely different in other respects due to attendant factors.

The House Where the Ruler of the 1st Stands

In interpreting Fred's horoscope we studied the meaning of the ruler of the 1st in the 9th; Paul, too, has this house connection. But, as we have already seen, Paul has expressed this meaning differently. He has immersed himself in study and has a lively interest in psychology (the latter does not come directly under the 9th house, but does so indirectly as a form of study), in philosophy and in similar 9th house matters. The freedom of the 9th house plays another role in Paul. As long as he can keep happily working on his own interests, he cannot be bothered about where the outside world has set up its boundaries. Like Fred, he sets great store by the freedom to form and propagate his own opinions.

The placement of the house ruler shows how the promise of the house will be realized. Paul, like Fred, has the opportunity to make sense of his life, by building up his own philosophy of life or vision of society; and he may travel in order to gain in maturity or to escape from his problems. Paul "chose" the way of philosophy and psychology. He has a good understanding of his own behavior on many points; but this does not get rid of his need to struggle with himself in the areas he understands. As he grows older, it will become apparent whether he has made constructive use of his inclination to explain things and to place them in a wider setting, improving his comprehension of himself and others, and tackling his problems, or has used this inclination to explain things in such a manner that he explains them away and neatly avoids his problems. Even though he has already set out on the "open way" and has engaged in confrontations with himself, there is always a danger that he will wriggle out of something with clever arguments.

Aspects of the House Ruler to Planets

Paul's ruler of the 1st (Pluto) is conjunct Venus and sextile Neptune, two connections also found in Fred's chart (Venus and Neptune both sextile the ruler of the 1st). In Paul's case, the aspects influencing the realization of the promise of the 1st house are friendly. Venus conjunct the ruler of the 1st makes us very much inclined to create and maintain a friendly atmosphere. We wish for social and emotional contacts in general, move easily in society and are not without charm. Just as in Fred's case, some snags occur, however, due to the native's habit of digging into things. Because this penchant for investigation and delving beneath the surface is strong in Paul, he is liable to spoil the atmosphere by tactlessness and asking awkward questions (Pluto square the Ascendant, etc.). But Paul already has an aspect of Venus in the promise of the 1st house, i.e., Venus square the Ascendant. Now Venus seems to be associated in a friendly manner with the ruler of the Ascendant, so we may rest assured that the square in the promise receives plenty of support from the ruler so that its energy will not be too unsettling.

The ruler of the 1st sextile Neptune increases the rather vague friendliness already given by the square between the ruler of the 12th and the Ascendant. The ruler of the 12th and Neptune belong to one another's sphere and have a similar effect, although we must never forget that their background influences are different. Fred has no aspect of the ruler of the 12th or of Neptune—either in the promise or in the realization of the promise. But Paul does have something to realize, and thus strengthen, a promise here—which is an obvious difference. Therefore Paul's sensitivity and vulnerability at this point will be greater than those around him can see or even imagine. And he will feel much more insecure than he—with his Scorpio Ascendant— will choose to reveal. Although the aspect to Neptune is harmonious, the planet is (and remains) the formless and sometimes chaotic Neptune, which is more at home in the world of infinity than in delineating a fixed role and identity. But, with the Sun and ruler of the 10th trine the Ascendant, Paul desperately needs a well-defined identity to feel he is functioning properly.

Just as we saw in the case of Fred, Neptune can give an appreciation of music and art, also for such things as mysticism, religion, films, the sea, etc. With Paul, it is not Fred's passion—music—that is so important, but religion. Paul was not much of a churchgoer, preferring religion as experienced by himself to more formal instruction. Not surprisingly, he held some "heretical" opinions on a number of points (remember his ruler of the 1st in the 9th!). This is another way in which he differs from Fred—but also a similarity—because Paul "chose" something that would fit the picture of his horoscope.

Aspects of the House Ruler to Other House Rulers

The ruler of the 1st is conjunct the ruler of the 7th, the ruler of the 11th and the ruler of the 12th (Venus) and sextile the ruler of the 4th (Neptune). In interpreting this, we remain in the same sphere because we have already encountered the ruler of the 7th, 11th, and 12th in the promise. If she was a problem there, here we see a harmonious connection. In principle, we could go over the same ground of the desire for friends and social contacts, the need for a partner and the response to one, the longing for harmony in a relationship, the need to give shape to an experience of unity and make room for intuition and empathy. In itself, this implies that the above-mentioned needs and abilities will be strengthened, since aspects already considered point in the same direction. What is now important are the relationships of these aspects to one another. Because the realizers of the promise are harmonious, we can say here that Paul has more potential for adaptability in himself, can learn to handle the giving and taking of affection better, and finds it easier to cope with his emotions and with problems in his relationships, than if the aspects had been disharmonious, or there had been no further aspects in the same sphere.

Therefore, in several respects, Paul has a much easier time than Fred in realizing the promise of the 1st house. In Fred's case, attempting to realize the promise always produced fresh problems, and initially this could only increase his uncertainty. Owing to the reasonably harmonious situation surrounding the realization of the promise of the 1st house in Paul, somewhere deep inside him is the knowledge that he is going to fall on his feet. And this usually happens, too, although not always in the way he anticipates. Paul's philosophy of life and his religious faith can help him in this.

The sextile between the ruler of the 1st and the co-ruler of the 4th can confirm Paul in his friendly paternal behavior; but, at the same time, increases his desire to earn the affection and goodwill of those around him. And this desire is fulfilled, in spite of his above-mentioned problems with contacts. The friendly nature of the aspects means that these problems are solved or reduced to manageable proportions.

In Fred's case, we saw in the promise, the Moon trine the Ascendant, with the realization of the promise coming through problems over authority and a desire for centrality (which themselves were involved in further problems). In Paul's case, we see in the promise the desire for authority and for a pivotal function, besides contactual difficulties, especially on the emotional plane, but the promise is realized in a friendly manner. Paul will eventually seem to be a more calm person than Fred, who is always intense about the way he works things out. Certainly, Paul is the more restful of the two, and radiates his basic confidence that everything will turn out all right in the end. Fred's restlessness seems to be saying to us, on the one hand, "I must see what happens," and, on the other hand, "I must attend to it myself." And the latter is the creative approach which Fred is urged to make by his hard aspects.

Summing Up

When we work with houses and house rulers we need to bear the following points in mind:

1. Each sign has a planet belonging to that sign—the day ruler (or day dispositor). In some signs there is a second planet, subordinate to the first. The second is called the night ruler (or night dispositor);

2. Each house has its own ruler. Its ruler is the day ruler of the sign on the cusp of that house, even if the cusp is in the last degree of that sign;

3. If a sign is intercepted in a house, then the house gets a second ruler, namely the day ruler of the intercepted sign. This secondary ruler must definitely not be overlooked in the interpretation, although it is rather less important than the main ruler;

4. Through its placement in sign, but much more through its placement in a house and through its aspects, a house ruler supplies extra information about the house over which it rules;

5. A house ruler produces both a psychic effect and an effect on the circumstances in which the matters belonging to the house must express themselves;

6. When we treat a planet as a house ruler, it loses its properties as a planet for the time being. Thus it does not matter which planet the ruler of the 6th is, as a house ruler it carries a 6th house significance and nothing more;

7. Planets in a house contain a certain promise (either hard or easy), but it is the house ruler that determines how this promise will be realized;

8. A house ruler indicates, by its placement and aspects, individual, character-forming experiences of the native;

9. In placements of house rulers in houses, it is always the house in which the house ruler stands (and this is usually not the house over which it rules!) that is decisive. The house ruler is deployed in *that* house, and is an instrument of it. The house is its end-point, so to speak. But because it rules over a whole house, *all* the contents of that house (forming, in their entirety, its "promise") serve the purposes of the house in which the house ruler is placed;

10. The house in which the house ruler is placed, is itself ruled by some planet. And so we can construct a chain of houses and house rulers. In such a house cycle, one house will function as pivot

(end-point). If that house turns up most often as end-point or pivot in all the house cycles, then it is the strongest house in the sense that it has a key position;

11. Each house has an individual ruler, but also a collective or mundane ruler. Aspects between these two can throw a clear light on the progress of affairs in all sorts of small happenings in the life;

12. House rulers usually have aspects with other planets. We may interpret each of these aspects as an aspect with another ruler as well as an aspect with another planet, thus as two or more separate aspects, regardless of the question of the number of houses a planet rules. Unaspected house rulers have to be interpreted in the same way as unaspected planets.

When we have learned how to deal with house rulers and house connections, we shall observe that they often show a resemblance, likeness, or relationship to factors of a completely different origin elsewhere in the chart, and that they strengthen or underscore these, irrespective of whether the repetition is harmonious or disharmonious. The value of this is very great. It provides us with one of the most reliable means of assessing what will really come to the fore out of the many aspects and meanings of planets in signs and houses.

If we confine our attention to the planets in the signs and in the houses, and to the aspects of the planets among themselves and to the Ascendant and Midheaven, then we frequently find too little confirmation of things that actually come to the fore. House rulers and house connections then throw a clear light on the whys and wherefores, because we shall often find the confirmatory factor in them. There is no necessity for a precise repetition of the same aspects, as long as the connections belong to a related or similar sphere and color. Even squares in one case and trines in another case can be regarded as supporting one another. For example: persons A and B both have Mercury in Libra, they are tactful and they have a friendly way of speaking; but, in practice, A is *much* more easily upset by difficulties, is much more irresolute, and is more prepared to compromise with people than B is. This could very well happen when A, besides having Mercury in Libra, also has Mercury conjunct the ruler of the 7th, and the ruler of the 3rd in aspect with Venus or with the ruler of the 7th. If B does not have these aspects, the greater sensitivity of A is explained. In the years that I have been studying house rulers and house connections, I have become convinced that exceedingly helpful factors in interpretation are to be found in just this sort of difference, as we have seen here in the—at first sight—very similar-looking first houses of Fred and Paul.

But the fact of the matter is that most students require time in order to feel thoroughly at home with the subject of house rulers. Therefore, in Part II of this book, I have given short examples of the interpretation of house connections. A complete analysis of all the possible aspects of the house rulers with planets, or among themselves, is impractical.

Here are a few tips meanwhile. If, for example, we have the ruler of the 6th in aspect with the ruler of the 9th and we do not know how to set about making an interpretation, the best thing to do is the following. We know that an aspect is a connection. So the first thing to consider is that there *is* a connection; the second thing to consider is the type to which the aspect belongs. If, for example, we have the ruler of the 6th square the ruler of the 9th, then by turning to Part II we can gain some idea of what the ruler of the 6th in the 9th does, and what the ruler of the 9th in the 6th does, and the way in which the two house rulers interact. To work out what the aspect means *as an aspect*, we add the coloring of the square. In this way we can practice judging the aspects and, after a while, we shall notice that we no longer need the short specimen interpretations. All we shall need to do is to follow the rules.

PART II

HOUSE CONNECTIONS

6

How the House Connections Work

It is impossible to deal with every facet of all the house connections here. Life is much too complicated to be summarized in a single review. The aim of this chapter is merely to give the reader a start, and to point him or her to the right method of interpreting the house connections. What follows is a brief listing of the character of the houses.

Brief Characterization of Houses

1st House

Psychological: our immediate attitude to the outside world, our undifferentiated mode of reaction, both mental and physical, to all possible external stimuli. The start of, the tackling of, something new; the personality, the vitality, the health (the latter also in connection with the 6th house), and the stamina. The degree to which one is able to hold one's own psychologically.

External: the external characteristics of the native, his or her appearance and gestures. The public aspect of any person or thing. The outer form, and its beauty or defects.

Physical: the head.

2nd House

Psychological: our attitude toward values and objects that provide our security. Our feelings of satisfaction and dissatisfaction and the motivations arising from them. Ability to secure our means of subsistence; for example, the ability to earn an income. Our need for solid security and the means by which we give shape to this. Economic insight. The way in which we handle matter.

External: money and goods, everything to do with possessions and materials. Our spending habits and our method of earning. Debts, wealth, profit, and loss.

Physical: throat and nape of neck.

3rd House

Psychological: our practical thinking, our impulse to examine and classify all the facts and affairs we encounter on the path of life. From this comes our ability to make plans and arrangements. The 3rd house is also the house of connections, not only as a means of welding facts into a whole, but for linking people with other people and with things through communication and contact—for example in trade (in which people exchange money for goods with one another). Practical, analytical thinking, classifying, arranging, brief communications, and quick, short, but not too deep, contacts. Our need for news and for telling news, our dexterity and general attitude to facts.

External: letters, postal communications, publications of all sorts. Short journeys, means of transport, documents, agreements and contracts, telephones, the neighborhood or the immediate surroundings. Numbers and mathematical studies. Brothers and sisters. Education.

Physical: lungs, air passages, and hands.

4th House

Psychological: our need of emotional security and safety, our inner emotional basis. Our attitude toward and our experience of domesticity. Our need to care and cherish. Our feeling for the source of things, thus for tradition, family and descent. Our heredity. Also our youth and our old age, and what we make of them. The final solution or conclusion.

External: land, houses, agricultural land, hotels, heirlooms, the parents and the running of the home.

Physical: stomach and chest.

5th House

Psychological: the desire to structure our lives around the things that make us happy, such as games, sport, having a good time, pleasures, and amatory interests. The need to be ourselves, to develop self-confidence and place ourselves at the center of affairs. Our creative ability and the urge to be productive — either in such things as hobbies or art, or in procreation, in which the sexual drive leads to the creation of children. Our need of leadership and exclusivity.

External: all places of recreation, such as cinemas, theaters, casinos, circuses, concert halls, parks, golf clubs, etc.

Physical: heart and back.

6th House

Psychological: our need to consider, analyze and understand, in order to make good and concrete use of what has been analyzed. Our attitude to work and the working environment, especially toward working as a subordinate or menial. Our enjoyment of work or the frustration it brings. Our attitude to the body, especially to the physical reactions that have to do with our health. Thus our attitude to diet, disease, and related matters. Our critical acumen and ability to view facts objectively. The degree to which we can and will function within a given social system, and the degree of self-criticism associated with this.

External: the circumstances in which we work. Thus the office, factory, surgery, shop, restaurant, police station, barracks. In addition — servants and personnel, the harvest.

Physical: intestines.

7th House

Psychological: our behavior toward our partner, our pattern of expectations regarding a partner, and our experiences within the partnership (married or living together). Our behavior when joining in a united effort with others and how we experience this. Our need for harmony and beauty, for equilibrium and for a friendly atmosphere. Also our open enemies and how we behave toward them.

External: the marriage service, the contract, the peace settlement, the fine arts.

Physical: the kidneys and the lumbar region of the back.

8th House

Psychological: the urge to live on the razor's edge, to dig deep right down to the core of things. Therefore also: delving into hidden depths in the areas of psychology, parapsychology, magic, and occultism. Our unconscious attitude toward our partner and toward joint ventures. Our creative urge. Our love of life and fear of death. Our attitude toward sexuality. Complexes and the potential for psychic regeneration. The will. Inner struggles. Hidden gifts and talents, and the longing for power.

External: legacies, funerals, the dead, psychological crises, (life-) insurance, wills, shared finances (with the partner or a friend), taxation, postmortem examinations, cemeteries, hidden places.

Physical: the genital organs.

9th House

Psychological: our need to spread ourselves and to expand our vision and our horizon. Our need to travel — both physically and mentally. Therefore our attitude toward higher education, studies, and foreign countries. Our attitude toward religion and metaphysics, the philosophy of life. Ideals and sense of justice. The propagation of knowledge and convictions. The formation and expression of opinions. The ability to place facts and phenomena in a broad framework.

External: long voyages, foreign countries, everywhere situated outside one's own town or district, textbooks, embassies, global contacts, the high court, exports, publications, universities and high schools, transport, science, religion.

Physical: liver and hips.

10th House

Psychological: the need to differentiate an ego, and to form a picture of oneself and of the outer world. Striving to reach a certain social status. The mask we consciously wear in order to feel we are functioning well in the outside world. The need to find acceptable limits and structures for ourselves and others. The degree to which we possess authority and the way in which we react to authority. The need to submit to rules and regulations.

External: government buildings, the career, fame or the lack of it, the position in the social or business world, the reputation. The law and all rules and regulations. Status and promotion. One of the parents.

Physical: bones, teeth, hair, nails, knees, and other joints.

11th House

Psychological: the need to break through fixed boundaries and to experience the other as oneself—not as superior or inferior. Attitude toward friends and friendships and what is experienced as such; also hopes and wishes arising from contacts with friends. The need to associate with people with similar thoughts and feelings, but without stifling the spirit of free discussion and debate.

External: the premises occupied by institutes and associations, clubs, political parties and their offices, the White House, Congress, the House of Representatives, democracy. Organizations in general. (International) friendships, advisers.

Physical: calves and ankles.

12th House

Psychological: the need for retirement and detachment, the hidden fears and inhibitions that can paralyze us (even to the extent of liquidation of the personality), but which also can form the drive to seek an inner, mystical union. Thus, transcendence of the personality. In each case, the 12th house represents the attitude toward the merging of the personality in the collective or the unconscious. Our deepest unconscious inner life, our dreamlife. Experiences in infancy. The desire for a solitary existence, escapist tendencies. The relativization of consciousness. The link with the collective unconscious, and the sensitivity to undercurrents and unconscious processes in society and in the surroundings.

External: cloisters, institutions, prisons, hospitals, and other public buildings. Hidden places and lonely regions. The sea. Secret societies, drugs, poison. Clairvoyance and the like. Meditation, charitable institutions, sleep, hypnosis, dreams, social work and social institutions, sanatoria. But also: bribes, difficulties, pain, defamation, murder, suicide, scandals.

Physical: feet.

Never follow these interpretations blindly! I say this, indeed, for a number of reasons, the chief of which is that each connection interpreted here is only one of many horoscope factors, and no significant conclusions can be drawn from just one connection. Other factors can give the matter such a new turn that we have to say completely different things about one and the same house connection appearing in two different charts. In this introduction to the process of interpretation, I have kept matters on a psychological level as far as possible, in order to give the reader some insight into the mechanisms through which we will and act. Although, when speaking of the 8th house, it is perfectly possible to babble about "the partner's money," we shall notice that in many 8th house connections the native is not in the least concerned with the partner's money. This external detail does, in fact, come under the 8th house, but is only one of many such details and is not bound to be expressed in every chart. So this is the emphasis where mechanisms are concerned: the main purpose of a chart is to give us a better understanding of ourselves and others. The external details can be left to take care of themselves.

Although I am well aware of the danger that the following interpretations could be used like cookery book recipes, I have nevertheless set them down—with the express warning that they must not be used in this way. Many years of teaching experience have convinced me that there is a great need for something like this to give the student a nudge in the right direction. What is more, with the help of the rules in Part I, and the brief characterization of the houses listed earlier in this chapter, the reader can make his or her own interpretation, which can then be checked against the examples we will now explore. If the present chapter is used as training material, and as a source of ideas for elaboration, it will have served its purpose.

To make optimum use of the following examples, we should study both connections between two houses, so that the distinction becomes clear. In fact I have done my best to describe the differences and similarities as plainly as possible. Thus, if we want to know the effect of the ruler of the 11th in the 8th, we should read not only about the ruler of the 11th in the 8th, but also about the ruler of the 8th in the 11th. This will speed up the learning process, so that soon we no longer need to consult the book, but can reach our own conclusions.

The 1st House

The Ruler of the 1st in the 1st

Our activities and manifestation are centered on ourselves. In practice, this means that we are very self-involved in what we do and in what we refrain from doing, that we are impulsive. How this affects others does not matter to us so much. Not that we ignore them altogether, but often we just blurt things out and rush in where angels fear to tread. Primarily, we are interested in ourselves and in our own impulses and sudden desires. Therefore, we appear to be rather egotistical at times. However, this self-centeredness is not usually ill-meant, but often seems very natural and naive, so that people seldom take it amiss — unless factors elsewhere in the chart indicate otherwise.

Because the 1st house indicates our approach to the outside world and our reaction to outside stimuli, any concentration on the 1st house can mean that we look for attention and reassurance in the world around us, either through our bearing, gestures, and behavior, or through the care we bestow on the way in which we present ourselves; for example, in our style of clothing.

Dependent as we are on our environment, we take our chances as they come. In this respect, we have a certain amount of ambition, but it is not the sort of ambition that is determined to achieve its goal whatever the cost. We are not out to do something special, but simply to be ourselves; at least, that is usually the case. Also, our attitude is mostly one in which we see ourselves engaged in lively competition with the environment. This is a role in which we can be very stimulating to those around us, but also very tiresome, because we rarely stop to think whether our impulsive desires and actions happen to come at the right moment for them. Whether we are aware of it or not, action and reaction are very important to us — especially as we do not take too well to being on our own without someone to stimulate us. We look for a stimulus not so much within ourselves as in the reaction to the way in which we present ourselves. Then we are very good at taking matters further on our own initiative, and giving others an added stimulus.

With this connection, we need to be careful not to rush people. There is always something boisterous and inconsiderate about the 1st house, although the degree to which this is true largely depends on the planets and signs concerned.

The 1st and 2nd House

The Ruler of the 1st in the 2nd

The 1st house is an instrument for giving form to the 2nd. Personal activity and manifestation is concentrated on our desire for security, both in the figurative sense of having firm ground under our feet, and in the literal one of becoming well-established in material things. This connection used to be interpreted as "the love of money," but that is only one of the possibilities and certainly not the main one. The 2nd house shows the part that matter plays in our lives, and this can mean manipulating it skillfully just as much as it can mean using it commercially. Thus we may want to keep close to matter and to knead and shape it for ourselves. Therefore, with the ruler of the 1st in the 2nd we may like to collect material things in order to gain a sense of stability, or to do something creative (not seldom something artistic) with materials — anything from knitting to sculpture. The point is that, in manifesting ourselves (1st house) we direct our attention to our need for security (2nd house) in all its facets.

Stimuli from outside, to which we react and which we need (1), frequently excite feelings of satisfaction or dissatisfaction and these can impel us to take certain steps or to do certain things. But we ourselves can be a motivating force in our contacts with others. With this particular house connection, the stimuli we give and the stimuli we receive in return where the external world is concerned, work powerfully through us in the sphere of pleasure and displeasure.

The Ruler of the 2nd in the 1st

The 2nd house is an instrument for giving form to the first. Our need for security and to handle materials is concentrated here on the need to manifest in the outside world. Often the ruler of the 2nd in the 1st can give us an air of confidence; we appear to be purposeful and self-assured, even if we do not feel that we are. There is nothing particularly surprising in this show of certainty, because the 2nd house (like its analogous sign Taurus) also has to do with tenacity, and with feelings of satisfaction and dissatisfaction. Planets and house rulers in the 1st house color the way we present ourselves, and in this case we do so rather obstinately, we insist on what we want with more perseverance than usual, and so create the impression of being more sure of our facts than we may actually be. Essentially, the ruler of the 2nd in the 1st implies that we will look for security in the outside world. We need something solid to go by, and will gladly offer it to others; how this is expressed can vary from being prepared to give money or goods to charity, to standing like a rock in a storm for those who need psychological support. However, where the giving of financial help is concerned, there is a danger that, without realizing it, the natives will fall into the habit of waving cash around in an attempt to buy contacts or affection.

The ruler of the 2nd in the 1st can induce us to find satisfaction in the world and to try to motivate the world to do what we want. But, if we simply consult our own feelings, we shall run the risk of neglecting the real needs of those around us. On quite a number of occasions I have also observed that, with this house connection, we may tend to overcompensate in times of uncertainty, and to concentrate too much on our physical needs (by taking snacks or eating candies), or to be seized with a sudden mania for buying clothes, and so on. But much depends on the rest of the horoscope of course.

The 1st and 3rd House

The Ruler of the 1st in the 3rd

The 1st house is an instrument for giving form to the 3rd. In what we do, we concentrate on our need for communication, exchange, brief contacts, the gathering and arranging of information, and the like. We enjoy busying ourselves with this sort of thing, and feel happy when we can chat with people naturally, indulge in give-and-take, or pursue some hobby or profession with a 3rd house flavor. Another possibility is a fondness for keeping in touch with brothers, sisters and/or friendly neighbors (if this is not contradicted elsewhere in the chart), as these, too, come under the 3rd house.

With the ruler of the 1st in the 3rd, we are usually inquisitive, and like putting two and two together. We classify all stimuli from the outside world, as they play a role in our thoughts and exchanges of information. We shall be attracted to such things as journalism, writing, teaching or learning, making short journeys, reading books, and we like talking about these topics. Also we enjoy clever conversation and jokes. Generally speaking, we possess commercial acumen and selling abilities. Our reactions to, and our dealings in, the outside world are chiefly aimed at eliciting a mental or informative response, which continues to fuel our thoughts and our association of ideas. Because our need for this sort of exchange gives us a smooth approach to others that avoids being too ponderous, we can become everyone's friend, with the danger of superficiality and blowing with every wind. However, with this connection, we can keep talks going under all kinds of circumstance, or can get them started again, and this can do a great deal of good in the social sphere.

The Ruler of the 3rd in the 1st

The 3rd house is an instrument to give form to the 1st house. We bring our need for contacts, communication, and the gathering and arranging of information, directly to the outside. Often, this produces a certain openness to those around us — at the very least, communicativeness. We talk to others readily, find it easy to make contacts, and are quite prepared to go along with people (both literally, in the sense of a short trip, and metaphorically in the sense of ideas and new concepts). Our curiosity is aroused by everything that happens. We came across inquisitiveness in the previous house connection, but there our dealings with the outside world were a means of gathering more facts and information, and this stimulated our curiosity. Here, however, our curiosity influences our behavior, and poking our nose into everything is our way of approaching the outside world. Often, we start conversations with direct or indirect questions designed to elicit information.

With the ruler of the 1st in the 3rd, we need not always seem very communicative (although this is not foreign to our nature), because we can turn to reading, for example, to satisfy our interest in the outside world. When the ruler of the 3rd is in the 1st, making contacts is an instrument for presenting ourselves to others. Certainly, we may enjoy reading, but then our main aim is to be well-read and to impress people with the fact. In various instances, I have observed, both with the ruler of the 3rd in the 1st and with the ruler of the 1st in the 3rd, that experiences during play with little brothers and sisters or other playmates, have been very influential on the approach to the outside world later in life, as well as on the way in which impulses from outside are assimilated. To say the least, they have been more influential than in the normal case.

The 1st and 4th House

The Ruler of the 1st in the 4th

The first house is an instrument for giving form to the fourth. Our personal activity and self-manifestation is concentrated on our emotional basis, on emotional exchange with the environment, on the home and domestic circumstances, and on caring and cherishing. We like being at home, as likely as not, or use our home as our base of operations. Often we find a need, wherever we are, to create a snug, homely atmosphere or situation — at home, in the office, even at the holiday resort.

Caring for and supporting others also comes into our pattern of needs in quite a marked way. Generally there is a strong link with one or both parents and the strongly charged emotions involved can be either pleasant or unpleasant.

The 1st house puts us fair and square in the outside world. Our contact with the latter and the stimuli we receive from it, can have a great influence on our feelings of safety and comfort, when the ruler of the 1st is in the 4th. Hence the need to create domesticity — as a defense against any feelings of insecurity. With the ruler of the 1st in the 4th, we need not shut ourselves away. Sometimes this house connection expresses itself symbolically, as for example in a lively interest in genealogy, folklore, history, or in some other thing that has to do with the roots of the family, the race or the culture. This connection represents the desire to experience one's roots emotionally.

The Ruler of the 4th in the 1st

With this connection, the contents of the 4th house are more an instrument than a goal. With this connection, we can use our need to care and cherish as an attitude to the outside world; which makes us rather fatherly or motherly in our approach. Our need for domestic and emotional security can be actively expressed by giving others sympathetic help and care, etc. Emotional ties with those around us are often important as far as we are concerned. In fact, both house connections between the 1st and the 4th can make us occupied with emotional ties and emotional security. The difference is that with the ruler of the 4th in the 1st we let our feelings show, and we incorporate them in our attitude to the environment, whereas, with the ruler of the 1st in the 4th, all impulses from ourselves and from the outside world are allowed to have their effect on us and are liable to cause emotional calm or disturbance. Also, with the ruler of the 4th in the 1st there is frequently a strong emotional bond with one or both parents, but here the situation in respect of the parental home has a greater effect than usual in determining our approach to the outside world.

The 1st and 5th House

The Ruler of the 1st in the 5th

The 1st house is the instrument that shapes the 5th house. Our activities and manifestation are concentrated on the areas of pleasure, sport, games, creativity and self-affirmation. This connection often occurs in people who want to go through life as professional hobbyists. When our behavior toward the outside world is a means of finding self-affirmation, of fulfilling our ambitions, a desire for leadership, and a central position, then there is generally an overemphasis on the ego. We use ourselves as a standard of measurement, and often make sure that we are in a position to more or less do what we feel like doing.

More often than not, we possess leadership qualities with this house connection, and the sort of poise that impresses children. In any case, the 5th house represents our attitude to children; and, with this connection, I have often encountered a love for and a playfulness with children, plus a natural gift for keeping them in order.

The pleasure-element in the 5th house can vary from a great fondness for (amorous) escapades, frequent visits to discos and similar entertainments, to dedication to a very serious hobby from which a great deal of pleasure is derived. So, by no means is everyone with this house connection a Casanova. But there is definitely a need for self-expression in the broadest possible sense — from chasing compliments to artistic creativity.

The Ruler of the 5th in the 1st

Here, the 5th house is an instrument for giving form to the 1st house. With this connection, our bearing toward others is one of benevolent authoritarianism. We assert our need to be central within our immediate surroundings, and possess leadership qualities. Also, with the ruler of the 5th in the 1st, we will not hesitate to make a bid for power of any sort within our immediate circle, in order to play a central role.

Playfulness in the broadest possible sense can be used in our contacts with the outside world — for example by acting as an entertainer — both for the sake of having fun and for the purpose of achieving an important and valued status. But naivety and childishness can be present; also a sense of rivalry, which can be put to good use in sporting contests. Hobbies and pastimes can be a means by which we make contact with the outside world: we are more than willing to share our interests with others.

The 1st and 6th House

The Ruler of the 1st in the 6th

Our personal activities and manifestation are concentrated on the need to analyze and systematize in order to be able to give everything a more useful and effective function in the great wheel-work of life. This explains why, with this house connection, we often like to occupy ourselves with practical, concrete matters, and usually have a well-developed eye for forms, relationships and details. This can lead to neatness and orderliness in external things; but I have also seen very sloppy people with the connection, who have said to me with a friendly smirk that what mattered to them was to keep everything nice and tidy inside their heads. And, indeed, they all seem to be very systematic, orderly, and even fussy, in their own way.

Work and service come under the 6th house; and, with the ruler of the 1st in the 6th, we often feel impelled to work, to do things for the community or, in any event, to make ourselves useful one way or another. This can find us in subordinate jobs, in the health service, or possibly in the armed forces. We look at things with a critical eye, and are inclined to put ourselves and others under the magnifying glass for a careful examination. Often we are quick to notice the little mannerisms of others.

We have no wish to assume a very provocative role in society; our criticisms are applied in a small way, to ourselves and to individual things, without attacking the functioning whole. In many cases we feel a need to be conformist; but, note well: it is entirely possible that we are strongly opposed to current social standards, but meticulously observe the rules and values of the subculture or group to which we belong.

The Ruler of the 6th in the 1st

Our needs to analyze and systematize, our critical ability, and capacity for service become instruments in contacts with the outside world. Our initial reaction to the latter can appear to be rather coldly critical and analytical; firstly because we have a good eye for detail and regularity, but sometimes secondly because of a need to scrutinize things and take them on their merits. On the other hand, we can be exceptionally helpful, as if helping others gives us some sort of status. Thus the native with the ruler of the 6th in the 1st can get into situations where he or she has no time to attend to personal affairs, as so many other folk have been promised assistance.

A critical attitude to the environment can cause tensions. Those around may express irritation, or we ourselves may feel nervy and a lot less calm than others may suspect, for the ruler of the 6th hides everything behind an impassive mask.

The 1st and 7th House

The Ruler of the 1st in the 7th

Our own activities and manifestation are concentrated on the sphere of life of our opposite number (especially a life partner or close friend) in our chart. In practice, this comes near to letting the partner lay the law down on how we behave in the outside world. We attach great importance to what they think and do. And, even though there is evidence of so much independence in our horoscope, we cannot help referring everything to our partner for a direct or indirect decision, and we let the partner become involved in all our affairs. As a matter of fact, I have often seen a certain docility toward the partner where this connection exists.

However, partnership involves giving and taking and, in a positive sense, the connection gives us the ability to reach acceptable compromises and to create balance in all kinds of relationships. The disadvantage of this position is the doubt that can arise, on the question of whether or not to choose a partner in preference to living alone; especially when independence is strongly indicated elsewhere in the chart.

The 7th house also shows what our attitude is to our opposite number, and with the ruler of the 1st in the 7th we are inclined to let this person (7) absorb us (1), another indication of how significant he or she is in our life. And we must remember that this can apply to the worst of marriages. Nothing is shown about the quality of the union; all that is revealed is that a union of one sort or another has a decisive effect and that the partner governs our behavior and directs how we shall present ourselves to others, as likely as not.

The Ruler of the 7th in the 1st

With this house connection, the relationship with our opposite number is very important; but with this difference that, with the ruler of the 1st in the 7th the person represented by the 7th house has the last say, whereas with the ruler of the 7th in the 1st the person represented by the 1st house does—that is to say, we do. With the ruler of the 7th in the 1st we need a relationship in which either we play first fiddle and boss the show, or else have no feeling that our own activities or manifestation are being hindered by the other person. We prefer to have a partner who leaves us free while being strongly attached to us, going along with whatever we want to do or enjoy doing. Yet even here the partner is very influential regarding our approach to the outside world (the ruler of 7 is always an "instrument") but his or her influence is usually transformed by us, because independence is a craving with this house connection.

The desire to keep the peace, restore balance, make compromises, and the like, can be expressed in our attitude when we have this house connection. And so we often appear rather friendly. Certainly, we are interested in others and have the ability to make contact with them; however, we put priority on being able to express ourselves freely.

The 1st and 8th House

The Ruler of the 1st in the 8th

Our activities and manifestation are concentrated on that area of life in which digging and burrowing, in the widest sense of these words, are the main modes of operation. Thus, we may delve into ourselves and others (psychology), into hidden realms of the mind and spirit (parapsychology), or into the mysteries of matter (for example, in experimental science); we may go deepsea diving, study archeology, or probe into matters of life and death as in surgery, pathology, undertaking, or detective work; also we may interest ourselves in occultism. The 8th house is the house of deep-lying causes, of backgrounds, and of the whys and wherefores of things.

With the ruler of the 1st in the 8th, we are inclined to look into the motives underlying our own actions, and even more inclined to study the motives of others in regard to what they do and do not do, because our behavior is often a reaction to our environment. Therefore it is sometimes said that, with this house connection, we keep getting in deep with ourselves and others. We have a certain reserve; our findings have to be brooded over or assimilated before we will show our hand, and this makes us appear rather wary. It is possible that we would make a fine strategist. However, since the 8th house is also the house of our repressions and hidden conflicts, our own activities and manifestation in and our contact with the outside world (1) will continually face us with this difficult side of ourselves. The result can be defense mechanisms, caution, sometimes "playing at hide-and-seek," and mysteriousness. Generally, although we would not admit it at any price, we feel unsure in our contacts with the outside world and sometimes we find it hard to decide whether we should do a thing or not. This uncertainty is part of the reason why we seek to identify people's motives—we want to secure ourselves against surprise attack. In a constructive sense, this can contribute to a knowledge of human nature, but it can also lead to a love of power in order to gain as much control as possible of everything the outside world could throw at us.

This (generally quite unconscious) need is also found when the ruler of the 8th is in the 1st; but there is a big difference. With the ruler of the 1st in the 8th, our own activities and manifestation and all contacts with the outside world give us the need to reflect and to take time to look into motives and underlying reasons, while the ruler of the 8th in the 1st produces a penetrating, investigative attitude right from the start as a form of personal manifestation. Therefore it is perfectly possible that, with someone who has the ruler of the 8th in the 1st, you will quickly get involved in conversation on 8th house subjects; whereas, with someone who has the ruler of the 1st in the 8th, you may not notice straight away that he or she is also interested in such things.

The Ruler of the 8th in the 1st

All the properties and equipment of the 8th house are now an instrument for helping us form an attitude toward the outside world. Sometimes, indeed, it is asserted that the person with the ruler of the 8th in the 1st will commit suicide or will become a murder victim; and sometimes this is also said of the person with the ruler of 1st in the 8th. To be sure, cases in which the natives are murdered or commit suicide are known with this house connection, but there are numerous other cases in which no such thing occurs. Therefore we should be very wary of jumping to conclusions in the matter, while even to hint at such a possibility to the native is utterly wrong and irresponsible.

Our need to challenge, unravel, and unmask things reveals itself in our attitude to the outside world. This means that everyone and everything we meet is put through a series of tests to see what might be wrong with them, before we bother to look for their good points. This imparts an air of secretiveness and, in addition, something that may best be described as a watchful, challenging scrutiny. The latter form of behavior can be found sexually attractive by others.

Under the 8th house we also find the struggle we have with ourselves and with factors hidden inside us. Sometimes the struggle shows, however hard we try to conceal it. Others can tell that something is going on, even though we do not breathe a word of it. What is more, with this position, we experience our vulnerability so strongly in everyday life that we act forcefully quite often in order to disguise our uncertainty. Frequently we attempt to obtain a position of authority (sometimes small but often big) within our circle.

The 1st and 9th House

The Ruler of the 1st in the 9th

Our activities and manifestation are concentrated on the area of life that relates to our need to expand and to widen our horizons, both literally and metaphorically; that is to say, either by travel and going abroad or by study and forming opinions. The 9th house also gives us a sense of justice, and with the ruler of the 1st in the 9th we often feel drawn to affairs in which wise and just decisions are taken in the promotion of a good cause. Idealism and dreams of the future are prominent features of the 9th house. Sometimes the scales will be tipped in favor of one of these things; sometimes more are in evidence. One individual will make plans to emigrate, another will become a champion for some such idea as that of continuous education.

We experience a need to place whatever we encounter in a fairly wide framework; the 9th house is always the house representing the search for a synthesis. What is more, the desire for freedom is very great and we need to lead a life that does not seem to enmesh us in rules and regulations.

With the ruler of the 1st in the 9th we cannot say that therefore we shall take up academic study, or therefore we shall be given to travel and shall live life on the go. That is much too black-and-white. There are plenty of people with no more than an average education who have the ruler of the 1st in the 9th. But they may have fairly wide interests (for example, they may love watching as many TV quiz shows as possible, even the most scientific ones, and educational programs), or they may spend more than average on holidays and the like.

What is more, we are strongly inclined to form our own opinions and to trust our own judgment. And, with the ruler of the 1st in the 9th, we are always liable to speak our mind, either in an irritating or in a constructive way. Because we are inclined to follow our own opinion once we have formed it; although, seeing the house is a mutable one, our concern is not to cling to our opinions and judgments, but to put them to the test and improve them.

The Ruler of the 9th in the 1st

The characteristics of the 9th house are now the instrument of our approach to the outside world and contribute to our typical behavior in it. Thus we are always ready to say what we think, and have a view to express on every topic that arises. Sometimes we are moralizing and admonitory, and feel called to convince others of the "truth" we have discovered. Opinionatedness can be one result, although it may have a positive side. What we mean by this is that standing up for what we believe to be right is a trait of the ruler of the 9th in the 1st: we are prepared to let the world know how it must or should behave.

Often we are fond of sport and of free existence. Contacts may interest us only when they have something more interesting to say than the gossip of the day, or when we can unburden our own thoughts and reflections. The latter should not be underestimated: with the ruler of the 9th in the 1st, we like to hear ourselves talk, and quite often we are able to convince ourselves of what we have found only by trying to convince others of the truth of it. Therefore, with this house connection, we often make a poor listener. But, if we can put ourselves in proportion in developing a philosophy of life, we may be able to adopt a genial and sympathetic approach in which we willingly lend an ear to others and offer them well-considered advice.

In any case, with this position, we need to be expansive in what we say. The danger being that we may be too expansive: for example, by mentioning in an offhand way how many fascinating exotic person-alities we know, for example a paramount chief we met on safari, or an Icelandic minister, a leading educationalist, or a religious leader, etc. With this house connection, we want to lay hold of whatever lies beyond the limits of our horizon.

The 1st and 10th House

The Ruler of the 1st in the 10th

Our activities and manifestation are concentrated on our (external) social manifestation and on our (internal) carving out of an identity. Quite often, with this position, we have a very great desire for recogni-tion within the established order, either in the community as a whole or in some subculture. We are ambitious to obtain a prominent posi-tion; but a clearcut position that fits our ego-image is also acceptable. We want to have a certain amount of power, authority and structure, and we enjoy creating rules and regulations for others which we too must observe. Provided other factors in the chart do not contradict it, we generally have a great sense of responsibility and prefer to express it in our profession and our daily life. Egotism frequently shows itself with this position, although this need not take a negative form. A great deal depends, in this connection, on how purposeful and effec-tive are our behavior and our contacts in the outside world, and on how far they contribute to a stable, and preferably influential, social position, or to a position that at least gives us recognition. The soloist, both in the arts and in professional life or in "high-flying" circles, can be found with the ruler of the 1st in the 10th.

The Ruler of the 10th in the 1st

Our need to regulate, structure, and demarcate (10) plays a significant part in our primary attitude, which can result in a certain degree of authoritarianism. There is nothing very mutable about the 10th house; it is stiff and starchy, and the ruler of the 10th in the 1st can make us fairly unbending. In a positive sense, this means that we tend to stick to our guns in difficult circumstances; but, in a negative sense, there is a danger that we shall leave others little room for maneuver and will accept their good suggestions only when it suits us to do so.

And so, with the ruler of the 10th in the 1st we are very self-oriented and, on the credit side, can become a selfmade man or woman; or, on the debit side, can be very hard and forbidding because we are determined to achieve our goals at all costs. Now, when the ruler of the 1st is in the 10th, we have a situation in which we wait to see how our outside contacts measure up to the requirements of our 10th house; but, when the ruler of the 10th is in the 1st, we are already so rigidly structured that all sorts of contacts are weeded out right from the start. I have quite often encountered leadership qualities in this house connection, and part (sometimes a large part) of the native's contacts have consisted of followers or hangers-on.

The 1st and 11th House

The Ruler of the 1st in the 11th

Our activities and manifestation are focused on the area of life that involves sharing the company of people with similar views and a similar disposition to our own. The 11th house shows how we get on with them, what we expect of them, and how our friendships develop from this. When the ruler of the 1st is in the 11th we have a great need to be on the same wavelength as others, so as to exchange ideas with them and can share all sorts of activity with them. We are eager to belong to their circle and are interested in everything that goes on in it. Of course, this does not imply that we spend all our time at the club, or that we are always surrounded by a crowd of friends. A single friendship can satisfy the requirement of this house—the houses represent qualities not quantities.

The 11th house reveals the extent to which we appreciate the self-expression of others, however much it conflicts with our own way of doing things. Frequently, the ruler of the 1st in the 11th shows that we are very much involved in the ups and downs in the lives of those we care about, and that we are able to develop side by side with them. A certain humaneness also belongs to this position.

But the 11th house is not all friendships and parties. It contains the basic premise of the equality of all human beings, and there is a readiness to proclaim this truth in the community somewhere along the line. Often the 11th house reveals the reactions of the public to our behavior. With the ruler of the 1st in the 9th we interest ourselves in these reactions and are usually prepared to take notice of them, because it is very important to us to form relationships with those who share our outlook.

The Ruler of the 11th in the 1st

Here too, great significance is attached to contacts with people on the same wavelength as ourselves; but, with the ruler of the 11th in the 1st, we are always inclined to impress them with our own significance. However, our decisions to do or not to do certain things are always colored by notions of equality, free expression, and friendship. We raise the banner of equality and fraternity in the world, are friendly in our approach and behavior, and believe that we are all equally valuable.

We are an advocate of equal opportunities yet, because the 1st house is the endpoint, there is something in our attitude that says, "But this is better than that. . . ." This can make us decidedly domineering, in spite of our affability. Owing to the informality by which we greet a minister no differently from how we greet a road sweeper, we can start to get above ourselves and can even become deliberately provocative, but seldom with bad intentions. We have a wish to adopt an approach that will do no more (in our eyes) than test the value of fixed conventions and, if necessary, break them. We are liable to be inquisitive about others, their motives, wishes, and desires; in fact we are interested in people in general.

The 1st and 12th House

The Ruler of the 1st in the 12th

Our activities and manifestation are concentrated on that area of life that involves the experience of unity, quietness and isolation, the collective and the unconscious, but also hidden fears and escapism. In practice, this means that we are somewhat reserved, even shy, toward others; very often due to a much greater sensitivity and vulnerability than they are able to realize. Even we ourselves are unaware of this sensitivity at the time, but in the first instance feel vaguely uneasy about stepping into the limelight. Usually we have no problems about being left in peace and quiet on our own; in fact we regularly seek this in order to "recharge our batteries." Our vulnerability toward our environment often results in our being overinfluenced by it; but then a short period on our own will often correct this effect.

With this house connection, we must beware of being too easily manipulated, especially by people who try to play on our emotions. Our sensitivity can find a better outlet in work or hobbies to do with 12th house matters such as intuition, empathy, dreams, hypnosis, meditation, yoga, religious or welfare work, and so on.

Often we are in search of something incomprehensible or universal; but, if we find a stopping place, say in some faith (not necessarily traditional) or creed that attaches importance to transpersonal unity, then we have the opportunity to lay a solid foundation on which we can cope with the most difficult circumstances. If we do, we can come into possession of that inner peace that shines out into the environment.

Our strongly developed intuition can guide us in the sense of learning to guess the needs of others, or of adopting the right attitude in a given situation. Or we can enter into, and put into words, the unspoken feelings of individuals and groups. We prefer to remain in the background if we have the ruler of the 1st in the 12th, but our influence can spread out to the front lines. The danger is that we can place such a disproportionate gap between ourselves and others that we demotivate ourselves, and then the more undermining and anxiety-laden facets of the 12th house begin to show.

The Ruler of the 12th in the 1st

With this house connection, intuition, empathy, compassion, vulnerability, and other 12th house qualities, are ingredients of our attitude toward the outside world. We sense atmospheres and, even as we enter a room, can feel underlying tensions and the like. Our reactions may be totally unconscious in this respect. Quite often, we shrink in anticipation of trouble to come or feel thrown on the defensive when we detect these hidden tensions. We do not know the cause of the tension, but are so hypersensitive that we can easily jump to the conclusion that those present do not like us or that something else is afoot, and so we prefer to leave. Sometimes we can feel things physically, such as another person's headache.

The 12th house dissolves form, and this comes over in our attitude as something indefinable often enough. People have difficulty in making us out, with the consequence that they react to us in all sorts of different ways, because each one forms a different picture of what we are about. This can undermine our self-confidence to some extent, because if we never know how people are going to respond to us, we have nothing to go on. Some folk will find us mysterious and therefore attractive.

With the ruler of the 12th in the 1st, just as with the previous house connection, we tend to fit in with what is going on in the unconscious, in the sense that we feel what attitude we should adopt in a certain atmosphere. The danger is that we shall talk and act like "the last book we have read." Our sensitivity makes us suggestible, but we ourselves can influence others by suggestion. Questions to do with infinity, unity, religious faith, spiritual life, the needs of humanity and of the oppressed, belong to this house connection. We occupy ourselves with such themes in a big or in a small way, and others see this interest as part of our very nature. The same questions come to the fore when the ruler of the 1st is in the 12th, but then we prefer to deal with them on our own, and they hardly enter into our dealings with the outside world.

The 2nd House

The Ruler of the 2nd in the 2nd

If the ruler of the 2nd house is posited in its own house, we have an unusually strong urge to acquire security and to have firm ground under our feet. We have a special talent for creating stability; which is just as well, because we do need a solid base in life, and to possess some form of wealth, either spiritual or material. Generally speaking, we experience comfort and discomfort acutely. In a positive sense, this can motivate us to learn the skills to earn an income, and we can motivate others when necessary. But, in a negative sense, we can all too readily indulge a desire for possessions, luxuries, money, and a life of ease.

However, on a higher level, we may have a feeling for matter and materials (which can take us into such occupations as a buyer, broker, artist, etc.); and we seem to know by instinct when to play safe — for example, whether or not to sign a contract containing a penalty clause.

As always, if a ruler is posited in its own house, the role played by that house in our character is strongly emphasized. This means that, even with a complete absence of indications elsewhere in the chart, we like to have something to fall back on, either in the form of tangible possessions, or in the form of the knowledge or skill required to earn a living, so that we shall never be left in want.

Obstinacy and stinginess are other characteristics of the ruler of the 2nd in the 2nd, and reflect our powerful desire for a secure existence.

The 2nd and 3rd House

The Ruler of the 2nd in the 3rd

Our need to create and acquire security is concentrated on the area of thinking, planning, transferring and connecting, and of contacts and communication. We seek security in these things, and that is why people with this house connection often earn their livings — either wholly or partly — by using skills belonging to the 3rd house (although we have to look elsewhere in the chart to discover the actual profession). The search for security, and for something to go on, by means of contacts, ideas, analysis, and so on, can make us seem very positive and self-assured in our approach to others, even though we do not feel this. With the ruler of the 2nd in the 3rd, we have such a forthright style of speaking that people think our opinions are unshakeable. Unfortunately, there is a good chance that we shall become so obsessed with security that we leave no room for anything really new. Or we cling to data that are no longer valid, having been rendered obsolete by the march of progress. The 3rd house shows our attitude to facts; and, with the ruler of he 2nd in the 3rd, we may be inclined to confine recognition to those facts that fit in with our idea of stability, and confirm certain fixed values or, at least, do not contradict them.

Unless the rest of the horoscope denies it, our thinking is concrete and practical; the concreteness and certainty of the 2nd house are always the instrument of our thinking and planning.

The Ruler of the 3rd in the 2nd

In this house connection, too, we find practical thinking and planning, but the perspective is different. In the previous case, the search for security was expressed mainly in our thinking and communicating; but, in the case of the ruler of the 3rd in the 2nd, the reverse is true: here we use our thinking, analyzing, communicating, and transferring, to obtain the utmost possible stability, or even material wealth. Here we find concrete and practical thought in a more pure form than with the ruler of the 2nd in the 3rd, because in the latter case our thought-world and our contacts have the last word.

With the ruler of the 3rd in the 2nd, as with the ruler of the 2nd in the 3rd, we can earn our living with 3rd house matters, which invariably serve as a means for creating security; and we have the motivation to gain proficiency in them. People with a very restless spirit can profit by this position because the 2nd house will keep on insisting on composure and caution. However, with the ruler of the 3rd in the 2nd, the native can be more obstinate and less flexible in what he or she has to say than with the ruler of the 2nd in the 3rd; he or she always seeks solid worth in the processes of thinking and communicating, but finds it difficult to abandon anything that matches the personal pattern of values.

The 2nd and 4th House

The Ruler of the 2nd in the 4th

Creating and winning security is a way of fulfilling our desire for hearth and home, an emotional basis, and union with the family, the past and tradition. Our own household, home, or family, or indeed any place where we feel emotionally secure, are very important to us: they are each and all means for feeling firm ground under our feet, for being able to find our own values, and thus for obtaining stability. We certainly do not need to be fond of our relatives with this house connection, but this is a definite possibility. The crux of the matter is that we must have somewhere where we feel safe and at home, either literally in a house or in our own room, or metaphorically in some other sphere of life. Whether or not people such as parents or children are part of this cozy environment is of secondary importance.

Often we need to spend a great deal of money or to use many of our skills in order to create and maintain a secure place like this. Because houses 2 and 4 are the pillars of our security (the 2nd is our existence, and the 4th is emotional life), a house connection between the two always gives a great desire for a fixed abode or place of work. People with this house connection attach more than usual importance to "good form," provided the rest of the horoscope concurs.

The Ruler of the 4th in the 2nd

With this connection, it is our emotional basis, and our home and family ties and attachment to the past, on which reliance is placed for obtaining solid security. Often we have a powerful need for physical closeness to those who are dear to us; the 2nd house is always focused on sensory perception. Because of the bias of the 2nd house toward what is material, we can also become emotionally (4) involved in the acquisition of concrete security, possibly in the form of possessions and an income (2), although I have met people with this house connection who liked to occupy themselves with the shaping of matter (artistically), mainly from emotional impulses — and found a sense of peace in doing so. In fact, craftsmanship and working creatively with matter (in anything from sculpture to needlework) are quite often engaged in for their soothing effect by natives with this position. But with the ruler of the 2nd in the 4th and with the ruler of the 4th in the 2nd, I have known cases in which business people had their offices at home and/or earned an income by selling and buying real estate, or by working the earth (as farmers, miners, etc.).

The 2nd and 5th House

The Ruler of the 2nd in the 5th

Our desire to provide and obtain security is focused on the area of sport, games, pleasure, creativity and children. A secure subsistence is a means of gaining a feeling of self-confidence. Very concretely, we can spend a great deal of money on things that we enjoy, such as hobbies, sport, and our children.

Because skills and motivations (2) are also instruments of the 5th, we can invest so much energy in our hobbies that we may even make money from them. In the area of amusement (5) we can seem so self-assured that people do not realize that we are diverting ourselves to build up our confidence. This house connection gives us the desire to do something, either great or small, to amuse and please ourselves and others. Not that we want to serve and entertain others for their own benefit: we intend to have fun — *and* recognition. And recognition is something we seek in order to have a sense of security, if the ruler of the 2nd is in the 5th.

Sometimes, with this house connection, we see parents who look for a great deal of support and security from their children. Frequently, having children is enough to give a sense of worth and assurance (certainty in caring for the young ones). All sorts of 2nd house activities can be turned into hobbies by the person with this house connection — such as finance, collecting (preferably valuable articles), gem-cutting, and also singing (the 2nd house is the counterpart of Taurus), etc.

The Ruler of the 5th in the 2nd

Although the ability to turn hobbies into a source of income was present in the previous house connection, it is even stronger here. Hobbies, sport, games, pleasure and creativity (5) are the invariable instruments for giving shape to our need for security and an income (2). Because sensory perception (2) is so important to us, we may well choose hobbies that lead to something visible or tangible (collecting, model building, etc.). But the need for concrete security can play a part in other 5th house matters, too. For example, there is a danger that we will see children as possessions, and may be inclined to make our own children conform to our own value pattern.

The element of rashness in the 5th house, speculation and gambling, can sometimes contribute to our income, but I have seen many horoscopes of people with a 2nd-5th connection who had never won anything to date. This connection has absolutely nothing to tell us on the subject of profit and loss. There is a difference that should be noted at this point: those with the ruler of the 5th in the 2nd are more likely to take a chance if they are in a good position to win or if they feel fairly safe in some other respect, whereas those with the ruler of the 2nd in the 5th usually take greater risks. People in the first group would probably be playing marbles (2) when people in the second group were playing cards (5).

The 2nd and 6th House

The Ruler of the 2nd in the 6th

Our need to create and acquire security is concentrated here on the area of work and service, of criticism and analysis, and of sickness and health. With this house connection, we wish for security and stability at work, and can toil away long and hard (the obstinate 2nd house as an instrument for the 6th). Often, people with the ruler of the 2nd in the 6th and people with the ruler of the 6th in the 2nd, are prepared to roll up their sleeves whatever the circumstances; work, service, and security are closely interwoven. This is a fine house connection to have in times of high unemployment, because our urge to work can help us to find a position exceptionally quickly. With the ruler of the 2nd in the 6th, we are prepared to invest all our skills and (financial) resources (2) in our work and working environment, also in things to do with health. The latter can vary from the outlay of (much) money on patent medicines and health products to the acquisition of knowledge regarding health and disease and having a healthy life style. We may even find work in the medical field. Also, serving others in our work, whether or not in the medical profession, is another common outlet (both here and with the ruler of the 6th in the 2nd).

The 6th house does not specify what we shall do or how we shall serve others; all the same, the ruler of the 2nd in the 6th does show the desire to be of service. The armed forces, restaurants, politics, etc., are possible spheres of activity. Now, with the ruler of the 2nd in the 6th, we express a need for security and for finding our own values in the work we do; this puts its special stamp on our service. Nevertheless, the critical outlook of the 6th house has the final say in our values and our certainties. And we like to play safe in matters of sickness and health.

The Ruler of the 6th in the 2nd

This is another house connection in which the themes of work and security are blended. But here the 6th house — representing our mode of working, our attitude toward sickness and health, and our powers of analysis — shapes the way in which we express our need for security. Perhaps we wish to work, or actually do work, in the field of services, relief work, medical work, and the like. Although it has been said that, with this house connection, we demand concrete payment (2) for all services rendered (6), which may well be true, we are not purely materialistic. Often, with this connection, we have a good sense of material values and know how to make capital out of our work, and how to earn a good income. And yet idealistic, unpaid work is also a possibility when doing good gives us a feeling of earning an established place in the community. Thus someone once told me that he was glad he learned so much from what he did; it motivated him to undertake even more. And, after all, the 2nd house is involved in non-material things, such as skills and motivations.

Sometimes we find a practical, useful, objective approach with connections between the 2nd and the 6th house, if the rest of the horoscope does not contradict it. With the ruler of the 6th in the 2nd, whatever is matter-of-fact serves our own value-pattern, and with the ruler of the 2nd in the 6th it can also serve the general good; however, we have to remember that the 2nd house always acts as a pivot for our self-interest and personal security. This shows up more clearly in the ruler of the 6th in the 2nd than in the ruler of the 2nd in the 6th, yet in the latter we often see that we judge our own interest by the general good; so that, even though the manner is rather indirect, we are still looking after ourselves.

The 2nd and 7th House

The Ruler of the 2nd in the 7th

Here our need to create and acquire security is concentrated on the area of life represented by the life-partner and companion. A partner is indispensable to our concrete well-being; we are inclined to follow our opposite number's lead in many things in order to feel that we have solid ground under our feet. Also we make a point of offering the other person security in the relationship (in some cases we are prepared to earn their living for him or her) in exchange for the reassurance of having them with us. Through our involvement with our life-partner, or through firm contact with a companion — and sometimes even through our social functioning in general — we can be confronted in such a way by our personal values and need for security that we can get into perspective what it is that makes us dependent on something or someone else, namely our uncertainty and search for certainty. As we learn to cope with this discovery, we can develop greater self-reliance. Thus with the ruler of the 2nd in the 7th we sometimes see a certain amount of docility to begin with, because the partner must offer us security; but, as time goes on, we are able to offer him or her security and support, and so there is a greater opportunity for comradeship.

Sometimes I have observed the desire to set up in business with a partner, or to work alongside one. But there is invariably a need to find security in serving the other, and this plays an important part in our certainties, motivation, and satisfaction.

The Ruler of the 7th in the 2nd

With this house connection, our personal security and our partner are very much tied in with one another, and we often find that the partner is expected to give us security, but not in the same way as in the previous connection. There we ourselves offered our means (2) to the partner, here the partner (7) is the instrument for providing our means (2). And so, sometimes, the partner literally contributes to our well-being. This can lead to a marriage with a well-to-do partner, but there are many other possibilities. So the partner can form an important link in our motivation or in the expression of our feelings of satisfaction and dissatisfaction. Or we may seek a partner who shares our (fixed) values and has a similar need for security to our own; and, if not, we are inclined to try and force these values on our opposite number. However, this can bring us into conflict with ourselves, because we do need our partner or companion to give shape to our desire for stability—the ruler of the 7th being an instrument for the 2nd house. In a positive sense, we also find cooperation in working for a motivating, common ideal (whether or not this ideal is spiritual or material makes no difference).

The 2nd and 8th House

The Ruler of the 2nd in the 8th

Our need to create and acquire security is focused here on the area of life that contains the greatest amount of insecurity. It is the area where we struggle with ourselves, where we look for intensity and depth and come face to face with the causes and consequences of our repressions, fears, and so on. Thus, with this house connection, we go looking for security (the need for security expresses itself here in 8) in a terrain that gives us the necessary confrontations. The 8th house is also the house of power. If we have enough power, we can guide what happens to us to some extent and avoid confrontations. The effects of this house combination can vary considerably. We can try to satisfy our need for security by handling "big money" (as a banker, insurer, etc.) or by occupying or making a bid for some position of power (in politics say). But we can become an authority in any number of different areas.

The 8th house also contains great intensity, in addition to our hidden talents. With the ruler of the 2nd in the 8th, we can find security in intense self-involvement. One example is an interest in psychology, another artistry. What matters to us is to challenge ourselves and life with controlled intensity; this makes us feel more assured. We are like the entertainer who is never sure of a good reception, but saves the day by "giving it everything he or she has got" and sweeping the audience along.

Even on a small scale, the ruler of the 2nd in the 8th is confrontational: every so often security is sought in a terrain that is insecure. Thus, paradoxically, we can gain some hold on life by concerning ourselves with the problem of death. As regards sexuality, which also comes under the 8th house, we note the following. Security can be sought in provocative behavior, but this is true of the ruler of the 2nd in the 5th, too. The difference between the 5th and the 8th is that 5 contains the element of pleasure and risk-taking, but in 8 we challenge the other person to see how far we can go, and in this way challenge life itself—no fun-and-games are involved here. Now because the main theme of the 8th is the struggle between the life-urge and the death-wish, and sexuality only mimics this, sexual provocation is not a characteristic of everybody who has the ruler of the 2nd in the 8th.

The Ruler of the 8th in the 2nd

Everything to do with the 8th house can be used to obtain security and may be an income as well. The 8th house digs below the surface, and therefore archeology, deepsea diving, the occult, surgery, (para)psychology, experimental science, investigative work in research and in the secret service, and similar activities, are useful to us in the formation of our pattern of values (the 8th house is the instrument here) and also in the confirmation of our values (by providing us with an income for example). Big financial interests can enter into the picture, too.

We can obtain a feeling of security by uncovering the things that make us insecure (as is typical of the 8th house). The search for what is hidden can motivate us strongly. When it comes to handling material things we can be very intense. Thus, as a banker, we would keep an eagle eye on customers' accounts, and, as an artist, we would have an enormous amount of emotional involvement in and would put a lot of energy into our creative work, to preserve our peace of mind and to strike a balance between our conflicting feelings.

With either connection between the 2nd and the 8th, we find problems (8) being solved by handling and shaping matter (2). With the ruler of the 2nd in the 8th, manipulating matter is a means of identifying our problems (for example, by occupying ourselves with creative work we can sense where our problems lie, even though we may not be able to put the discovery into words); whereas, with the ruler of the 8th in the 2nd, we use creative work on matter in order to rid ourselves of problems we already see and know, or we convert our problems into a creative pursuit because it eases the tension for us and gives us fresh motivation to do something new. Sometimes, too, the representation of our problems (in a concrete or symbolic manner) is a healing process with the ruler of the 8th in the 2nd, a process that helps us to recover our equilibrium.

The 8th house is liable to work compulsively, by way of overcompensation for example. Therefore, the ruler of the 8th in the 2nd can mean that owing to an insecurity felt all the more intensely because the ruler of this confrontational and insecure house is posited in a house that seeks security, we can seek material security by becoming a compulsive hoarder. In a positive sense, however, we can find peace by integrating in our life the restlessness, the confrontation, and the struggle with ourselves.

The 2nd and 9th House

The Ruler of the 2nd in the 9th

Here our need to create and to obtain security is concentrated on the sphere of travel both physically (abroad) and mentally (in philosophy, study, religion, and so on). Although we may actually spend a great deal of money (2) on the things mentioned, the main effect of this house connection is to give us clear-cut opinions and ideas. Our need for security and our attachment to certain values (2) are the instrument here of the house of journeys, persuasions, and judgments (9). Therefore fixity and fixed values find expression in our ideals, our conceptions, and our sense of justice, and in all the convictions we try to convey to others. Therefore the danger that we will find hobby-horses to ride is not imaginary; but steadfastness in opinions and beliefs has a positive side. Once we have taken up some study, we can pursue it with marvelous perseverance. Generally speaking, the things we want to know, and to tell others, are very down-to-earth and practical.

However, the effect of the 2nd house is not always materialistic. If we are taken up with the practical needs of the world, the desire for security given to us by the ruler of the 2nd in the 9th can also express itself as the wish to raise the subsistence level of others in the world, and therefore to make it a more stable place in which to live. But it must be said that the things on which we form a judgment or opinion are based on preconceived values and certainties. Often we find that our means of subsistence (2) and working in travel, education and philosophy, or in some other 9th house matters, somehow go together.

With the ruler of the 2nd in the 9th, the emphasis is placed on bringing our security and stability elsewhere in our world or on imparting it to the realm of the mind; whereas with the ruler of 9th in the 2nd, it is 9th house activities themselves that give *us* a sense of security, and they are especially useful in reinforcing our own system of values.

The Ruler of the 9th in the 2nd

As we have already seen, the 9th house is focused here on our own security and material safety. This can mean that we use our ability to convey our knowledge, ideals, and opinions to earn a regular income. However, what is more important is the attempt to employ our studies, religion, or a sense of justice to identify those things that will give us a sure footing in life, either literally or metaphorically. From the same background, 9th-house matters can strongly motivate us to learn new (often diverse) skills, and the fresh insights and ideas we gain can open up further paths to us.

Here, too, there is a danger that we may cling to a specific conviction with blind stubbornness (2) because of the security it offers, or may fanatically stand in the breach if we are naturally very insecure. But if our character is fairly stable, there may be a desire to pass on our new-found certainties to others in a manner that, far from being fanatical, is practical and level-headed.

The 2nd and 10th House

The Ruler of the 2nd in the 10th

Our need to create and acquire security is concentrated here on that area of life that, externally, has to do with the struggle for a certain social position and, internally, has to do with the forming of an identity based (unconsciously) on what we think we are able to do and to be. With this connection we desire a stable social position. We are more than likely to plan our career, and to look for a recognized position of authority in the outside world. In any event, we put on a show of being strong and self-assured.

For preference, we express our fixed values (2) in the community and in our work, and, given the chance, we are inclined to turn these values into rules and regulations that are binding on ourselves and others. Having a solid position, both in the inner and in the outer world, is so important with this house connection that we are prepared to create it ourselves.

At the same time, when it comes to carving out an identity for ourselves (10), we have a great need for a clear-cut picture of ourselves; which is why we have an even greater need for an equally clear-cut picture of the outside world. Otherwise, we run the risk of failing to fit in with the outside world.

We are often strongly motivated to work for—and to apply—our skills to all those things that we think belong to us or can help us socially, as well as those things that will give us a definite value in other people's eyes or will give us an authoritative role—because, with this house connection, we frequently possess managerial qualities, although these need not be exercised in a prominent place. Also we are prepared to spend a great deal of money on anything that will further our career or improve our status.

The Ruler of the 10th in the 2nd

With this house connection, our social position serves our security mainly. And so we have a great need for a stable career. For our part, we can restore stability to the work from which we earn an income. Stability and security are the goals behind many of our efforts. The forming of an identity for ourselves (10) always turns on the question of security (2). On the one hand, we run the risk of clinging to all sorts of security purely because, if our security is lost or modified, we feel as if we have lost a piece of ourselves. But, on the other hand, we have the need to form a self-image that is practical, sober, and realistic, a self-image with which we can do something; so that, as we become more self-satisfied and better able to accept ourselves (10), we are motivated in other areas of our lives—after all, with a properly functioning self-image, the ruler of the 10th in the 2nd gives us an incentive for activities of every kind (the 2nd house also contains our feelings of satisfaction and dissatisfaction).

The 2nd and 11th House

The Ruler of the 2nd in the 11th

Our need to create and acquire security is concentrated here on friends and on those with similar ideas and tastes to our own. With this house connection, we are liable to let our sense of values and our notion of stability and security depend on the understanding and esteem accorded to us by this circle. In the 11th house lies our need to encounter others as our equals or comrades — not as superiors or inferiors. Yet, with the ruler of the 2nd in the 11th, we can look up to others, because we need them so desperately in order to feel safe and to have a sense of stability. Many of our values, opinions, and motivations can turn out to be borrowed from or, at least, approved by, our friends and colleagues.

Although it is said of this house connection that we spend our money freely on friends and clubs and the like, this is certainly not the rule but simply one possibility. We can use our powers of persuasion and our skills in a wider circle in order to find the security we seek through providing this circle itself with security in a certain way.

There is a great desire for firm friendships; and I have quite often seen, both with the ruler of the 2nd in the 11th and with the ruler of 11th in the 2nd, that an income is earned in a joint venture with friends — we may go into business with them, and so on. But it is equally possible that, with either connection, we do work in which we can give shape to our values and ideas within a greater whole, helped by or for the benefit of people of a like mind. Work in politics or in some communal organization is therefore a distinct possibility.

The Ruler of the 11th in the 2nd

There are more possibilities with this house connection than have already been named. The core of the situation is our need to let friends and like-minded people share our values. Here, too, we seek security in our circle of intimates, but in a different way from the above. Here we are more likely to have preconceived opinions and to find friends for ourselves among those who share these opinions, while with the ruler of the 2nd in the 11th we are more inclined to make friends first and then to arrive at a (sometimes new or modified) pattern of values.

With the ruler of the 11th in the 2nd we are therefore not so dependent on others for the satisfaction of our need for security. Friends and people on the same wavelength as ourselves can give us a big incentive to do or to learn certain things. They stimulate our feelings of satisfaction and dissatisfaction (2) quite powerfully and, by their presence, stir us into activity, provided what we do leads to a sense of security, or to visible results (2).

The 2nd and 12th House

The Ruler of the 2nd in the 12th

We attempt to create and find security in an area of life that is immaterial and in many respects even incomprehensible. To all appearances this is a difficult point: a connection between one of the most material houses and the least material house in the horoscope. However, it need not cause any serious problems. In our search for security, things that others may find hard to understand—such as yoga, meditation, hypnosis, religion, dreams, creative visualization and so on—can give us a sense of safety and stability and, in fact, we can obtain palpable benefits from them.

However, the 12th house is also concerned with less mysterious things, such as self-sacrificing service (voluntary work in the third world, for example) or work in hospitals, prisons, institutions, etc. And, with the ruler of the 2nd in the 12th we can channel very many of our skills and motivations into these activities. In several instances I have observed that, although not working in any of the above spheres, the native did help out in them from time to time because it made him or her feel good. In other instances, the native has had a sympathetic and unselfish attitude regarding work, due perhaps to religious sensibilities or to a social conscience.

The 12th house has something extra-special about it. In this house lies our ability to intuit and enter into what is going on in the stream of time as it flows between past and future. People in whom the 12th house plays an important part often have presentiments. I have frequently found the ruler of the 2nd in the 12th (and the ruler of the 12th in the 2nd) in people who, without being able to say why, did practical things or transacted a piece of business with what later turned out to be perfect timing; all at once, the time was ripe in the community to do something, and they just did it.

With the ruler of the 2nd in the 12th, we can give (much) money to charitable institutions on behalf of good causes, relief work, or the religious needs of humanity; and we seek personal security (2) in the sense of unity with all mankind (12). In some cases, this search for unity can lead to the misuse of alcohol or drugs, or to religious fanaticism. But, in a positive sense, the person with the ruler of the 2nd in the 12th can take an interest in the plight of the underprivileged and can devote his or her means and abilities to helping many of them.

The Ruler of the 12th in the 2nd

With this house connection, 12th house matters are the instrument that can serve to obtain security, but not as in the previous house connection. Here our need to experience unity and to explore the unseen world is subordinate to values, security, and practical requirements. Here, too, we can be gainfully employed in or with things of the 12th house, but the idealistic need to experience unity within ourselves and with others that was so prominent in the previous connection, is directed to more practical ends. "Cosmic consciousness and all that sort of thing is fine," says the ruler of the 12th in the 2nd, "but it must lead to something." However, it is not so easy to shrug things off like this, because on the negative side all sorts of elusive and invisible factors (frustrations, fears, unrecognized collective needs conflicting with personal security) can attack our safety and our material situation. And so one can encounter surprising extremes: uncertain chaos as against a clearly defined motivation in which intuition plays a valued role.

In a negative sense, I have met people with this connection (and also with the ruler of the 2nd in the 12th) who have irresponsibly drawn money on the dole, or did little to help themselves, because the state "has heaps of cash." But, more positively, I have seen the yoga instructor, the dream analyst, and others mentioned in the previous house connection; although, it must always be remembered that personal security and motivation are the ends for which service to others is only the means.

Often, with this connection, there is a great deal of creativity. In fact, the 12th house seems linked to emotional expression in art and music. Anyway this sort of thing (where the tender feelings of the public are stirred) can lead to a sense of security, or even produce an income. There is no need to associate the 12th house with fraud and imprisonment; the number of cases where these occur is very small!

The 3rd House

The Ruler of the 3rd in the 3rd

Our need to examine and classify as many as possible of the facts that we encounter on our path through life, and our thinking and arranging, are concentrated here on their own terrain, besides being the instrument it uses to express itself. This can produce considerable acumen in thinking and analyzing, quick-wittedness in conversations and debates; but, undoubtedly, we do "think for thinking's sake, and speak for the sake of speaking." Because this house is concerned mainly with the way in which we deal with individual facts without co-ordinating or synthesizing them, we are able to master an enormous quantity of impressions and data, but at the risk of not being able to see the forest for the trees and of losing the train of thought. Therefore although, with the ruler of the 3rd in the 3rd, we are usually a mine of information, we do have problems seeing what lies behind all the facts and figures we have accumulated.

This house connection is very helpful in professions demanding flexibility in speech, writing, and gesture, and the mental gift for absorbing new details quickly. Such professions are those of journalist (where a great number of facts have to be taken in at top speed), educator (where we must always be prepared to answer unexpected questions from students and to cope with unscheduled interruptions), and representative (where we need to see the implications of every word the client says and must never be caught napping).

With this house connection we are liable to have a restless, inquiring mind, so that we need to read a lot, to write and/or talk, to transmit facts or goods, to make short contacts, and so on. As a result, we can be very well-read, can discuss any subject, have plenty of business acumen, and are always open to new impressions and indeed welcome them. Unfortunately there is a danger that we shall remain superficial and be quickly distracted, so that we fail to complete anything and are prepared to abandon yesterday's sure thing for the sake of today's top attraction. We can miss making solid contacts because we flit around chattering. Exchanging information comes so easily to us that we are inclined to use it as a mask. Nevertheless, with this connection, we are able to lift people from a deadlock with our unassuming cheerfulness and easy flow of conversation, and to save many an awkward situation with a humorous remark.

The 3rd and 4th House

The Ruler of the 3rd in the 4th

Our thinking and planning, and our need to examine and classify all the facts and things we encounter, are concentrated here on the area to do with home and hearth, our emotional basis, and our ties with family, the past and tradition. Facts, information, and brief contacts (3) play an important part in our emotional life or, more specifically, in family life, so that, for example, a free open exchange of opinions and a flexible contact with other members of the family are very important for our emotional comfort and to make us feel "at home," both literally and metaphorically.

With the 3rd house as the instrument of the 4th, or as a source of emotional security, we can become involved in all sorts of 3rd house activities. For instance, I have often seen the building of a small library in the home, or a collection of magazines or newspapers, a passion for using the domestic telephone, or various people being brought home for a cozy chat. Brief contacts with people of every kind, taking cognizance of the most diverse facts and information, and things that occur to us when we marshal our thoughts (all 3rd house matters) exert a big influence on our ideas of emotional ties, the past, tradition, and so on. The 3rd house also has to do with trade and transport. So a link between the 3rd and the 4th house (the ruler of the 4th in the 3rd in this instance) can give the desire to deal commercially in things involving the home, whether they be houses themselves or the contents and interiors of houses. Sometimes, too, we like writing at home (3) in order to feel emotionally at ease (4). The nature of the writing is not particularly significant, and could be a novel, a poem, a newspaper report, a letter, or a diary.

The Ruler of the 4th in the 3rd

Here our need for emotional security, and our capability for giving warmth and care, are a means of determining our attitude towards facts. In actuality, our subjective feelings play a big part in the way in which we arrange and approach facts, even though we imagine that our thinking is very objective. In a positive sense, we can use our feelings to ascertain or appreciate certain facts, but we can use the same feelings to ignore valuable facts that do not suit our book.

In itself, the 3rd house is very neutral and objective; but, with a 4th house connection, it loses something of its neutrality. With the ruler of the 4th in the 3rd, thinking and analyzing, talking, and writing are not determined by our emotional well-being and the need for emotional security *alone*. Generally speaking, the environment most closely involved in our emotional health, namely the family in which we grew up and the family we ourselves have started, has a strong influence on our attitude toward the mental and contactual activities of the 3rd house.

However, there are so many other possibilities, such as an interest in, or writing about, things such as the manners and customs of one's country, folklore, genealogy, family psychology, history, and everything else to do with the country, the native soil, and one's roots. Perhaps there is a gift for the imaginative representation on paper of an emotional atmosphere in the form of folk tales and fairy stories, or an interest in sayings and proverbs. In short, the varied 3rd house is protean in its possibilities. But with the ruler of the 4th in the 3rd, it is our feelings and our need for emotional security, and our capacity to be loving and caring, that form the basis. Facts themselves (3) remain the endpoint.

The 3rd and 5th House

The Ruler of the 3rd in the 5th

Our thinking and planning, and our need to examine and arrange all the facts and things that present themselves to us, are concentrated on the area of gambling and pleasure, creativity and children, and on all the things that give us a sense of self-confidence and authority. We are preoccupied with recreations such as hobbies and sport, with what brings enjoyment (from family outings to interests demanding a lot of hard work), or with things that gratify us because we can put something of ourselves into them (as an entertainer, for example), or we can use them to prove our worth (perhaps as the member of some board of governors or directors).

Writing, drawing, calligraphy, linguistics, trade, transport, quizzes and intelligence tests, and many other 3rd house concerns can become favorite occupations. Also we may approach various 5th house matters, such as looking after children and playing sports and games, in a 3rd house manner; in other words, we may think about them, enjoy reading, writing, or talking about them, and so on. Often, with the ruler of the 3rd in the 5th, we desire to discover as much as possible about subjects that fascinate us and, in this way, to increase our self-confidence. What is more, we like the contacts and give-and-take (3) that give us reassurance. Sometimes, too, we prefer to trace ideas in broad outline rather than to pore over their details, and are more concerned with organization than with practical performance.

The Ruler of the 5th in the 3rd

With this house connection, the need of self-confidence and authority, and of entertainments, games and hobbies, is an instrument both of thought and speech. We desire to impart an air of authority to our words and to make our presence felt in brief contacts, and frequently do so with ease. The 5th house always seeks the agreeable and romantic side of life, and this is an attitude we can express in words and gestures. That is why we meet the ruler of the 5th in the 3rd in individuals who can sweet-talk others so charmingly that the latter are unaware that the conversation is being manipulated. Taking a lead in 3rd house activities can be another outlet.

The need for playfulness in our thinking and speaking often puts us in a good position to understand the fun-thinking of children, and therefore this house connection is helpful for teachers of toddlers and younger children (the same is true of the ruler of the 3rd in the 5th). The 3rd house is inevitably concerned in the transmission of knowledge and information, and teaching material can be presented in an entertaining and spontaneous way.

With the ruler of the 5th in the 3rd, favorite activities can sometimes influence or alter our thinking, either directly or indirectly. For example, by training hard for a certain sport, we can discover certain links between mind and body that give us a completely different outlook on all sorts of things. But contacts with children (5) or giving full rein to the playful element in ourselves, can switch our thoughts to another track and give us a fresh approach to facts and information.

The 3rd and 6th House

The Ruler of the 3rd in the 6th

Our thinking, planning, and a need to examine and classify all the facts and figures we encounter are focused on the area of life where we find our work and service. Therefore our thinking is mostly very practical and down-to-earth; we feel compelled to do something with information, contacts, and the like, and not seldom we possess a remarkably keen eye for details, and are good at filling in work schedules. In our work we can use all sorts of activity belonging to the 3rd house. Often, part of our work consists of the collecting and arranging of facts (library or journalistic work, etc.), or the transmission of facts and information (teaching, commerce, etc.), or marshalling facts and figures into a scheme (bookkeeping, programming, etc.).

However, the 3rd house possesses a certain restlessness and curiosity that can influence our behavior at work. We have a great desire for change and a constant flow of new impressions in our sphere of work, which can turn us into a Jack-of-all-trades and master of none, but can also give us a very flexible attitude to work and a liking for going on many small business trips.

There is often considerable mental interest in health matters, and a fondness for reading and talking about a proper diet and sensible living. But I have not always seen this knowledge put into practice. The 6th house also shows our attitude toward objective reality. The ruler of the 3rd in the 6th is found regularly in the charts of those who like to fit in and do what is generally accepted (although there must be nothing in the rest of the chart that contradicts this). With the ruler of the 3rd in the 6th, thinking is governed by objective reality, and the native's code of conduct is usually that one should do one's duty in a sensible and practical manner whatever it may be.

The Ruler of the 6th in the 3rd

Here the desire to apply our analysis of our situation in concrete and useful ways and our need to work and to be of service, are focused (internally) on our thought processes and (externally) on brief contacts. In other words, practical usefulness and attention to detail are the instruments of our thought, so that this house connection offers all kinds of opportunities for purposeful, systematic, and pragmatic thinking. We need suitable facts that we use in a practical way, which is different from the need to do something practical with facts that come to hand. There is a subtle distinction here. In the latter case, any facts whatever can be put to good, concrete use; but, with the ruler of the 6th in the 3rd, there is a prior choice of facts; above all, we seek practical and useful information.

Our desire to work and to be of service also expresses itself in the sphere of the 3rd house, so that we find all sorts of 3rd house matters turned into work. With the ruler of the 6th in the 3rd, our thinking (3) is often critical (6), and there is a danger of niggling and faultfinding, we need to make sure we are not going about rapping people's knuckles. With this house connection, work, service (6) and contacts (3) are fused, which can signify all sorts of things, such as brief contacts in which we make ourselves useful (the 6th is the instrument of the 3rd here) or which have to do with our work. In casual conversation (3) we can exchange ideas on all kinds of 6th house subjects, for instance on health matters, but also on work in the broadest sense, on the economy, or on how we ourselves make both ends meet, etc.

The 3rd and 7th House

The Ruler of the 3rd in the 7th

Our thinking and planning and a need to examine and arrange all the facts and figures we encounter, are concentrated here on the partner and on teamwork. Our partner or a close friend are therefore very decisive for the way in which we view the world; every form of exchange with them is very important. And so the partner has to be someone to whom we can talk. We need a partner who has a lively mind, whose interest is quickly aroused in all sorts of things; someone who continues to intrigue us even when satisfying our curiosity. Variety (the 3rd house is a restless house!) is also very necessary in the relationship. Not that we want many relationships, simply a partner who can keep us fascinated, especially on the mental plane (3).

Because the 3rd house (thinking) is subordinate to the 7th (the partner or companion), there is a danger of being too readily influenced by those who are close to us, and of trying to ape what they think and say. The other side of the coin is that we are prepared to listen to the thoughts and opinions of others without shutting our minds to them.

A link between two houses involved in contacts and communication usually gives a great need for give-and-take, both with specific persons and in general. If the rest of the horoscope is not too much at variance with it, we can, with such a house connection, have a good command of words and a knack of keeping in touch with people. For instance, in company, we know how to keep the party going by telling a joke or by giving an amusing turn to the conversation (we find this with the ruler of the 7th in the 3rd, too). In conversations and in other mental activities, we are concerned with creating a balance, with opening up stiff and formal talks, with preserving harmony, with maintaining contacts and a friendly atmosphere by diplomatic behavior and tactful speech.

The Ruler of the 7th in the 3rd

We find diplomatic speech and behavior with this house connection, too. Our need for harmony, balance, and a flexible and humane contact with the other person (the life partner, companion, or even the opposite number in general), is invariably an instrument of our thought and speech. As already said, friendly conversation, placidity, diplomacy and the like, are found here, too. Also there is a need for mental exchange with the partner; but, here, we are the ones who more often decide the topics discussed. Nevertheless, the partner's opinion is certainly valued, and he or she can always stimulate our contactual and mental activities.

In matters such as trade, traffic, the conveyance of facts and goods (3), we often see a concrete involvement with the partner, who helps us earn our living by them: the partner is then an actual assistant, or helps to supply facts and information, or gives advice. The partner's opinion and involvement is very important to us.

Sometimes the effect of this house connection is more abstract; and then the 7th house no longer represents the other person or our attitude toward this person, but rather a need for beauty, harmony, and balance. The potential of this connection includes cultured speech, fine writing, and the ability to improve the way in which one's thoughts are expressed in order to make them more flexible and pleasant to the ear, and so on.

The 3rd and 8th House

The Ruler of the 3rd in the 8th

Our thinking and planning—and the need to examine all the facts and everything we encounter—are concentrated here on the area of life involving confrontation with ourself, profound searching in general, and the desire to challenge life. Our thoughts are occupied with what lies *behind* phenomena, and with seeking the essence of things. However, by doing this, we confront ourselves with our repressions, complexes, and neurotic tendencies, which also lie in the 8th. The consequences can vary considerably: a fear of death we are unable to banish from our minds, fear of exposing our inmost thoughts when talking to others, persistent looking for hidden drives in ourselves and others—which, in the course of our lives, can give us a good knowledge of the human heart—and so on. Much depends on the approach to the solution of problems, but one thing is certain: with the ruler of the 3rd in the 8th, contacts, conversations, mental activity, reading and writing, are all instruments in carrying out the search for a solution. Quite often, while reading something, it does not have to be anything special, we can get a flash of memory or inspiration and exclaim, "This describes me and my problems exactly!" or something of the sort. Such confrontations can help us see the reason for our predicament and can assist us to resolve it.

Another keyword of the 8th house is intensity. We seek intensity through our thinking, and use facts to give shape to this intensity. However, this house also has to do with power, usually needed to mask our insecurity, and less often displayed as an expression of personal equilibrium by which we automatically radiate power and authority. On this account, our thoughts (3) can turn on themes to do with power; but sometimes the emphasis is on trading (3) in those things where important interests (8) are at stake, such as in the world of high finance (banks, insurance brokers, etc.).

Sometimes our way of talking and communicating is cynical or provocative, often because of our need to see how far we can go and whether we can draw the other person out.

The Ruler of the 8th in the 3rd

Our search for intensity and profundity, but also our confrontation with ourself, are the instruments here of the 3rd house, that is to say of our thinking, our contacts, and so on. Consequently, we are quite likely to look for facts and contacts that have more to offer than trivia and tittle-tattle. This connection brings composure to the restless and rambling 3rd house. We pursue a line of thought more persistently and consider matters in greater depth. However, our need for conversations that have some substance can cause problems. In itself the 3rd house gives easy-going, informal contacts; but, with the ruler of the 8th in the 3rd, we have little taste for such contacts, as they do not have much to offer us. This can produce taciturnity (seeing everything and saying next to nothing); it can also produce the use of our influence (power is a feature of the 8th) to steer conversations, possibly in a manner that is too forceful and manipulative.

The 8th house also has to do with problem-solving, and has an inbuilt mechanism for repressing whatever we cannot or will not solve. Often the act of repression gives us a desperate desire to hide our insecurity by showing ourselves to be well-informed. We may insulate ourselves by blocking genuine contacts and by insisting on imposing our own style on conversations.

Where we have more balance, we can, with the ruler of the 8th in the 3rd, encourage ourselves and others to look at the things mentioned in greater depth from fresh standpoints. We can carry out research into traffic and transport problems, or deficiencies in trade or education, etc. We use our abilities to tackle problems with thorough intensity in the terrain of the 3rd house so as to introduce or carry out improvements.

The 3rd and 9th House

The Ruler of the 3rd in the 9th

Our thinking and planning and our need to examine and arrange all the facts and figures we encounter, are directed toward the widening of our horizon, the synthesis of facts, the framing of a philosophy of life and the formation of our own opinion. All that we see, hear or read, contributes, in this house connection, to our personal vision, and we try to fit it into our existing view of life and society. If the new facts do not fit, with this connection, we are usually prepared to accommodate them by modifying our views.

We have a great need to discuss things that transcend everyday cares: things such as religion, philosophy, distant lands, freedom, study, and so on. What is more, the 9th house also represents the propogation of knowledge and truth. With a connection between the 3rd and 9th houses, we are particularly keen to write on certain subjects, or to deliver lectures, or something to the same effect; and, in doing so, we hate to leave any fact unused. Knowledge and information are instrumental in the formation of our judgment and we use them as a vehicle for our opinions. This can have various results. It can bestow a pseudo-objectivity: we let the facts "speak for themselves," but forget that (because what we are doing is finally in the interests of the 9th house) we may well be employing these facts as a mouthpiece for our opinion, so that they are "colored." But with this connection there can also be a need to share some vision, symbolic picture, or ideal when writing, speaking or lecturing and the like. This could apply to political pamphlets, or to fairy tales containing a moral. For the message of the 9th house demands a hearing. This house connection often gives good powers of expression, but with a danger of tactlessness (9th house).

The Ruler of the 9th in the 3rd

With this connection we already have a preconceived opinion, vision, or philosophy of life (9) to use as an instrument of our contacts, thoughts, conversation, and research. This colors the facts for which we are looking; we keep a sharp lookout for things which will help us widen our horizon. From a somewhat different background from that of the ruler of the 3rd in the 9th, the native's opinions can be biased with the ruler of the 9th in the 3rd. Incidentally, this has nothing to do with dishonesty: generally speaking, it is just the result of a strong attachment to a certain idea or ideal that we have wholeheartedly espoused and therefore plays an important part in our informal contacts (3). We must take care not to adopt a lecturing style of speaking or set ourselves up as guardians of our neighbors' morals. On the other hand, we can make outstanding use of our stimulating powers of persuasion to convey knowledge and information; so this is a good connection for educators. With the ruler of the 3rd in the 9th, all sorts of facts contribute to the formation of a judgment, opinion, idea, or ideal; with the ruler of the 9th in the 3rd, we start with an ideal, idea, opinion, or judgment and look for the facts that will substantiate it.

The 3rd and 10th House

The Ruler of the 3rd in the 10th

Our thinking and planning, and the need to examine and arrange all the facts and figures we encounter, are concentrated here because we desire to carve out an identity, to form a (clear) self-image on the basis of what we are able to do. We also desire to present a certain picture to the world, a picture that will enable us to function in society. All sorts of 3rd house matters, such as the gathering and classifying of information, talking and exchanging, can become our means of approach to the outside world. Often, with such a connection, we make an effort to be communicative; we start conversations easily and give the impression that it is easy to talk to us. The rest of the chart will show the extent to which this impression is true.

Planets in the 10th quite often provide information about the type of work we do (the 10th house is the house of social position), and the ruler of the 3rd in the 10th can indicate a profession in which communications, contacts, information, analysis, and above all variety, play an important part.

With this connection, our thinking (3) is used to build structures (10) and, with the ruler of the 3rd in the 10th our analytical ability will be devoted partly to structuring, and also to the laying down of rules.

Our ideas tend to be practical and concerned with our social life; they are also concerned with the formation of a personal identity.

The Ruler of the 10th in the 3rd

With this house connection, too, thinking and the need for structure go hand in hand. Here the desire to sort, define, and classify finds an outlet in the arranging and ordering of facts and in making practical use of them. I have often observed very purposeful thinking and speaking with the ruler of the 10th in the 3rd (and, for that matter, with the ruler of 3 in 10). With the ruler of the 10th in the 3rd, the process of forming an identity affects the way we interpret and codify facts; also we try to exercise authority in affairs of the 3rd house in order to impose ourselves on society.

We can be communicative, but not in the same way as in the previous house connection. With the ruler of the 3rd in the 10th contacts, communication, talking, and thinking are means of approach to the outside world; but, with the ruler of the 10th in the 3rd, we seek the identity and the resource to take part in community life in the sphere of contacts, communication, talking, thinking, and—what we must not forget—our aim is to find and recognize ourselves in the 3rd house area of life, so that it becomes more especially a goal. As with the ruler of the 5th in the 3rd we may be guilty of talking down to people, because we want them to share our picture of ourselves and of our place in society. This, and the fact that we sometimes identify with our knowledge, can lead to rigid opinions and hobby-horses on the one hand, but to soundly structured lines of thought on the other.

That we tend to speak in an authoritative manner can stand us in good stead in the world of commerce, for example, because our down-to-earth eloquence carries conviction (with the ruler of the 9th in the 3rd, we have the power to pass on information convincingly; with the ruler of the 10th in the 3rd, we are much more direct, and have aims to achieve). With the ruler of the 3rd in the 10th, facts, contacts and information can help us to acquire authority, while with the ruler of the 10th in the 3rd, our authority, or rather identity, is something we wish to express in contacts or in our handling of facts, so that we can prove our worth in these things. So, once more, there is a difference in background even though the effects are practically identical.

The 3rd and 11th House

The Ruler of the 3rd in the 11th

Our thinking, planning, and the need to examine and classify all the facts and figures that present themselves to us are focused on a desire for contacts with people of similar thoughts and outlook, with friends, and with those to whom, somehow or other we feel inwardly related. Our thoughts are taken up with these people, with the possible result that we all too readily accept their opinions and modes of thought and let them determine the way in which we see and interpret facts, that is to say, the way in which we arrange and elucidate our thoughts. We long to engage in mental give-and-take with others, and have a great need to converse with friends and to exchange information with them. In itself, this connection shows good contactual ability.

In the 11th house, we also find the power to break through fixed forms and limits to discover the value of people who are completely different from ourselves. And so, with the ruler of the 3rd in the 11th, we can introduce a certain originality into our thinking, speaking, and analyzing, because our thinking is an instrument in transcending forms in the widest possible sense. Also we eagerly make contacts because of a belief in equality. However, our so-called equality can end up looking very much like inequality if we give way to the tendency to let others guide our thinking. If we manage to avoid this danger, the ruler of the 3rd in the 11th can provide a two-way stimulus for a living exchange of impressions and opinions with friends and mentally congenial companions.

Sometimes, due to restlessness (3), we can expect too much of our circle of friends, and can become fickle and changeable. Less hurtfully, we can seek friends who are themselves full of change and variety. Sometimes this connection (and also the ruler of the 11th in the 3rd) can indicate a liking for less usual forms of communication, such as sign-language for the deaf, the decipherment of old scripts, the decoding of secret messages, and so on.

The Ruler of the 11th in the 3rd

Our need of friends, of contacts with like-minded people, and of equality as such, and our need to break through fixed boundaries, are the instrument for our thinking, analyzing and ordering of facts. This frequently leads to an uninhibited, even provocative, approach to people who are high up the social ladder. Since the 11th house is the instrument, considerable stimulus can be derived from the circle of people with the same mental outlook as our own; nevertheless, our own thoughts and ideas (3rd house) will always come first with us. The essence of this connection is that our genuine friends are restricted to those who share our mental and contactual preferences.

As we have just said, friends and those who are congenial spirits can serve as mental stimuli: we look for exchange of information and enjoy talking to them. Sometimes this gives a desire to have many friends, each of whom can arouse and satisfy our curiosity in some special field of interest; the danger being that too many contacts for the sake of information and impressions will lead to superficiality, and that we shall fail to make the sort of friends from whom we can adopt values that will give direction to our thinking in a highly individual manner (11). A single friendship, based chiefly on mental exchange, can help to deepen our thinking and can impart originality to the way in which we gather and classify facts. Independent thought, combined with a willingness to listen to others who are on the same wavelength, remains one of the characteristics of the ruler of the 11th in the 3rd.

The 3rd and 12th House

The Ruler of the 3rd in the 12th

Our thinking, planning, and the need to examine and classify all the facts we encounter, are brought to bear on a longing for unity, a need for detachment and isolation, and an interest in a rich inner life. Very often, with this connection, we are concerned with such things as dream-life, meditation, yoga, fairy tales, myths, and legends, especially for their symbolism and deeper meaning. We are able to sense, understand, and often explain to others, the more esoteric aspects of life. Perhaps, due to our feeling for the emblematic, we write poetry or prose that touches a tender chord in our readers.

There is a danger that we may confuse dream with reality, because our fantasy and powers of imagination are so well-developed. Although some astrologers assert that, with this connection and also with the ruler of the 12th in the 3rd, we are somehow lacking intellectually. My own experience shows that this is wholly without foundation. Certainly, with these house connections, linear, causal thinking can mature rather later than usual, because of the need to dwell longer in the mythic phase. However, it is striking that people with this connection possess a remarkable type of memory and, by making cross-connections and putting two and two together, can fill in details that they do not know for a fact.

If we have this connection, then we are capable of being perfectly happy on our own, enjoying 3rd house pursuits such as reading, writing, poetry, or prose, preparing lessons or lectures, and so on. It is during these solitary hours that we often get our best ideas and inspiration. On the other hand, with the placement of the ruler of the 3rd in the 12th, communication is not a strong point. With this connection, we are sometimes inclined to react not to what is said, but what is probably intended. We can divine what is left unspoken; but it is not always wise to blurt out such things. Sometimes we find it hard to concentrate because we are easily distracted by our rich inner life.

The Ruler of the 12th in the 3rd

Our longing for unity, our sensitivity and sympathy, our need for isolation and detachment, and our desire to enjoy the things of the spirit, are instruments of our thinking and planning, our speech and gestures, and our need to exchange goods and ideas. This gives various results. We can make outstanding use of our empathy (12) in trade, where a knack of spotting fast-selling lines and of knowing what arguments a customer will find persuasive are very important.

What is more, intuition plays a significant part in all our contacts, because we are more or less inclined to react to the emotional content of words and intonations, and thus not to what is actually said but to what may well be intended—just as with the ruler of the 3rd in the 11th. But with this difference that, with the ruler of the 3rd in the 12th, contacts and conversations sometimes lead to inexplicable feelings that determine our reactions although we do not have a proper hold on them; while, with the ruler of the 12th in the 3rd, we already have an uncomfortable feeling when entering into a conversation that we ought to be on our guard. So we are quicker on the mark.

With the ruler of the 3rd in the 12th, there is a lack of concentration because our fantasy runs away with us all the time. With the ruler of the 12th in the 3rd, there can be a similar lack of concentration, but now because our approach to things is rather chaotic (12), or because we have to settle down and collect our thoughts. And sometimes we are so good at reading between the lines that we tend to become sidetracked. However we can also discover valuable information in this way.

All sorts of 12th house matters can play a part in our thinking and talking. Thus we may feel the need to correspond with others on various (sometimes Utopian or unrealistic) ideals. Collective needs, the care of the aged, of the mentally disabled, of drug addicts, and of others requiring help (12), can interest us, and we may teach or write about them.

Frequently, with a connection between the 12th and the 3rd house, we approach facts in a naive or childish manner. With the ruler of the 3rd in the 12th, it is the facts themselves that sound a certain chord in us and we try to harmonize this with religious sentiments, a need to experience unity, or some ideal to which we devote ourselves. But, with the ruler of the 12th in the 3rd, we are already inclined to look at facts in a somewhat unrealistic way — through rose-tinted glasses.

Secret anxieties also lie hidden in the 12th, and these can feed our thoughts with the ruler of the 12th in the 3rd. On the other hand, our thoughts can draw inspiration from the measure of idealism and religious feeling found in both connections. With the ruler of the 3rd in the 12th, we can use all sorts of information, facts, and contacts, to inspire us. With the ruler of the 12th in the 3rd, a certain inspiration is already an instrument of our thoughts and contacts.

The 4th House

The Ruler of the 4th in the 4th

Our need for emotional security and comfort, the desire to care and be cared for, to cherish and be cherished, and the longing for domesticity can all express here in undiluted form. We have an unusually strong need for emotional warmth and safety which we also like to give to others. Our attitude is probably a very caring one. This can be good or bad. For example, on the one hand, we can be a loving parent who builds a safe and cozy nest; but, on the other hand, we can be a chivvying parent who holds children and everyone else in the home in a firm and almost smothering embrace, ostensibly for their own good, but mainly for our own emotional reassurance. Wherever we are, we have the ability, if we will, to create a warm air of domesticity, and will really be in our element when we are in surroundings where we feel at home and have the opportunity to make our neighbors, acquaintances, and friends welcome, so that we can mother them. The mainspring of our actions is a powerfully developed desire to look after others and to mean something to them.

Quite often there is a strong attachment to the old home or to one of the parents. The rest of the horoscope will show whether this attachment is felt to be agreeable or oppressive by the native. In this connection, we should note that to make a special stand against the influence our parents have had over us is a form of psychological attachment to them. With this house connection, we often bestow much time, money, and/or energy on things to do with family, hearth, and home. In real terms, this can mean a house in which attention is paid to the appointments, but more with a view to comfort than to decor. Sometimes (if the rest of the chart does not contradict), people with a prominent 4th house like to furnish their dwellings as trendily as possible in order to win general approval.

Frequently we have an interest in, or a feeling for, folk art, tradition and so on, or we are extremely patriotic or nationalistic.

The 4th and 5th House

The Ruler of the 4th in the 5th

Our need for emotional security and comfort, and the desire to care and to be cared for, to cherish and to be cherished, are focused on the area of games and pleasure, creativity, children, and on all those things that give us a sense of self-confidence and authority. The creation of a warm, comfortable environment gives us pleasure, makes us more self-assured, adds to the enjoyment of our hobbies, and so on. With a house connection such as this, we may be adept at organizing things for children, and may also be involved in the management of other things that have to do, either directly or indirectly, with caring for others. We may be entrusted with looking after the needs of people in other areas beside our own. We throw ourselves heart and soul into running charity events, bazaars, and so on. Here, unlike the previous house connection, the good cause (in which we are emotionally involved) is a means to an end; our own satisfaction and assumption of a leading role is what matters to us most.

Also we can arrange our domestic life (4) in such a way that it revolves around our many hobbies. With this placement, I have regularly seen that the native's environment, even in youth, has encouraged hobbies and creativity. Sometimes home life suffers from an overemphasis on sport, amusements, gambling, or pleasure. With this connection, we can spend quite some time away from home looking for the emotional satisfaction to be derived from adventure or romance. Then the house we live in is simply a point of departure and return. In the vast majority of cases, home and hobbies are blended, and, with the ruler of the 4th in the 5th, our house and household are subordinated to a desire for entertainment or our absorption in some serious pursuit.

The Ruler of the 5th in the 4th

Hobbies and home are linked by this house connection, too, but now much more in the sense that the hobbies give shape to domestic life and, figuratively, provide us with an emotional base. The same is true of the other 5th house matters, such as amusements, sports, children, creativity, and ambition. Also these primarily serve to improve emotional well-being, and they show how we set up our home life. Hobbies may be used directly or indirectly to improve home and environment.

The attachment to hearth and home is often great: we take pleasure in expressing ourselves in the domestic sphere. Quite often, people with this placement convert their residence into a sort of home base for their operations. If, with the ruler of the 5th in the 4th, we wish to experience a sense of emotional security, then it is virtually essential to have a regular opportunity to do—within the home environment—certain things we like doing, such as rummaging through our papers and spending time on our hobbies (free from any responsibility), while displaying a certain measure of authority. For all these things are instruments for building up a sense of security. In both house connections (the ruler of the 4th in the 5th and the ruler of the 5th in the 4th) I have seen people who proudly put their homes on display; then the ostentation of the 5th house and the actual domestic environment are combined. But in most cases there is merely a great attachment to the home and an interest in doing everything possible to make it a pleasant place in which to live.

The 4th and 6th House

The Ruler of the 4th in the 6th

Our need for domesticity, emotional comfort, safety, and our desire to care and to be cared for, to cherish and to be cherished, are focused here on work and the working environment, on service, and on the sort of contemplation and critical analysis required for useful activities. We want to be occupied in looking after and mothering others and in creating a homely atmosphere. Usually we try to bring an air of cozy informality to our work. This is an outstanding connection for all kinds of housekeepers and those holding similar positions.

We have a great need to be happy in our work, and are more inclined than others to mope if the atmosphere is uncongenial or if the job is repugnant to us. On the other hand, we can throw ourselves heart and soul into work we enjoy and that gives us an outlet, whatever that work may be.

Because we look for emotional security in an area that represents our habit of critical analysis, subjective emotional impressions (as a means or instrument) can impair our objectivity. Our point of view is always subjective. With the ruler of the 6th in the 4th on the other hand, our critical ability is usually brought to bear on matters that interest us or in which we feel at home, so that it is not the point of view but the topic to be criticized that is determined subjectively.

With the ruler of the 4th in the 6th, there is sometimes a great emotional interest in health, disease, and diet. If we are active in one of these or in a related field, we can carry out our task in a warm, understanding, and caring way. Service to others and humane feelings are closely linked with this connection. With the ruler of the 4th in the 6th, the impulse to help others is usually emotional and we like to do so caringly, whereas, with the ruler of the 6th in the 4th we use helping others (and may even need to help others) in order to feel good and to know we are wanted. In the latter instance, we are not so paternal or maternal in our behavior.

The Ruler of the 6th in the 4th

Service to others is the instrument of our search for emotional security. We can use expressions of various 6th house characteristics to improve our home life. Service to others can take the form of helping, or making the house attractive to them, and can give us a feeling of satisfaction. It can also take the form of slaving away at constant cleaning and polishing, but this is simply a possibility, not a rule. Working at home or doing work in which our own house plays an important part, will often be found with this connection. Also, we frequently feel a need either to take work home because it is more agreeable to do it inside our personal environment than it is outside, or to do work that puts us in touch with ourselves and our feelings, and makes us more serene. Whether the work is writing, bookkeeping, sweeping, or polishing is immaterial.

Sometimes, with this connection, we wish to do something particularly useful (6) for our country or our family (6); which is just as likely to lead to political activism as it is to cultivating the kitchen garden. The keynote is the psychic need; the practical results can take many forms.

The 4th and 7th House

The Ruler of the 4th in the 7th

Our need for domesticity, emotional comfort, and security, and a desire to care and to be cared for, to cherish and to be cherished, are focused here on the life partner. Our peace of mind depends largely on the happiness of our relationship, because our opposite number (7) is the end-point in this house connection. We hope to obtain emotional warmth from the other person, look for a fatherly or motherly type, and ourselves show care and concern in the relationship. Domesticity, emotional warmth, and the like, are all needed to make the relationship meaningful.

At the same time, we run the risk of losing something of ourselves, because we are inclined to wrap our opposite number in cotton wool or to meet the partner more than halfway in some other respect for the sake of the emotional tie and emotional response. If we have independent traits shown elsewhere in the chart, we shall find this something of a problem. The 7th house indicates companionship. With the ruler of the 4th in the 7th, sometimes the result is teamwork with a close relative or someone who is like a member of the family to us. In this case, our affection for this other person is very great.

The Ruler of the 7th in the 4th

With this house connection, just as with the ruler of the 4th in the 7th, we seek a domestic partner, one who is caring and kind, and who makes a big contribution to our sense of security. But there is a difference from the foregoing connection. There the way in which we try to give shape to our need for domestic and emotional security is subordinate to the wishes of the partner; whereas, with the ruler of the 7th in the 4th, the partner has to fit in with, or be resigned to, our way of doing things. That is why we are liable to find this aspect in people who have, or wish to have, a docile, caring partner, one who offers a safe home port, irrespective of whether the native spends much time in it or not. Sometimes, too, we find collaboration with a close relative when this connection appears in the chart; in which case the collaboration often has to do with family possessions and interests, or with other things that have to do with home and hearth, security, or maybe tradition and the native land. With the ruler of the 7th in the 4th, the partner has to fit into our sphere. With the ruler of the 4th in the 7th, we are more likely to fit into theirs.

The 4th and 8th House

The Ruler of the 4th in the 8th

Our need for domesticity, emotional security, and a desire to care and to be cared for, to cherish and to be cherished, are focused here on the area of life and death, inner struggles, repression, and hidden gifts or talents. Generally speaking, this means that the field in which we are seeking security has little security to offer in the first instance.

On a number of occasions, people with a 4th house-8th house axis (both the ruler of the 4th in the 8th and the ruler of the 8th in the 4th) have confided to me that, in their youth, they suffered some trauma or experienced an emotional upheaval which left deep traces, although what happened was later repressed. With the ruler of the 4th in the 8th, we feel emotionally vulnerable, and find it very difficult to show our hand. Therefore we tend to allow few, perhaps too few, to share our inner and our emotional life. We need tender care and affection but find it hard to let this be known; and so we often keep at arm's length the very thing for which we long. Nevertheless, even though our emotional sensitivity is so acute, we can achieve a great deal with this connection.

We may display enormous application and intensity when we are emotionally involved: the 8th house always has to do with depth and intensity. Our emotions and a desire for companionship and home life, that our sensitivity makes us hide, can prove to be the incentive to get through to ourselves and others and to gain deep psychological insights. Inner peace (of mind), or a place where we feel at home, or emotional involvement (4) are invariably a key for unlocking unconscious and repressed problems.

Now, in fact, the fourth house can have a good effect here. I have often observed that people with the ruler of the 8th in the 4th or the ruler of the 4th in the 8th are prepared to give psychological support to people with family troubles. Insight and understanding, with the ruler of the 4th in the 8th, flow mainly from the fact that we ourselves experience (or have experienced) very strong emotions, which are the point from which we set out in search of answers.

With this connection we can experience a powerful emotional attraction to esoteric and secret teachings, parapsychology, or the subjects of force and strategy.

The Ruler of the 8th in the 4th

When we discover a way to deal with repressed or unconscious problems we gain a feeling of emotional stability. We need to dig deep and penetrate to the core of things, and we have a desire to confront ourselves with everything: our complexes, neuroses, hidden gifts, and talents. We focus here on comfort and security both emotionally and, more concretely, in the home. Here, too, we find an initial situation that is insecure. Events or situations in our youth have left deep traces behind (whether or not we are prepared to recognize this is another matter). We have an enormous need for an intense emotional link with our environment. Frequently, this need is more than the environment can satisfy. Sometimes we are too demanding; sometimes there is little or no rapport with those around us. The quest for emotional comfort and security can be conducted so unconsciously that we have no idea what claims we are making on others, or why they are grumbling.

Another effect is that we feel so vulnerable that we insulate ourselves by devoting ourselves completely to a certain avocation — usually something to do with caring, in the broadest possible sense.

Sooner or later, with this placement, we make huge changes in our lifetime. I have seen big changes (usually for the better) in people with the ruler of the 8th in the 4th, subsequent to a change in attitude toward their childhood, the past, their home and family, or emotional ties in general.

We can develop a fine appreciation of child and family psychology; but, when we ignore emotional problems when they arise, we may still resort to forcefulness and manipulation. This forcefulness then becomes an instrument for expressing our feelings. Only when we have a secure position of authority, in small things as well as in great, do we dare to display affection and domesticity. Therefore, with this house connection there are two extremes (besides all the nuances in between), namely the (fortunately rare) domestic dictator and the family psychologist.

Finally, it often happens that we invest a great deal of effort or money into a plot of land, our own house, or our own domestic surroundings, with resulting peace of mind, however restless the ruler of the 8th in the 4th may be initially.

The 4th and 9th House

The Ruler of the 4th in the 9th

Our need for domesticity, emotional comfort, security, and our desire to care and to be cared for, to cherish and to be cherished, are expressed here in the area of travel, both physical (to foreign countries) and mental (study, philosophizing, etc.), and in the area of the formation of opinions and the passing of judgments. Although we sometimes see a literal fulfillment in the form of a home (4) abroad (9), or parents (4) associated in some way with another land (9), as foreign nationals for example, foreign places need not enter into our situation at all. Psychologically, this connection often signifies that we try to express our feelings, especially our caring ones, in opinions and judgments that relate to the kind of (self-)education we pursue, or our philosophy of life. Our feelings on some subject, or on how we think things ought to be play a large part in our psychological development.

Since the 9th house also has to do with the propagation of our own views, the ruler of the 4th in the 9th sometimes gives such an emotive style of exposition, that philosophical views are explained in a theatrical or dramatic way. The 9th house is also involved in the search for a synthesis. Apart from the fact that our emotions are directly involved in the way in which a synthesis is attempted, the ruler of the 4th in the 9th can also mean that we want to include our feelings in a wider, sometimes comic, context, with the danger that we may rationalize them. With the ruler of the 4th in the 9th, domestic life and the family can loom large in the native's (self-)study or spiritual evolution.

The Ruler of the 9th in the 4th

With the ruler of the 9th in the 4th, the family is not an instrument of our spiritual evolution, but we use our philosophy of life and our religious or social convictions as materials for our family life in a literal sense and as an emotional basis in a figurative sense. In this connection, we often meet people who advocate a certain freedom (for parent and child) in rearing children and in family relationships. Both with the ruler of the 4th in the 9th and with the ruler of the 9th in the 4th, I have seen that, in his or her immediate environment (the family) the native found the necessary encouragement to study or develop in some special way.

With the ruler of the 9th in the 4th, we can sometimes experience a liberating peace of mind when we feel or intuit for ourselves the meaning of life, love and sorrow; the meaning of things lies in the 9th house, and here that house is always the instrument that helps in the formation of the 4th. With the ruler of the 4th in the 9th we saw that peace of mind contributes to the native's spiritual evolution. But, with the ruler of the 9th in the 4th, the spiritual evolution contributes to the formation and maintenance of domestic and emotional security.

We can devote ourselves to a certain ideal, or else in the background prepare the way for others to devote themselves to it. Sometimes such an ideal becomes a part of us very early in life, forming the climate in which we grow up (religious climate or humanistic climate), but that is not always the case. Even in our later years, more recently formed ideals and opinions are important in this connection.

The 4th and 10th House

The Ruler of the 4th in the 10th

Our need for domesticity, emotional comfort, security, and our desire to care and to be cared for, to cherish and to be cherished, are concentrated here on our need to carve out an identity, and to strive for a certain degree of authority and a certain social position, in keeping with the image that we have of our place in the outside world. This house connection can be encountered in people who invest a great deal of energy in furthering their careers, while the whole family has to help (willingly or unwillingly) or suffers temporary neglect. For some, the work relates to hearth and home, and caring activities, and contributes to the social position in some way. For example, the nursing profession, interior decoration, "meals on wheels" for the aged, and so on, can provide a function in the community. Often we want work in which we can become emotionally involved. Sometimes, in spite of the need to build a career, we are so sensitive and vulnerable that we prefer to play an important part behind the scenes rather than to step into the limelight.

The 4th and 10th houses also represent parental influence; and, both with the ruler of the 4th in the 10th and with the ruler of the 10th in the 4th, our parents have had an important influence on us. Irrespective of the rest of the horoscope, we find in both placements either a strong bond that leads us to follow in the footsteps of our elders, or else a strong reaction that impels us to go the opposite way.

The Ruler of the 10th in the 4th

Here our need for social position, a desire to carve out an identity for ourselves, and our craving for authority and autonomy are focused on house and home, and on our wish for emotional comfort, security, kindness, and care. Often, with this connection, the career can literally blossom at home, so that everything begins and ends there. There are many options of course, but 4th house activities tend to come to the fore: for example, housekeeping, social work, interior design, estate management, and farming, are all possible.

However, we try to use social status to give a feeling of comfort and security to ourselves and members of the immediate family. This can lead to overdriven ambitions. If the domestic situation is warm and happy, ambitions can usually be expressed in a balanced way. This is more difficult when our homelife is unsettled. With this connection our social position can flourish or suffer based on what happens at home. We are more sensitive with this than with most other house connections. There is something rather subtle about it, as there is with the ruler of the 4th in the 10th. So, family, house, home, and emotional basis are the objectives of the ruler of the 10th in the 4th, and therefore our self-image and social status are strongly under the influence of both the present domestic situation and the environment of our childhood.

The 4th and 11th House

The Ruler of the 4th in the 11th

Our need for domestic and emotional commitment, security, a desire to care and to be cared for, to cherish and to be cherished, are focused here on contacts with people who share our attitudes and interests — with friends and with those for whom we feel an inner affinity. We seek emotional security in their company, which can mean that we are seldom at home. For whenever we feel a need for emotional support, we think of staying with some good friends. Because we are inclined to fly to them for comfort, their ideas and opinions, their insights and way of life can exert a powerful influence on us. In order to preserve peace and harmony with them, we tend to follow them, and, usually, this makes us feel good.

We look for like-minded people who can give warmth and have something motherly or fatherly about them, while we ourselves have lots of warmth and care to offer. Emotional ties, security, and friends who can be regarded as a surrogate family are much more important with this house connection than friends with whom we can share intellectual interests, although the latter are not ruled out. The emotional sphere takes precedence.

The 11th house also represents a need to break through boundaries. With the ruler of the 4th in the 11th we can let home and family play a part in the breakthrough process; for example, by accepting brand-new social ideas on raising children and on everything to do with the home, by rejecting certain role patterns (if the rest of the chart is in agreement), or by setting aside ethnic, cultural, or other barriers by throwing our house open (it is the instrument here) to various activities in this field.

The Ruler of the 11th in the 4th

Openness toward the new and different and breaking down boundaries and fixed forms are also found when the ruler of the 11th is in the 4th, but the background is different. Here we are just as willing to accept the new and unusual provided it strikes a chord in our feelings. The new and unusual must not threaten our secure base but it may help broaden this base or even replace it. Thus "open house" can be a feature of both connections. With the ruler of the 11th in the 4th, the door is always open to friends and kindred spirits. But although friends are an important factor in our emotional health, we are less inclined to follow them than with the ruler of the 4th in the 11th, because with the ruler of the 11th in the 4th our own feelings and opinions have the last word. In any case, our friends will already have been chosen because they are in broad agreement with us.

With this connection, our domestic circumstances can be changeful and turbulent, also we can have frequent visits from and contacts with friends—in fact we may need these. An old-fashioned, dull domestic routine has absolutely no attraction for us.

The 4th and 12th House

The Ruler of the 4th in the 12th

Our need for domesticity, emotional comfort, security, and a desire to care and to be cared for, to cherish and to be cherished, are expressed in the part of us that longs for unity; it combines with our need for isolation, detachment, and a desire for a rich inner life where the role of worldly values and temptations has become unimportant. With the ruler of the 4th in the 12th we are usually sensitive and vulnerable on the emotional plane. We have an enormous need to provide and experience warmth and safety but, for one reason or another, do not immediately succeed in doing so on a personal level. Sometimes this is a consequence of a sense of insecurity or of being unsettled in our youth; but, in other cases, we are disposed to retreat to an emotional island, and to concentrate on being caring in collective areas such as the third world, social minorities, the oppressed, the underprivileged, and other groups in need of help. We can excel in this, but find it hard to display the same warmth and care to individuals.

We may feel very vulnerable as a person with this house connection. This has not always been an easy house connection in our Western culture with its one-sided emphasis on being positive and empirical. On the other hand, there are numerous opportunities for finding a form of emotional security in the field of the unseen, the indefinite, and the incomprehensible. Among the areas in which we can find relief — areas for which we have an unmistakable affinity — are dreams, dream imagery, meditation, yoga, hypnosis, creative imagination, music as emotional expression, and many other things to which we can turn our attention in our quiet moments or which put us in touch with our inner world or religious sentiments.

Both the ruler of the 12th in the 4th and the ruler of the 4th in the 12th are regularly encountered in people with stronger than average intuition. The 12th house, which can be dreaded for its impersonal activities, is not a stranger to fear. The attempt to experience emotional calm in a potentially threatening area can trigger flight mechanisms such as addiction to drink and drugs, retreat into a dream or fantasy world, and so on.

Often with this connection (and with the ruler of the 12th in the 4th) we have initial difficulty in knowing what to do about homelife.

This can give us a sense of alienation, a feeling of being lost, or a feeling of discomfort in a home we may have been living in for years. And yet, quite frequently, as we become more sure of ourselves (using music or imaging or visualization techniques), we find we have great resources because we can draw direct from our unconscious life-source (12) for emotional security and, in this way, can introduce warmth and humanity into our home life.

The Ruler of the 12th in the 4th

Much of the previous listing also applies to this house connection, although the background is different. Here the need for an experience of unity, our feelings of detachment and isolation, our need for a rich inner life is an instrument for laying our emotional base and for giving form to hearth and home. As a result, we may need a quiet room in the house where we can unwind, be ourselves, and recharge our batteries. The laying of an emotional base, to which reference has just been made, can be brought about by such things as meditation and hypnosis, mentioned earlier, but also by other things belonging to the 12th house, such as the sea and all that is associated with it, service for the community, the religious or spiritual side of life, etc. Thus one individual will feel at home when gazing into a large aquarium, while another may want to hold seances at home, to mention just two very different possibilities!

Sometimes, as with the ruler of the 4th in the 12th, we are not sure how to shape our domestic lives. With the ruler of the 4th in the 12th, the reason for this uncertainty is having to find our emotional security in a collective context; with the ruler of the 12th in the 4th, the reason is that we bring all sorts of emotional needs to the surface when constructing our emotional base. For a time, we can fall prey to inner restlessness and become a kind of wanderer—literally, by leaving home to visit foreign lands, or metaphorically, by traveling in other emotional worlds. We certainly have a feeling for the past, for parapsychology, for dreams, for fairy tales, etc.

Not seldom, humanitarian impulses (the instrument) prompt us to care for others (the goal)—perhaps by supporting foreign relief, perhaps by helping a member of the family. Also with this connection, I have often observed a shorter or longer period in youth when we felt insecure or were not accepted, or when chaotic tendencies were at work and there was no steady routine due to bouts of illness or some other disturbing influence in the home. There was a lack of suitable soil in which a sense of security could grow. We need to provide this soil for ourselves, but may lack the confidence to do so. Taking refuge in flight is a possible response; but we can also make creative use of the potential of this house connection, as hinted earlier.

The 5th House

The Ruler of the 5th in the 5th

Being ourselves, developing and radiating self-assurance, finding ourselves at the center of attention — through creativity and through doing things that give us pleasure, such as sports, games, and hobbies — are both a means to an end and the end itself. Not only are these strong needs, but the drive to satisfy them is strong. The associated character traits will come to the fore (if the rest of the chart concurs). We long to exercise authority, can perform functions that put us in the lead, and can organize all sorts of events to make us feel important. Thus we can aspire after an executive role in some enterprise — possibly as an unpaid administrator in a charitable organization, or in a sports club or the like. Our role has to be a central one because we have such a need to be reassured.

However, reassurance can come to us in other ways. If we devote adequate time and resources to things that give us pleasure, and if this brings recognition (sincere praise is often all we ask), then in many cases we are not so obsessed with becoming the center of attention elsewhere. It is hard to say what our favorite pursuits and hobbies are likely to be, there are many choices. The chief requirements are that they give us pleasure and that they earn us a degree of approval and respect. If these are denied, we feel an urgent need to obtain this somehow or other. In which case, our behavior can be fanatical and coercive, and even imperious or tyrannical. Those around us may accuse us of egotism, when what we are seeking is enough space and recognition to help us develop self-confidence.

Creativity is often prominent: with the ruler of the 5th in the 5th, our creativity ranges completely from art to amusement if the rest of the horoscope supports this. Procreation — producing the next generation — is another expression of this house. Looking after children, whether they are our own or not, can be second nature with this house connection. And should children play a very minor role in our lives, which is entirely possible of course, then we ourselves may have a disarming but childish confidence that everything will turn out all right in the end; and this can lead to the taking of (sometimes unnecessary) risks. Work and play can be treated as a welcome challenge, and the notorious gambling fever of the 5th house can also break out.

The 5th and 6th House

The Ruler of the 5th in the 6th

Our need to do the things that bring us pleasure, to engage in hobbies and creative pursuits, and to have a central role and to be self-confident, is concentrated here on the domain of work and working conditions, and of the kind of analytical and critical thought that has useful applications. Our hobbies can become our profession. Often with the ruler of the 5th in the 6th and with the ruler of the 6th in the 5th, hobbies merge with work; with this difference that, with the ruler of the 5th in the 6th, we use our favorite pursuits to shape our work, whereas with the ruler of the 6th in the 5th, we try to confine ourselves to doing work that will be a credit to us or work that suits us. With the ruler of the 5th in the 6th, we look for a measure of independence (preferably within the context of service), or, at any rate, some say in the work that we do. Possibly we think of work as a hobby and express our ambition in the field of work and service. Sport and games, children, or amusements, may relate to our work, although other chart factors will naturally contribute to our choice of occupation.

There is a degree of tension with the ruler of the 5th in the 6th, in the sense that the pronounced self-interest of the 5th house has to serve as an instrument for the (self-)critical, often reserved and unassuming, 6th house. Therefore, in spite of our ambition in the area of work, etc., we can toil long and hard at routine tasks and keep out of the limelight for a period. The fur begins to fly when the work no longer meets our expectations. The 5th house also sometimes exhibits a love of ease, in which case we are happy to let others run round for us. Needless to say, such an attitude at work will cause problems, although serving others is still our goal.

The Ruler of the 6th in the 5th

The above-mentioned tendency to sit back and let others get on with our work for us is as strong—if not stronger—with the ruler of the 6th in the 5th. Everything to do with work and service invariably serves our purpose to make something of ourselves, and especially to enjoy life. Not only do we need, more than anybody, work that is a hobby, we cannot do without it. I have seen people with this house connection lose an incredible amount of energy in overcoming various internal blocks before they were able to tackle work they did not like. But when a job appealed to them, there was no holding them.

With the ruler of the 6th in the 5th, all sorts of things belonging to the 6th house can arouse our interest or become hobbies. What we mean are such things as plans and projects (an eye for detail belongs to the 6th house and creativity belongs to the 5th), breeding and herding cattle, allopathic or alternative medicine, manual work, repairs and odd jobs, and so on.

Also, with this house connection, we strive for a certain independence, for a measure of control over our work, and prefer to be an executive or a self-starter; for here the 5th house represents the nature of our goal. We can toil hard and long to win social acceptance. However, I have also encountered this connection in mothers who were completely satisfied with being maternal and raising their families. Their services were literally given to their children in a very positive way. Whatever we do, the crux is whether or not we like doing it.

The 5th and 7th House

The Ruler of the 5th in the 7th

Our need to do the things that please us, to spend time on hobbies and creative pursuits, and to play a central role with self-confidence, is focused here on the part taken by our opposite number or partner. With the ruler of the 5th in the 7th, we need the other more badly than we might care to admit. We put on a display of verve and eager ambition, but mainly so that they can reassure us. Independent though we may seem, with this house connection, we cannot cope without our opposite number, because we derive our self-confidence mainly from the partner. Sometimes dominating behavior creeps into the relationship, but this flows from our insecurity. If we possess only a little self-confidence, our behavior toward the other person will be characterized by warmth and charm.

Because we like to do things together (the same is true of the ruler of the 7th in the 5th), we easily become involved in the partner's tastes and interests. The partner's hobbies often become our hobbies. However, our personal ambition and egoism inevitably tend to spoil things, because the placement of the ruler of the 5th in the 7th implies that we will want to achieve our ambitions in our partner's terrain. And the above-mentioned dominating behavior can raise its ugly head once more. But our need of a partner and the consciously or unconsciously felt dependence on them, does not always leave much room for such a central role in a relationship. The placement can also make us want to let the world see how very kind we are to a partner, or it may give us the desire to have a good-looking or sophisticated partner to strut round with, and so on.

Sometimes we take up hobbies in the fields of sociology and interpersonal relationships; on the other hand, we may have a love of fashion, clothing, or other things with which we, with our desire for harmony, can make life more pleasant and beautiful.

The Ruler of the 7th in the 5th

With this house connection the partner also plays an important role which can improve our self-confidence, but here the role is more obviously a supporting one. If at all possible, the partner must do or take part in the things we enjoy as hobbies, and from which we can gain credit or reassurance. When the horoscope shows elsewhere that we are subservient, we can make ourselves very useful to our partner, although this is not something one would naturally envisage with this house connection. Even so, we reckon on receiving a certain amount of praise and encouragement in return. Although we can act in an authoritarian manner toward the partner, the reverse is also possible. The essential point is that whatever our relationship with our opposite number may be, it must give us pleasure and a feeling of reassurance. The pleasure may go hand in hand with a romantic attitude (and, in extreme cases with the behavior of a Don Juan), but this need not always be true.

The 5th and 8th House

The Ruler of the 5th in the 8th

Our need to do things that give us pleasure, to engage in hobbies and creative pursuits, and to play a central role with self-confidence is focused here on an intense area of life, the terrain in which we struggle with ourselves in order to conquer repressions and complexes and to uncover our hidden gifts and talents. Owing to this complex duality, the 8th is a difficult house to interpret. And here, because the 8th house plays an important part in winning self-confidence, much of the effect of this connection depends on the state of affairs within ourselves.

Our interest can be captured by all sorts of 8th house matters, from high finance, and life and death, through sexuality. We have a tremendous desire to prove ourselves: our ambition is expressed here in an intense house. Yet the insecurity that accompanies our drive to succeed can cause us to overdo things. A lust for power, treating life as a gamble, stubbornly trying to get our own way without any consideration for others, are possibilities; but there can also be totally different results, such as a keen interest in matters of life and death, hobbies that help us to make personal progress by confronting us with ourselves, creativity arising out of our most deeply hidden, unique gifts (8). These activities need not always be deeply investigative; what characterizes them is their intensity. For example: ready-to-assemble kits for our hobbies come under 5; but hatching out something of our very own and transforming it creatively, with blood, sweat and tears, as if we were on some "holy crusade," is something that comes under 8. With the ruler of the 5th in the 8th, we tap this deeper creativity through our hobbies. Activities we enjoy are bound to give self-confidence (5), particularly when we come face to face with a (grimmer) more substantial reality, one that demands we abandon ourselves to our true inner self (together with its shadow). In this sense, sexuality is also linked with the 8th house, its fun side lies in the 5th, its elements of surrender and intensity lie in the 8th.

The ruler of the 5th in the 8th can result in sexual obsessions, and some astrologers even go so far as to highlight the theme of death found in the 8th and to brand the native as a potential sex murderer. But, although I have come across one sex murderer with this house connection (he has the ruler of the 8th in the 5th and the ruler of the 5th in the 8th), we must never generalize this. I have seen the same connection in the charts of a sexologist, and of people with no special calling but with what seems to be a completely individual approach to life, determined by a large part of their total self—that is to say, by their complexes as well as by their gifts, and by the desire to delve deep into themselves. Connections between the 5th and the 8th often run to extremes.

The Ruler of the 8th in the 5th

Here our desire for intensity, our need to delve into the psyche, to confront ourselves and others in order to get to the root of things, to face complexes and repressions—not to mention hidden gifts—are an instrument for gaining self-confidence and for deriving enjoyment from the things we do. Again we see a certain duality, for the path to pleasure and self-confidence can be thorny. The ruler of the 8th in the 5th will probably confront us, sooner or later, with the necessity for self-examination; if not, we run the risk of becoming isolated. Fear and defensiveness (8) can make us determined to take and keep the reins in our hands; we want everything to revolve around us and we upstage everyone else while we bask in our imagined glory. But this leaves us feeling lonely, which eventually may cause us to open our eyes and start taking a less superficial view of things.

All sorts of 8th house matters can become hobbies; for example, (para)psychology, archeology, deep-sea diving, detective work, or scientific research, in short anything that uncovers, unveils or exposes what is hidden.

Because the battle between a love of life and a fascination by death is fought out in the 8th house, those who have the ruler of the 8th in the 5th feel happy only when they are challenging life and seeing how far they can go (stunts and recklessness). Another unconscious drive is to conquer death by enshrining our own unique individuality in something creative—a noble deed, a work (of art, for example) executed with passion, and so on. Indeed, with the intensity and true creativity of the 8th house, we can become highly original, if wayward, artists (or practitioner of the art of living), provided we are not incapacitated (temporarily) by 8th house problems.

The 5th and 9th House

The Ruler of the 5th in the 9th

Our desire to do the things that give us pleasure, to engage in hobbies and creative pursuits, to have a central part and to be self-confident, is focused here on our need to travel either literally and/or mentally, to be expansive, to widen our horizons, and to form our own opinions and judgments. This house connection often goes with a great love of freedom. Not that we are dissolute or profligate (although there is a slight risk of this), but that we need to be active after our own fashion and without being forced (5) in areas where we are completely free to develop, either in broadening the mind or in traveling, while dreaming of the future.

Therefore a teacher with this connection (the 9th has to do with imparting information) can be very stimulating with his enthusiasm and animation when he is talking about a subject that lies close to his heart, which is the rule rather than the exception with this house connection. He (or she, of course) can dream of an ideal process of education, and can expect to be given the liberty to work toward it.

The 9th house is the house of synthesis and anticipation of the future; if, then, we are looking for self-affirmation in it, we need a great deal of freedom, enthusiasm, and opportunities for development and for broadening the mind—and we gladly reciprocate by providing these things for others. With this house connection, we do not hide our opinions, because speaking our mind is a confidence-builder for us. In fact, we are so emphatic about what we think that other folk's ideas tend to go by the board. Possibly we exercise a managerial or organizing function, in politics, institutes of higher education, law courts, and the like.

The Ruler of the 9th in the 5th

The earlier-mentioned executive functions are sometimes found with this connection, too; but here the fact that we manage and organize is more important than what we manage and organize, whereas the reverse is true with the preceding connection. Here the 9th house is always the instrument of the 5th, so that everything to do with the widening of our horizons, with study, travel, philosophy of life, and forming opinions can serve to reassure us and to make us feel good.

Our recreation can be travel or study (of one or several subjects), and we can enjoy giving lectures on the knowledge we have lightheartedly acquired. Of course, this will boost our self-confidence. With the previous connection, one would expect our hobbies to lead to further study and sometimes to higher education; but, with the ruler of the 9th in the 5th we tend to choose those studies which make us important or reassure us, or which amuse us enough to (be able to) play a part in the hobby sphere.

With this house connection we need plenty of freedom to feel comfortable. And we are always ready to accept a challenge; for the spirit of adventure in the 9th house is a means of self-expression for us. This may give an adventurous or free-for-all attitude, or can lead to revolutionary concepts in creative matters, so that new trends and fashions are born before we are aware of it. Usually they just emerge from the way we are.

No matter whether the function we perform is important or relatively unimportant, we do need space. With this connection, a top executive in big business will want a free hand to take risks and to be original. Also, with the ruler of the 9th in the 5th, we like the sound of our own voice: airing our opinions builds self-confidence.

The 5th and 10th House

The Ruler of the 5th in the 10th

Our need for pleasurable occupations, for creativity and amusement, for self-confidence and an important role in life is the basis for forming our identity, for achieving social status, and for obtaining a measure of autonomy and power. With a ruler dedicated to self-confidence and authority placed in a house that majors on authority, considerable ambition may be expected. Our desire is to hold an important or influential position or to operate independently. We have to be able to think of our work as our own.

If the rest of the chart does nothing to prevent it, a married woman with this connection will have a home that runs like clockwork. She will think of plenty of things her husband can do for her while she looks on and supervises.

Quite frequently, 5th house matters have a say in our professional or social position, and may even form the whole of our work, which can vary from show business, management or self-employment, through artistic activities or caring for children. I have observed, in a number of individuals, that working with children has produced subtle but far-reaching changes in their self-image, their mode of functioning in the outside world, and in the associated pattern of expectations. Children (5) can serve as an instrument for building our identity (10). Nevertheless, in the final analysis, our attitude, our expectations, and our status will determine the extent to which we are influenced by children. Our self-image is the goal in this house connection.

The 10th house is not a particularly flexible house and, with this connection there is a risk that we shall be very unyielding when our identity and authority are called in question. We are quite prepared to make a fight of the issue.

The Ruler of the 10th in the 5th

Here too, ambition is strongly developed. We need a clear-cut self-image, social status, and desire autonomy and authority. So, once more, this placement indicates a big wish to be important. Now, with the ruler of the 5th in the 10th, the main aim was to win a solid position in the outside world; but, with the ruler of the 10th in the 5th, social position is subordinate to what we experience as pleasurable or important, and this may sometimes bring us into conflict with what society expects or requires. What is more, with this connection, our social position is often determined by 5th house matters, as in the previous connection. But whereas there these 5th house matters could form part of our social behavior and position, here our whole social behavior is generally speaking oriented toward creativity, ambition, hobbies, and amusements. And so, very often, our profession and/or public image are tied up with activities in the area of the 5th house.

Very often there is a certain natural ascendancy over others, partly due to the way in which we make our assumption of authority seem self-obvious. However, if there is anything elsewhere in the chart that undermines this, we can find ourselves in executive positions where we are ill at ease because we accepted them without thinking.

We can be very fond of children (our own or those of others) and we may be ambitious for them. This can stimulate their development, but if we are too dominating it can inhibit them.

The 5th and 11th House

The Ruler of the 5th in the 11th

Our need of pleasurable things such as hobbies and games, our need for a central role, for self-confidence and creativity, are focused here on a desire for contacts with people that we like. We want an important place in our circle of friends and in society in general; yet, because the 11th house calls the tune here, we are to some extent dependent on the other(s)—we readily adopt their thoughts and desires in order to have (and to preserve) a sense of belonging. Now, although this represents a form of insecurity (of which we are not always aware, possibly because we do not wish to be aware of it), we usually make a very good job of disguising the insecurity from ourselves and others by the natural, pleasant, and amusing manner that we adopt in our social milieu. The 5th house imparts a certain pride, authority, and flair; and, with its emphasis on pleasure, can make a very good impression.

We look for esteem and boost our self-confidence by participating in groups where we feel comfortable. We want to share our hobbies with friends and with other kindred spirits, but we also allow ourselves to be influenced by their tastes and preferences. Sometimes this leads to problems, for our own self-expression lies in the 5th house and the self-expression of others lies in the 11th. The ruler of the 5th makes us want to have the last word, but our need to make and preserve contacts is what tips the scales. Our creativity, among other things in an artistic sense (5), can therefore be strongly influenced by those with whom we are familiar. Sometimes we suddenly discover a number of new things in ourselves after making new friends.

With children, who also come under the 5th house, we maintain a chummy, open, and free contact; sometimes with the intention of making a break with current role patterns (our need to change forms also lies in the 11th house). We tend to instill into the minds of children the importance of social functioning, because the latter is so decisive in our own experience.

The Ruler of the 11th in the 5th

As with the previous connection, our circle of friends and social activities play a big part in our lives. Only here we are more decisive. Our fondness of the company of people with whom we have some affinity—friends, kindred spirits, and the like—is an instrument for and subordinate to what we take pleasure in doing and it does not deter us from putting ourselves first. To put it more delicately, we look for friends who feel they have an affinity with us. It is important to have friends who are on *our* wavelength; we are not interested in having friends who want us to be on *their* wavelength. We prefer them to like the things we liked before we met them. Others can certainly influence our ideas, but by no means as strongly as they would do if we had the ruler of the 5th in the 11th. Anyway, with this house connection, our friends are prepared to put up with our rather dominating attitude, or may scarcely notice it, because we have so much warmth and spontaneity to give.

Social behavior and creative expression are so closely linked by a 5th-11th house connection that, in both varieties of this connection, part of our act in our circle of friends and in society is liable to be sheer creativity.

The 5th and 12th House

The Ruler of the 5th in the 12th

Our need to do things that give us pleasure, to enjoy hobbies and creative pursuits, for self-confidence and the need to play a central role is concentrated on a desire for isolation and detachment, on a desire for unity and for a rich inner life in which worldly longings have become unimportant. This placement looks like we don't have any ambition because the 12th house has apparently blunted its keen edge. But make no mistake, we can focus our ambition on impersonal or collective goals while, behind the scenes, we feel amazingly important. It is just that we do not relish appearing before the footlights.

With this connection, we prefer to be on our own doing the things that give pleasure and build self-confidence. An artist with such a connection will withdraw completely during the creative process in order to work in isolation.

We can also achieve our ambition in 12th house matters, such as service to the community—in which we devote ourselves to the oppressed, the underprivileged, or others in need—or we can take an interest in everything to do with the unseen world, such as meditation, hypnosis, religion, or other spiritual interests. And sometimes we put a great deal of effort into things to do with water, and especially into things to do with the sea. Somehow or other, we want to shine in them or to find reassurance in them, for the 5th house is always ambitious.

In everything to do with the unseen world or community service or with what goes on behind the scenes (which need not be anything underhanded) we like to play an important role.

Often people with this connection have a feeling for dreams, fantasy, the conceptual world of a child. Other things that come under the 12th house are fairy tales, fables, legends, and the mythic phase of childhood. Sometimes the connection with such things results in writing—like the authorship of fantasy novels. The world of endless possibilities is also the world of the child, and we can explore this world creatively with the ruler of the 5th in the 12th. Here, too, there is the danger, typical of the 12th house, of being carried away (for a time at least) into fantasy land, addictions, or unrealistic ideals.

The Ruler of the 12th in the 5th

The world of the unseen and the unbounded plays an important role here, too; not because it is our only interest, but because it can enter into our hobbies and is a means of gaining self-confidence. At first sight, it may seem utterly nonsensical that anyone could gain confidence through things that have no solid material foundation; but the answer to this is that we are not looking for material security when the ruler of the 12th is in the 5th. With this connection, we can derive a sense of pleasure, self-confidence, and authority from the idea that there is more to life than earthly delights, and we are capable of feeling at one with the greater whole. This feeling can come to us in various ways; for example, during religious exercises, when we are undergoing hypnosis, or as we gaze in contemplative mood at the measureless ocean.

Our hobbies are quite likely to relate to service to the community or the world of the unseen. For instance, an artist may feel impelled to depict the unity of all living things (12), and a schoolchild can display the same sensitivity by reading or writing metaphysical poetry.

Although we can gain a feeling of confidence from this infinite world with the ruler of the 12th in the 5th, we often go through a (sometimes fairly long) period of insecurity first while we are desperately trying to find out who we are. Insecurity is generally experienced with the ruler of the 5th in the 12th, too, but in another way. With the ruler of the 5th in the 12th, the building up of our self-confidence (or even receiving a compliment) can create vague fears (12); whereas, with the ruler of the 12th in the 5th, we suffer from insecurity and these vague fears right from the start. However, once we have found some security, we can sometimes go to meet life with an almost child-like cheerfulness, because our confidence is not derived from transient material things but from deeper values. Yet, with this connection also, there is a danger of harmful habits and of going in search of inner reality by means of narcotics and mind-bending drugs and of losing oneself completely in the process.

What is more, with this connection, there is often an understand-ing of the fantasy world of the child, but we are sometimes inclined to limit the child's space because we think the collective fantasy world ought to be in keeping with our own, which is not always the case — certainly not completely so. It is possible to encourage children to use their creative imagination in such a way that we give them something that enables them to keep in contact with their creative unconscious right on into adulthood. However we must be careful not to introduce into their upbringing, or to present to their minds, ideas that are too idealistic, unworldly or eccentric.

The 6th House

The Ruler of the 6th in the 6th

Our need to consider and analyze things and to draw from them useful and practical conclusions, our critical ability and our willingness to serve, are not only our goal but also the road by which we reach that goal. Naturally enough, this leads to considerable emphasis on the above needs and characteristics, and makes us keen to satisfy or express them. Now, this can make us shine in 6th house matters, but it can also, in extreme cases, make us hypercritical, nit-picking, easily bogged down in fussy details, and apt to lose sight of the overall view. In a positive sense, this connection can indicate a practical and down-to-earth attitude and the desire to harness our energies to something useful (which can amount to working hard for a salary).

We can find and do work in any area of the 6th house; for example, in health care, in the army, in the fire department, in service, in restaurants, in shops, with animals, and as a dietician, but also by doing practical work (including odd jobs) with our hands— provided the rest of the chart does not block us.

Often, where our work is concerned, we are prepared to memorize a wealth of practical details and to make efficient use of them; and yet, in other areas of life, we can be slovenliness itself. Although the 6th house favors order, neatness, and regularity, I have found that these are not always sought on the outer plane. Our home may be a chaos, while we keep, with meticulous precision, a well-arranged mental note of the things that are important to us. Of course, external orderliness can leap to the eye with this house connection; all I am saying is it is not a law of the Medes and Persians. Nevertheless, we do find an eye for detail, precision, and regularity in external things quite often. The native can be a designer of useful objects such as pieces of furniture, but can also be a fashion designer with a fine eye for detail, or the sort of bookkeeper who will puzzle over the accounts after hours until they can be made to balance.

In rare cases, I have seen in very rich, idle people, a (sometimes too) critical attitude to workers and personnel, but in times like our own this attitude is not as common as it was formerly. It is important to us to be able to make good use of our analytical and critical faculties in planning, scrutiny, and research, at work and elsewhere, but sometimes we tend to overdo these things.

The 6th and 7th House

The Ruler of the 6th in the 7th

The need to consider and analyze in order to make useful and concrete findings, a critical ability and willingness to serve others, are concentrated here on union with our opposite number or life partner or companion. The ruler of the 6th in the 7th certainly highlights some sort of companionship: work and partner are always involved with one another by this connection, and in addition we tend to attach great value to the role of the partner. In a positive sense, this means that we like to settle things amicably, and this facilitates cooperation. And yet, with this connection, we remain very critical of the partner, because our eye for detail is turned on this person. Sometimes our critical faculty can conflict with our need to preserve a harmonious atmosphere in our working relationships, including our working relationship with the partner. For we make a certain set of demands on the partner on account of various trifles that appeal to us. However, on the other hand, harmony in the relationship with this other person is so important that we gladly relinquish our demands. Perhaps the best solution is a partner who indulges in criticism on his or her own account.

Also our objectivity (another 6th house trait) is applied to the other person, who may well be piqued by our coldly critical analysis of the relationship. Or we use our objectivity to hide our emotions during matrimonial disputes. On the credit side, there is the opportunity for a very honest relationship, in which the other is seen as an equal, not from ideas of fraternity, but from a hard-headed look at the association. Equality in this sense can result in concrete agreements concerning work, money, and living quarters. But the role of the partner has a decisive effect on the way in which we tackle these things.

The Ruler of the 7th in the 6th

Partner and work are linked by this house connection, too; but now, where collaboration is concerned, the emphasis is more on our personal ideas and conditions of work, although we do also seek harmony and balance in work. Sometimes, with the ruler of the 7th in the 6th, there is a relationship in which the partner (whether or not compelled by necessity) contributes to our work or makes it possible; and often practicality or usefulness underlies the relationship. The 6th house is invariably practical not playful, and precise but not very impetuous. This house connection, like the previous one, is firstrate for working with others.

It is said that, with this house connection, we run the risk of marrying someone who has poor health and needs to be waited on, or a partner who needs our help in some other way; but, in practice, we do not rush into a marriage of this type. However, it can be that we are content to serve our partner—as, generally speaking, we are with the ruler of the 6th in the 7th—but here we do so on our own terms.

If the previous house connection makes a person a critical life partner or companion, the ruler of the 7th in the 6th makes us even more critical, because the partner is subject to our critical examination (6) and has to be resigned to following our detailed prescription for life and work. Certainly we can possess objectivity — more objectivity than usual in fact. But, whatever the case may be, if we find a partner with whom to share a piece of work or a working agreement, and if we can be serviceable to the partner, then we can be very happy with 6th-7th house connections.

Finally, with the ruler of the 7th in the 6th, our working environment or actual job can involve 7th house matters of various kinds, such as diplomacy, the creation of a harmonious atmosphere, but also luxuries (cosmetics for example) and fine arts, contracts and the like.

The 6th and 8th House

The Ruler of the 6th in the 8th

Our need to consider and analyze for the purpose of making good use of our findings, our critical ability, the desire to serve, are concentrated here in the area where we struggle with ourselves in order to overcome repressions and complexes and to break through, as intensely as we can, to our hidden talents and to the core of things.

With this connection, we can use our critical acumen and our eye for detail in tracking and research in the widest possible sense. Often we are ultra-precise in searching into the kernel of things, which sometimes leads to significant discoveries after years of hard and careful work.

Another possible effect is when, through our work, our willingness to help, or our powers of objective analysis, we intentionally or unintentionally discover psychological laws and truths about the psyche in ourselves and others. This can encourage us to keep on researching, and often leads inevitably to confrontation with ourselves.

Situations in or around our work can suddenly bring us face to face with ourselves, too. And if we genuinely desire to look our problems and repressions straight in the eye, then this house connection can bring us work in which helping people at a psychological level plays an important part somehow or other. For even a salesperson in any line of business can, with insight and the right approach, give customers the little nudge they need to make satisfactory purchases. The ruler of the 6th in the 8th makes us good at this.

People with the ruler of the 6th in the 8th often find work in the terrain of the 8th house, work they do with dedication and with great intensity, and that frequently brings problems to light or demands digging and seeking. It can even be work involving power or finance, which always come under the 8th house.

If we are prepared to tackle our 8th house problems, then, with the ruler of the 6th in the 8th, we can gain a great deal of insight into the relationship between mind and body, and contact with disease can give us a better idea of the psychic functioning in ourselves and others. It is a big advantage to a physician to have this house connection (or the ruler of the 8th in the 6th). Such insights enable us to tap our hidden potential and to gain fresh energy and stamina. But if we shrink from coming to terms with our unconscious problems, we may get tangled in all sorts of defense and flight mechanisms, such as the urge to work and to make ourselves useful in order to get a grip on ourselves and our surroundings (the 6th as an instrument of the 8th) as long as we do not have to lay ourselves open to others. This can go hand-in-hand with ambition at work, but not with open ambition. So the 8th house develops its unconscious pressure here. We can take evasive action by taking intense interest in some facet of our work in order to avoid confrontation, which ultimately is almost unavoidable.

The Ruler of the 8th in the 6th

The ruler of the 8th in the 6th knows a similar flight mechanism. Here, too, we turn to our work as a means of escape from complexes and neuroses. But there is a difference from the ruler of the 6th in the 8th. There work, service, sickness, and health inevitably led to confrontation with ourselves, and gave us a choice between sticking our heads in the sand or facing up to things. With the ruler of the 8th in the 6th, we try to discharge the tension of these things in our occupation, irrespective of whether we take up the gauntlet or stick our heads in the sand. With the ruler of the 8th in the 6th we can put our shoulder to the wheel and work harder and longer than anyone, and we are very demanding on colleagues and subordinates because we also ask a lot of ourselves. The more fiercely we play at hide-and-seek with ourselves the more demanding we become; but the opposite is true if we have the courage to tackle our complexes and neurotic traits and tap our hidden resources. Then psychological insight, understanding of the problems of others, insight into the whys and wherefores of all sorts of things, insight into power structures, and so on, can help us to develop an adaptable attitude at work and trim our demands to suit the abilities and preferences of different people. Those with this house connection are often appreciated for their obligingness, their readiness to be always at the beck and call of others, and for their hard work; but, in many cases, such qualities attend and mask inner problems. This house connection often gives an interest in, and a growing insight into, the relationship between mind and body. Frequently there is an irresistible urge to investigate and analyze; even people who have had no more than an elementary education will inquire into the reason for things. The 8th house is a sphere in which we feel alone (but definitely not lonely); and, in fact, with the ruler of the 8th in the 6th, we are inclined to work on our own or to seek a function in which we are left largely to our own devices.

The 6th and 9th House

The Ruler of the 6th in the 9th

Our need to analyze, to ponder, apply our results usefully, our critical ability, a desire to serve, are all concentrated here on the need to extend horizons either physically or mentally, and to propagate our views. Sometimes this means quite literally doing business abroad, or working in institutes of higher education or in courts of law, etc. We set about learning things as systematically and as objectively as possible. The orderliness and regularity of the 6th house are an instrument of the 9th. When we have reviewed and analyzed something, we want to look at it in a wider context — philosophical or sociological — or to fit it into some concrete theory of our own. Whatever the case, we have clear-cut ideas on how we should understand our findings.

Often we have restless minds, and are always looking for opportunities (the 9th house is always seeking new pastures). This occasionally causes instability, but usually signifies no more than a love of change — which often expresses itself either in work that involves a lot of travel, or in the need to study and investigate.

Professionally (6) we can be characterized both by enthusiasm and by a certain opinionatedness. We are keen on looking for fresh opportunities. But since we trust our own judgment above all things, we are sometimes inclined to fling the advice of others to the wind even when it is good, and to convince ourselves that we know best. Work that demands a certain amount of bravery, flair, and exploration should suit us well.

With this connection, I have sometimes seen amazing casualness in the native's diet, living habits, and dress. The 9th house does not give an interest in such things, and the native will wear anything that comes to hand, eats at odd hours, and cannot get worked up over niceties. And so, with the ruler of the 6th in the 9th, we can encounter the rather striking contrast between external slovenliness and careful exactitude regarding studies.

The Ruler of the 9th in the 6th

Our need for expansion, for widening our horizons by traveling physically (abroad) or mentally (study, religion), and our need to hold our own opinions, are focused on a useful, concrete, practical and industrious area of life. Generally, this implies a practical, down-to-earth outlook; the plans we make must be profitable, and must have an obvious goal. Our insights must have real value and we like our judgments to be watertight. We sit and think about all sorts of things and analyze and sift them according to our preconceived opinions (the 9th as an instrument of the 6th). Also we are prepared to study for our work in order to improve ourselves, often without any external stimulus but purely out of interest and a love of learning.

As with the previous house connection, so here; we can do well in work that needs to be performed with courage and flair. With the ruler of the 6th in the 9th, being able to cut to the chase was the main point, but here it is only a means to be used when necessary, our work does not have to be permanently absorbing and challenging. The deciding factors, as far as we are concerned, are regularity and a solid basis (6).

With this connection, we can also do work involving travel or contact with foreign countries. This can mean anything from a career in a travel agency through bookkeeping for an export firm.

Our studies and training must be mainly practical or have some bearing on practical matters (economics, for example). Things that have a direct application are particularly important to the 6th house, and our need to widen our horizons is concerned with them. Passing on what we know can form part of our work, both in education and in other fields, such as writing a book on craftsmanship, old trades, the care of animals, and so on. The self-conceit of the 9th house is instrumental in shaping our work, and we like to be given a free hand in doing it, and do not set great store by the opinions of others.

The 6th and 10th House

The Ruler of the 6th in the 10th

Our need to reflect and analyze and to make good and concrete use of our findings, our critical ability and our desire to serve, are an instrument here for defining our personal identity, for gaining social status, and for obtaining a certain measure of autonomy and authority. There seems to be an element of contradiction in this house connection: the 6th is a subordinate house, but the 10th is associated with lawmaking. Nevertheless, a fusion of some sort is possible. For example, we can give our services and advice to gain standing in the community and to feel important. With this connection, we often strike others as being very obliging, because we keep coming up with viable solutions to their problems, thanks to our practical insight. We are able to promote our career prospects with our diligence, adaptability, efficiency and organizational skills. Besides earning us a commendation, these qualities can elevate us to a position of partial or complete independence.

We have fixed ideas about management, and these ideas are likely to be in conformity with the way things are done in our own part of the world. And so, we have much of the equipment necessary to rise to the top, from errand boy or gal Friday to company director. Our insight based on experience into how to run a company can give us an edge over managers taken on straight from college with heads full of theory and little else.

With the ruler of the 6th in the 10th, it is possible to take a critical and objective look at the picture we have of ourselves and of our place in society, and to do something constructive about what we see. But self-criticism, although it is an important feature of the 6th house, will not put in an appearance unless the courage we require to examine our shortcomings is found elsewhere in the chart. Failing this, the place of self-criticism can be taken by hypercriticism of others, by way of overcompensation for the criticism we are sparing ourselves. And then, with the ruler of the 6th in the 10th, we can be a nit-picker who, although extremely painstaking in activities demanding great precision, splits hairs with others and prevents them from attending to the main task. But the achievement of self-criticism can provide the constant feedback required for well-prepared work.

The Ruler of the 10th in the 6th

Our need for a well-defined identity, autonomy, authority, and a desire to achieve social status, are the instrument here for our need to make ourselves constructively useful and to develop our critical ability. It may sound strange but, with this connection, I have encountered a high degree of willfulness. The explanation is that the 6th house is critical and analytical and strives for objectivity, and therefore does not think much of preconceived opinions. If someone gives us advice, then the 6th house prompts us to analyze it to see how far we can trust this advice. With the ruler of the 10th in the 6th we are not impressionable as far as facts and figures and advice are concerned. We have a point of view, that is to say an image of ourselves, a consciousness of our position and a determination to rise in the world and to have our authority confirmed. And so we are inclined to make our mark on all 6th house matters, especially where work, analysis or service play a part. If our findings run counter to those of others, we are liable to "do our own thing" regardless, although always with a practical end in view. Thus the ruler of the 10th in the 6th is not always biddable; it reserves the right to make mistakes in order to learn from life. That this is often hard in practice does not matter too much to the native, who puts experience under the microscope. And, depending on whether the analysis being carried out is self-analysis or analysis projected on the outside world, he or she will either grow through personal experience or, alternatively, will take offense and be unwilling to learn because "the fault always lies with others."

I have also more than once observed, with this house connection, that the progress of the native's career (10) keeps bringing more work with it (6), and often this is accepted gladly because it helps to lift us up the social ladder. Anyway, the fact that the ruler of the 10th is in the 6th shows that genuine hard work is required. Like the ruler of the

6th in the 10th, the ruler of the 10th in the 6th can also give occupations in the services or in service industries, such as the armed forces, hospitals, health care, restaurants, public office, and so on.

The 6th and 11th House

The Ruler of the 6th in the 11th

Our need to ponder and analyze in order to make good use of our findings, and our critical faculty and our desire to serve others, are concentrated here on our contacts with friends and with people on the same wavelength as ourselves, that is to say with kindred spirits. On the one hand, this connection can imply a very critical and even demanding attitude toward these contacts; on the other hand, we prefer the company of practical people with a good critical sense. Quite often this results in the formation of friendships through our work, irrespective of whether we are working for others, for ourselves, or for charity. Our working conditions and working environment are conducive to meeting like-minded individuals. Conversations with people in these circles are important to us and we feel happy when the topics discussed are practical—topics related to everyday life, but also with politics, or with the organization of some society or club.

We like to be helpful to others and expect them to help us in return in certain respects, which they often do. We introduce objective attitudes into our circle of friends, but run the danger of applying double standards, namely our own based on our own well-weighed analysis, and the standards of others with whom we do not wish to fall out. Whatever the case, our concerns are mainly practical or business-like. We can find employment in 11th house terrains such as association work, politics, work in the sphere of contacts, or work in which we break through rigid limitations of form, either literally or in interpersonal relationships.

The Ruler of the 11th in the 6th

With this house connection friends and kindred spirits are closely associated with our work and/or our penchant for critical analysis. Quite often we are helped in our career by contacts or by the intervention of friendly people, are enabled to find work, or are put in a position to benefit ourselves and society in some other way. The opinions and ideas of friends and of like-minded people are quite important to us in our work, but our own analysis and our own practical insights have the last say in this and, indeed, in any other of our material concerns. In a number of cases I have seen people with this connection introducing something humanitarian into their work, or something that could contribute to the individual development of themselves or of others. This is not surprising when we remember that the 11th house represents the need to pull down barriers and to respect everybody's individuality, and that here it is the instrument of our work and service.

We also find this house connection in people employed in institutions where they work with many individuals to achieve a single goal, a state of affairs that produces a certain social atmosphere, perhaps even a subculture. Examples of such institutions are the armed forces (the professionals of course, not the conscripts), political bodies, trade unions, and the like. Comradeship is often something we need in order to enjoy our work, and we know how to bring a touch of informality even to the most sedate organizations.

The 6th and 12th House

The Ruler of the 6th in the 12th

Our need to reflect and analyze (in order to make good use of our findings), our critical faculty, and a willingness to serve are used to give shape to our need for isolation and detachment, and our longing for unity and a rich inner life in which worldly desires lose their attraction. At first sight, this looks impossible, for how can a very down-to-earth, practical house assist the development of a formless and, sometimes, even chaotic house? Nevertheless, there are a number of conclusions that can be drawn from this connection. In the first place, we need work (the means) in which silence (the end) plays a part, such as work on our own, in isolation, or work behind the scenes where we are less exposed to public criticism, or work in which inner quiet is important (e.g., hypnosis or meditation). On the other hand, we may become involved in work that touches our feelings or appeals to our sympathies; so that we can live an extremely self-sacrificing life with this connection. And sometimes we do something very practical, quite possibly something to do with the sea, or have a recondite occupation, such as analyzing narcotics and hallucinogens.

Psychologically, this house connection indicates that our critical faculty and eye for detail run the risk of being sidetracked or even of going astray in some way or another. The 12th house always blurs contours. Our self-criticism can be excessive without good cause, and so can our criticism of others. It is important for us to find a positive way of using our powers of analysis. For example, we can set to work helping people with addictions or with social problems where intuition and empathy are required. Then again, we might do artistic and creative work that touches the emotions, or we might try to make sense of the world of the unseen by carrying out objective research into spiritism, superstition, meditation and so on.

Dreams, feelings, sudden thoughts and other images from within can give us guidance in our work and in our critical scrutiny of ourselves. If we have this connection, the relationship between mind and body is at least as important for us as it is with the 8th and 6th house connections. Neither with the ruler of the 6th in the 12th nor with the ruler of the 12th in the 6th need we be afraid that we shall start suffering from all sorts of ailments at an early age. If we know how to use the unconscious forces of the 12th house creatively, we may well live longer than most. However it is possible for us to suffer from exhaustion because we do not know when to stop where our emotional involvement is concerned.

The Ruler of the 12th in the 6th

The world of the unseen, of seclusion, of dreams, and of the collective unconscious is an instrument here for our need to make a critical, useful and concrete application of what we have considered and analyzed. As in the previous connection, there is an element of apparent contradiction here: the chaotic and indefinable seem hardly suitable as an instrument for our common sense and analytical ability. Also, just as in the previous connection, we feel urged to use our intuition and empathy in our work; and, in fact, they are helpful in fields where, for example, we have to make social, psychological, or even medical diagnoses that require more than head knowledge. The difference from what we find with the ruler of the 6th in the 12th is that *there* the important thing was to satisfy our feelings, while *here*, with the ruler of the 12th in the 6th, the concrete application matters more to us. Nevertheless, the unseen world is still tied up with work and service. This is a fine connection for magnetizers and for people in similar professions, but the ordinary family doctor can gain a great deal of benefit from this aspect.

In our work we sometimes have very idealistic—and not always realistic—concepts. Indeed, in a few cases, there can be an aversion to hard work and a preference for profiteering. But we must not think the worst unless there are further indications of the same kind in the chart; in which case, the chaotic tendency of the 12th house can cloud our objective view of things.

We may have religious convictions that exercise an influence over our social behavior, our approach to work, and our attitude to sickness and health. But other convictions or ruling ideas can also play a part: we may have an emotional affinity with vegetarianism for example.

With the ruler of the 12th in the 6th, dreams, associations, feelings and the like (to which we can be immediately responsive if we choose), sometimes make a direct criticism of us. But if we shut our eyes to it, we can lose ourselves in senseless fault-finding and carping at others, and at society, in order to distract attention from our own failures. Again, as we stated concerning the ruler of the 6th in the 12th, there is no need to fear that we are unusually susceptible to disease. With the ruler of the 12th in the 6th, we can often draw a large amount of energy from within during quiet moments of seclusion, or during sessions of yoga, meditation, or prayer. And a definite religious attitude (not necessarily formal) can prove inspirational in our work as well as having a beneficial effect on our physical wellbeing.

The 7th House

The Ruler of the 7th in the 7th

Satisfying our desire for a life partner is both a means and an end with the ruler of the 7th in the 7th. Voluntarily or involuntarily, we have a great longing to be near our opposite number. How many times have I heard people with this connection sigh that they would not know what to do without the partner! The absence of the latter affects them greatly and makes them feel incomplete.

It must not be supposed, however, that the relationship will always be happy, regardless of the rest of the horoscope, and of the attitudes of those concerned; although, with the ruler of the 7th in the 7th, we tend to let the other person lead. The 7th house represents our willingness to compromise and, with the ruler of the 7th in the 7th, this characteristic is accentuated.

In deference to the other person, we can look for compromises or even give way, which can cause problems if it does too much violence to the rest of the chart. First and foremost, we try to keep the peace, to preserve a pleasant atmosphere, to share as much as possible with the partner (especially in social life), and to follow and understand the partner as much as possible. Unfortunately, this can mean papering over the cracks in our relationship for many years. On the other hand, we can really mature in a relationship with a companionable partner who comprehends but does not abuse our insecurity and our, often unmeant, dependence. Because the other person plays such a big role in our lives, he or she can be very stimulating, and can even set us on our feet and increase our self-confidence. But if the other person deliberately abuses us to make us docile, the world will see us as "cowed" or "hen-pecked."

We tend to display the same docility when collaborating with a companion, and we like to keep the peace or reach compromises. But once we have found ourselves, we can show a completely different side of our character, both as a companion and as a spouse. Little by little, and in a subtle and tactful way, we can put over our own ideas on the relationship until we achieve equality. However, if the other person takes what we are doing the wrong way, or if we fail to win the hoped-for concessions, the relationship can become very difficult because the balance will swing to the other side, and the enjoyment will go out of a relationship which does not come up to our expectations. Be that as it may, with the ruler of the 7th in the 7th, contact with a partner is vitally important to us for self-realization; sometimes extremes are experienced in the relationship, but usually we are tactful and ready enough to settle matters amicably.

The 7th and 8th House

The Ruler of the 7th in the 8th

Our need for and our attitude toward a life partner is concentrated on our need to live dangerously and to get to the bottom of our complexes and neuroses, as well as to uncover hidden gifts and talents. This is a very intense house connection for a relationship. We seek an ideal relationship with an all-or-nothing approach, in which we deliberately challenge the other person in order to see how far we can go — and how far they can go, too. Sometimes this ends in open warfare. But more often than not, it is just a matter of drawing the other person out for a time (usually quite unconsciously) until we know where the limits lie. And then the relationship can become solidly based; the lowest stone has been brought to the surface and we know where we are. Needless to say, with this connection we ought to have a forceful partner, and generally speaking we do; although, occasionally, the partner is no match for us, and then the relationship cannot be satisfying, for we need the tension of struggling with an equal in order to settle down.

Forming a relationship usually encourages us to grow and sometimes we are brought face to face (possibly in no uncertain terms) with the shadow side of ourselves. The partner is always instrumental in causing us to penetrate to our own depths, and our relationship with the partner compels us to abandon ourselves to life. Usually this is more concrete than sexual. Sometimes the most decisive thing for a woman is surrendering to the husband, or, for a man is loving submission to the wife, but other things may be more important.

Once the confrontation with ourselves is out of the way, we can become really dominant in a relationship; power (resulting from the build-up of internal pressure) always goes with the 8th house, and this is something with which the partner may have to reckon.

The same more or less applies to collaborations. I have seen many individuals with this connection who have undergone a radical change (very often to their advantage) due to an important collaboration or companionship, yet without any deep crisis. But I have also seen others "slave-driving" a colleague in an attempt to escape from inner problems. Anyway, a relationship can alter us significantly and can help us discover hidden gifts and talents; it can also degenerate into a power struggle if we do not come to terms with ourselves.

The Ruler of the 8th in the 7th

Power play, intensity, and an all-or-nothing attitude, are liable to be the means (and sometimes the weapon) in relationships that have the ruler of the 8th in the 7th, but in a different way from what we found with the 7th in the 8th. Problems within ourselves (8) have very direct repercussions on our relationship (7) and are not the consequence of that relationship. Although, of course, all of us have inner problems that affect our relationships, the fact is more apparent in those who have this house connection. There is a great need to intensify the relationship, and to enjoy many shared activities. Given honest self-appraisal, the ruler of the 8th in the 7th can give considerable inner growth through a partnership.

Although we want our own power and influence to be felt in a relationship, we seek a partner who is so strong that, to begin with, we ourselves may very well slip into their control, and it is only later on that we wake up and start struggling. Our struggles can be long or short, energetic or mild, depending on how much we think of ourselves and how much our partner thinks of himself or herself. With both connections I have found that the persons concerned were not only closely bonded but in almost paranormal communication with one another. But in less refined cases I have observed possessiveness and jealousy toward the other person, because the partner (7) is made the escape-valve for the nagging uncertainty arising from problems that have been neither tackled nor solved (8). With this connection, we can trespass so much on our partner's time and leave so little room for maneuver in the relationship, that, indirectly, we give the partner a great deal of power over our unconscious. Nevertheless, the other extreme is possible, too; that is to say, a relationship in which two strong characters stimulate one another to discover and develop their hidden gifts and talents.

The 7th and 9th House

The Ruler of the 7th in the 9th

Our need for and our attitude toward a life partner is focused on physical or mental travel, on widening our horizons, and on our need to make up our own minds and to form our own opinions. With this house connection, we long for a partner with whom to share our insights, philosophy of life, religious beliefs, or social vision. While we do not want to adopt our partner's vision, this can certainly help in the formation of our own. Discussions with the partner may help us modify our ideas, but we will not permit the partner to meddle with them too much.

The opportunity to grow and develop in a relationship is very important to us; not so much in regard to our psyche, but more in the sense of study, freedom, and a chance to improve in general. The 9th house represents our need of perspective and hope for the future, and we are least happy in a relationship that is not very exciting, or shows no sign of going anywhere but just ticks over. We require freedom of movement for ourselves and also gladly concede it to our opposite number. A relationship in which the partners support and encourage one another, and perhaps pursue the same studies, is one of the positive possibilities of this connection.

There can be a shared love of travel. Although it is sometimes said that, with this connection, marriage to a foreigner or to someone with a completely different ethnic, social, or cultural background often takes place, it is not a common occurrence.

With the ruler of the 7th in the 9th, we may well have a strong sense of justice, because the 7th house, as the house of peace and harmony, is an instrument here of the search for what is true and right.

When collaborating with someone we expect to have a fairly free hand and we accord the same privilege to our colleague. Foreign places, study, the dissemination of knowledge or the propagation of a belief, not to mention a fight for justice, can all play a part in the collaboration.

The Ruler of the 9th in the 7th

With this house connection, liberty, foreign countries, justice, breadth of outlook, knowledge, study, all contribute to collaboration. But here it is the partner or companion who is more likely to lead. There is the same desire as before to share a concept, opinion, or vision with the other person; but, whereas in the previous house connection, the emphasis was on our own vision, now we are inclined to go along with his or her vision and to say those things that will meet with our partner's approval. Of course, we do express certain ideas of our own, but the partner will guide us in the formation of those ideas. We can no longer make up our minds independently, but independence is not of first importance to us. As a matter of fact, this does have its good side: the 9th house influence always tends to make people very opinionated; however, with the ruler of the 9th in the 7th, we are prepared to climb down in order to fit in with our partner's notions, and so we gain flexibility in our thoughts and relationships. With the ruler of the 7th in the 9th, we tend to keep forcing our opinions on the partner. With the ruler of the 9th in the 7th, there is more chance of a dialogue.

Another feature of this connection is sharing a love of travel and study with the partner, and setting out to realize certain idealistic hopes for the future. We also have a great love of justice (as an instrument of our social sense), which sometimes comes out in our work (in a court of law, for example) or in our spare-time occupations (delivering lectures on moral issues, doing relief work, etc.). Given the opportunity, we often bring a lot of enthusiasm and idealism to a relationship. Possibly we advocate an open marriage (this goes for the ruler of the 7th in the 9th, too).

The 7th and 10th House

The Ruler of the 7th in the 10th

Our need of a particular relationship with a life partner is closely interwoven with the formation of our self-image and with social position and career. Our partner definitely plays a part in the creation of our identity and is very influential on our attitude about ourselves and society; but, because everything is focused on the 10th house, the degree to which we let them influence depends on our own limits, our own values, and our own ideas. With the ruler of the 10th in the 7th, the reverse is true, and the partner has the last word.

With the ruler of the 7th in the 10th, we prefer a partner who will support our ambitions and career, either directly by collaboration, advice, or stimulus, or indirectly by taking off our hands everything that does not immediately help our aims. There is not the slightest reason why a partner of this sort should be a slave. More than once I have seen a very capable, energetic partner with his or her own field of interest who seemed to support the native, directly or indirectly. Collaboration can be very fruitful with this house connection. However, a few conditions have to be fulfilled, the chief of which is that the partners in the collaboration should have their own tasks with clearly defined responsibilities; also, they should share some socially recognized goal. Although, with this connection, we give priority to our own values and (social) concepts, in a relationship or collaboration, the opinions, support, and application of the other person are things we prize, and sometimes we will not make a move without their whole-hearted approval. Therefore this is not a placement that signifies self-conceit and lack of attention to one's partner.

Because the 7th house has peace and harmony emblazoned on its shield, and because the 10th house is concerned with profession or career, facets of the 7th house often enter into our occupation; which may, for example, be in the diplomatic service, have something to do with harmony and embellishment, or involve the art of persuasion (or even flattery). Politics are another option.

The Ruler of the 10th in the 7th

Our social position, and the way in which we carve out an identity for ourselves are closely intertwined with the role of our life partner or companion in this house connection. But here we are more (and sometimes too much) inclined to heed and follow our opposite number. Although we may occupy the foreground while the partner remains in the background, the partner is usually the driving and guiding force behind us and he or she has the final say.

This is an outstanding placement for collaboration because we are a good listener as a rule, and are ready to compromise and behave in a reasonable way in the interests of peace and harmony. Of course the rest of the horoscope must endorse this and if, for example, we are full of inferiority feelings and are dependent on the life partner or companion for everything, we may lay such a heavy burden on his or her shoulders that the relationship runs into problems. The further development of the relationship is largely governed by the extent of our self-acceptance and ability to look at ourselves objectively. In good cases, the relationship is outstanding and successful because it is based on equality and sincerity. The partners can encourage one another's social aspirations; and, if only one of them is working, the other will gladly share their ups and downs and, where possible, help to clear bottlenecks for them. Here, too, the native's occupation often has a 7th house theme, such as diplomacy, harmony, agreement, art, politics, and social life, to name but a few possibilities.

The 7th and 11th House

The Ruler of the 7th in the 11th

Our need for and our attitude toward a life partner is, in this house connection, closely involved in contacts with friends and kindred spirits, or people with whom we feel an inner affinity of some sort. Both with the ruler of the 7th in the 11th and with the ruler of the 11th in the 7th, if we marry or live together with someone, we need their friendship and companionship. Tolerance in the relationship with our life partner counts for more than love-making and sex. Although it is very difficult to distinguish between the two house connections outwardly, there *is* a difference. With the ruler of the 7th in the 11th, this friendship and companionship are the main object, and (chiefly mental) contacts are what is important. If we have friends that the partner does not like (although, with this house connection, we do try to have the partner approve of friends), we will not abandon our friends — which is something a person with the ruler of the 11th in the 7th might well do. With the ruler of the 11th in the 7th, friendship is certainly very important, but it does not have overriding importance either in itself or in a relationship. In both cases we have a great need of freedom in the relationship. At any rate, we want to feel that we can develop our self-expression in whatever way we desire (and often we never make any use of it). Also we seek a partner with a similar idea of freedom. Contemporary forms of cohabitation could appeal to us if we have either of these house connections — with this difference, that the ruler of the 7th in the 11th definitely favors the breaking of role patterns and taboos, whereas with the ruler of the 11th in the 7th, any breaking of role patterns must serve the interests of the relationship.

The tendency, with the ruler of the 7th in the 11th, to see the partner as an important member of our circle of friends, brings with it the danger that we will confuse love and friendship and will marry or live with someone who makes us a good friend but a poor partner. We may try to kid ourselves that we are enjoying a modern, open relationship with no strings attached, but, for all that, we can be getting ourselves a raw deal — just comradeship without love.

Also, with this connection, we are inclined to let the form and content of a relationship be governed by the prevailing standards of the group for which we feel an affinity, because the ruler of the 7th in the 11th encourages this. Thus a conflict can arise between our desire for a companion who will leave us free and our actual dependence on our partner. Indeed this house connection runs from one extreme to the other, from the individualist in a relationship through the husband who has become completely absorbed in the environment provided for him by his wife. Naturally, we usually find that the native is living somewhere along the line between these two extremes.

The Ruler of the 11th in the 7th

In addition to what has been said above about this house connection, we see with the ruler of the 11th in the 7th that freedom and comradeship are an instrument for shaping our relationship. We prefer a situation in which our friends are those of our partner and vice versa, but here the partner has the final say in who our friends will be. Although, as in the previous connection, love can be confused with friendship, the danger is not so great, because we do not form friendships out of the desire for a relationship (as someone with the ruler of the 7th in the 11th is inclined to do), but form a fairly close relationship because of the importance we attach to friendship (the ruler of the 11th being in the 7th). Friendship here is an instrument of the relationship. With this connection, we tend to let the partner decide our attitude toward friends and friendship. But we do have a provocative and nonconformist streak in us which can lead to conflict. The challenge to fixed forms and the concern for the individual development of self and others, which are inherent in the ruler of the 11th, mean that rules in a relationship that are too strict usually go by the wayside.

We look for obligingness and comradeship on the grounds of equality in a relationship. With both the ruler of the 7th in the 11th and the ruler of the 11th in the 7th, there is a possibility of collaboration with friends, or of undertaking important things in some other way with the help of people belonging to our circle of friends. We seek a form of cooperation in which all are equal, and contribute according to their individual skills and experience.

The 7th and 12th House

The Ruler of the 7th in the 12th

Our need for and attitude toward a life partner are focused on our need for isolation and detachment, and on longing for unity and for a rich inner life in which worldly pleasures have lost their appeal. The connection is one, like the ruler of the 12th in the 7th, that can run to extremes. When a formless house such as the 12th has to give direction to a relationship, the result can easily be confusion or derailment. With this connection, we often view a relationship very idealistically, and are ready to sacrifice a great deal for it and to sink our own interests. The danger is that we will confuse love (7) and compassion (12), and will marry or live with someone we rather fancy who we (consciously or unconsciously) know needs us. Occasionally such an alliance is entered into out of vague feelings of guilt (12 again). Inspired by an ideal, a religion, or some other source, we can uncomplainingly continue to play the helpful role for a very long time; in essence we turn this into our own special form of relationship. But we do need some privacy: somewhere we can be on our own to recharge our batteries regularly. This can do the relationship good although, if the partner does not understand our behavior, it can worry him or her. Anyway, with the ruler of the 7th in the 12th, we need our quiet times in order to do our part in bringing music back into the relationship.

Because we have to give shape to our relationship in such a collective area of life, the ruler of the 7th in the 12th can also entail the risk that we are in love with love and not with our partner; in other words, that we prefer the intoxication of romance to the prosaic side of things that everyday life always brings to a relationship. It can be a long while before we really get to know the other person, because of all the dream images, ideals, and fantasies that we place between us and them, or project on them. Often, with this connection, we look to see what form we can give the relationship.

Nevertheless, the ruler of the 7th in the 12th does have a number of plus points up its sleeve for us if we open ourselves up to the world of the unconscious. We can forge a close and unbreakable bond with the other person, without being able to explain the nature of the link or the power of attraction. I have encountered an almost telepathic communication in such cases. It is also possible for us to meet in a spiritual (or other) 12th house setting, someone with whom we can share feelings we are unable to share with anyone else; this can form the basis of a true union. Actually, our affections embrace the whole world, which is symbolized for us by the partner; and the partner may feel that he or she has no hold on the relationship or on his or her part in it, and may experience frustration and a sense of being cheated. Be that as it may, although chaotic elements can steal into a relationship (or working partnership), this is an ideal connection for those who wish to join a partner in cultivating a rich inner life.

The Ruler of the 12th in the 7th

With this connection, we bring to bear our need for isolation and detachment, and our longing for unity and a rich inner life on our relationship with the life partner or companion. Here, too, idealization of the other person, or a relationship built on compassion, can play a part—but not in the same way as in the previous connection. We expect much of a relationship. Also we invariably introduce into it (collective) imagery of some sort as an instrument, and look for a partner in whom we can see this imagery; that is to say, we seek an idealistic partner with whom we can feel at one—but, in doing so, we run the risk of being completely swayed by this other person. With the ruler of the 7th in the 12th, we sought a partner who shared our own ideals. But, with the ruler of the 12th in the 7th, we tend to let him or her determine our particular brand of idealism.

Once we become more self-reliant, it can come as a great shock to see ourselves and our partner in a new light, and in this sense we experience a disappointment. With the ruler of the 7th in the 12th, the reverse is true. There our dream and fantasy world is the end-point and we possess the capacity to imagine that a bad relationship is good.

The ruler of the 12th in the 7th can promote unrealistic expectations too, but deep anxieties can play a hidden role in a relationship.

It has been said that, with the ruler of the 12th in the 7th (or with Neptune in the 7th), we shall marry someone who is often drunk. However, I have not found this to be a hard and fast rule in my own practice. Certainly, with such a house connection, we fear that our relationship is fragile and, because of this, we (usually without being aware of what we are doing) sink our own interests and do everything we can to make the other person as ideal as possible. And so the latter feels stifled, or unable to move, or is left guessing what we are up to. And then they can turn to the bottle; but the cause lies deeper. So, admittedly, a partner who takes to drink is one possibility, but it is by no means a rule. A strong spiritual union in which the outside world has no place, either literally or metaphorically, but which we find fulfilling, telepathic contact, dreams and ideals shared with the partner — these are all positive expressions of a house connection that has some difficulty in finding a recognized form.

The 8th House

The Ruler of the 8th in the 8th

Intensity in all respects is the key concept for the ruler of the 8th in the 8th. Our need to live dangerously, to challenge life as a symbol for challenging ourselves, our need to penetrate to the core of things and to bring to the surface what is hidden, our compulsion to tackle complexes and neuroses, and our desire to discover our buried gifts and talents — all these are both a means and an end in this area of life: intensifying the things mentioned and their mode of expression. We try to identify and remove the limitations to our personal power and ability; and, if we are not aware of this fact, then, all too often, we project our desire on the outside world, and see how far we can go with others by conducting a (clandestine) power struggle with them. (Incidentally, it is illusory to suppose that the entire contents of the personal unconscious, the 8th house, can be made conscious in such a way as to liberate us from our projections.)

Wherever we are, we feel a need to look into the business of all and sundry, and to poke about for the reason of things — sometimes more deeply than necessary, and we take other's words and actions the wrong way and so offend them. Nevertheless, if we restrain ourselves and adopt a more balanced approach, we can show considerable discernment and penetration and can display great insight, maybe as a top scientist, detective, or industrial spy, to name but a few possibilities. What is more, we aim to discover something of lasting value. It makes no difference whether our great discovery is a new atomic particle or the application of an important principle in the field of interpersonal relations to change somebody's life for the better.

And if people with the ruler of the 8th in the 8th dislike being challenged, the need can exist to do something, that, as it were, "raises the dead," or bestows power; and, because the 8th house hovers between the extremes of life and death, our contribution can be either very constructive or highly destructive.

Sometimes the urge to challenge life appears to manifest itself in events or situations that seem to say: "Prove that you have the ability to. . . ." Not seldom, I have seen individuals with the ruler of 8th in the 8th whose lives have been very intense in this respect, who have been very lonely; the main reason for their struggles was their difficulty in committing themselves to others.

Sexuality also belongs to the 8th house. And this is something in which we are likely to be very interested if we have the ruler of 8th in the 8th. Naturally, there are many degrees of difference between the sex maniac and the sexologist who tries to unravel everything to do with this theme, clinical, mental, and emotional. The sexologist, too, tries to bring to the surface whatever is most deeply buried. Our ability to surrender to life and to ourselves often expresses itself here in the degree to which we can hand ourselves over sexually to our partner. Certainly, the ruler of the 8th in the 8th can have a strong element in it of sex for the sake of sex; but in the long run the native seeks that form of sexuality that will enable him or her to plumb the depths in themselves and in the other person, thus sexuality is more a means than an end.

With the ruler of the 8th in the 8th, we want to prove and challenge life and to discover the extreme limits of our individuality. Therefore we can indulge in covert provocation, a sort of friendly but very decided independence where current norms and opinions are concerned. In fact there is much that can be achieved here if we simply go our own way; but not without a (for us, manageable) struggle. And we know how to act creatively when we will. We would not feel we were alive in the absence of stress and challenge.

The 8th and 9th House

The Ruler of the 8th in the 9th

Our need to experience intensity, and to dig down to the core of things, the urge to tackle our complexes and neuroses, and our struggle for power (over ourselves and, by extension, over others), are focused on travel both physical (abroad) and mental (study, philosophy of life), on the search for truth (which we often proclaim as THE truth), and on the formation and expression of our opinions and judgments.

With the ruler of the 8th in the 9th, we inject a certain amount of passion into our words, and often the enthusiasm with which we rehearse what we have learned or discovered can give others the feeling that they are obliged to do or read the same. Yet, usually, we are unaware of our compelling word-choice and intonation. We are carried away by our own fervor, and do not realize how contagious this is.

With the ruler of the 8th in the 9th, we like to immerse ourselves in things that lie beyond the horizon of everyday life and its vicissitudes; things that have to do with power, or with psychology, research, the occult, the laws of existence, life and death, and whatever is connected with them. Study (9) in these areas is entirely possible; and if we feel emotionally attracted (as the instrument) by the subject we are studying, we can sometimes display an all-or-nothing attitude, burning the midnight oil, and amazing others by our zeal and tempo. But, if the subject fails to interest us, then we have a powerful psychic resistance to overcome, and this costs us a large amount of energy.

The impression we make, and the topics that interest us, depend on how comfortable we feel with ourselves. If we play at hide-and-seek with ourselves by covering and denying our faults and our complexes, then the effect of the ruler of the 8th in the 9th can sometimes degenerate into a literal power struggle in 9th house terrains (such as religion, philosophy of life, scientific theories, and the like). We may become very fanatical on these topics, and may even go so far as to twist the words and pronouncements of others. Our dogmatism is in proportion to our insecurity and to our desire to keep the lid on Pandora's box (8)[1] and we are scarcely open to reason. We cling to our ideas and ideals with grim obstinacy.

But, to the extent that we achieve a measure of tolerance, we can apply ourselves, full of fire and enthusiasm, to our ideals and our dreams of the future, and can bring our ideas and concepts to the attention of others without manipulation or power struggles, yet generally without any impairment of our powers of persuasion. In many cases, we experience further development of the psyche (8) by occupying ourselves with travel, study, religion, metaphysics, or something of that sort; and, when we make discoveries about ourselves and our own functioning, we often feel the need to report them to others so that they can share the riches we have found. Therefore, the person with the ruler of the 8th in the 9th is a good propagandist.

The Ruler of the 9th in the 8th

Here the needs of the 9th house are an instrument of the 8th house, to which they give shape and in which they must find fulfillment. This means that it is very necessary for us to have some philosophy of life (no matter what) that stirs us deeply and makes a strong appeal to our emotions. Also we need to keep on deepening our convictions. The things that make up our vision, or fit into it, or the things we see and experience during our travels can have a big influence on us by starting up internal processes that bring our dark side to light. And we may be compelled to take a more profound look at the meaning of things and at our own role in the world. This can lead to confrontations and can change us completely from a characterological point of view (8).

The unconscious nature of the 8th house and the primitive urge to (deliberately) forget or repress things usually provide the necessary uncertainty in this terrain. It may well happen that we espouse a certain philosophy of life from which we draw a great deal of strength; and, with the ruler of the 9th in the 8th, are so afraid of losing it, that we defend it frantically, and strike others as being something of a stick-in-the-mud. Our sense of security always stands or falls with this vision. Its type—religious, philosophical, or social—makes no differ-

---

[1]In ancient Greek mythology, a box, the opening of which released all sorts of evils to plague the world. The one thing left behind in it was Hope. *Translator's note.*

ence. What we want is something to give us certainty. The 8th is always the end-point—the search for an inner core.

This connection often goes with an interest in things that are hidden, which may have to do with the occult, but may also be political undercurrents, or secrets and mysteries that need to be unraveled or fathomed, or deep-sea diving, or—for people who dig graves or comfort the dying—matters of life and death. We pursue these interests with great enthusiasm, are studious, and are eager to have good explanations or a synthesis in this area (the 9th house here is an instrument of the 8th). Once we take up a certain line of thought, we do not let go until we come to the end of it (this is true of both 8–9th connections). To those around us we may appear to be worrying, but all we are doing is combining our predilection for intense searching with our vision and our coordinating ability.

The 8th and 10th House

The Ruler of the 8th in the 10th

Our need for intensity, the desire to penetrate to and uncover the core of things, to tackle complexes and neuroses, and to gain power, are an instrument here of forming one identity, for gaining social status and coming into possession of a certain autonomy and authority. It will be clear that this is a placement in which, on the one hand, we are very preoccupied with ourselves and, on the other hand, we provoke confrontation. The suction exerted on the conscious by everything we have repressed or have attempted to ignore (8) will show in the image we create for ourselves in the outside world, on the basis of which we function in society (notwithstanding the fact that the urge to deal with these repressions also resides in 8). Often we feel an underlying vulnerability; but with this connection we possess the resources to hide the fact: the 8th house is well-stocked with defense mechanisms and the 10th house can provide a mask. One of the most effective defense mechanisms is the adoption of a powerful, authoritative attitude, or of some other form of behavior that commands respect. Be that as it may, we easily approach the world with our real self heavily disguised and give the impression that everything is under control and that it is going according to plan. And we may not wish to admit that we can shiver and cry inside—even to ourselves.

With this house connection, I have seen people undergo a radical change at some point in their lives, quite often after a crisis, which, strange to say, can be quite minor. Tackling our personal problems, and having the courage to face them, has great consequences for the way in which we look at ourselves and the world, and therefore for our functioning.

If we shut our eyes to our problems, the hidden anxiety we feel for ourselves can erupt into a power struggle that engulfs our whole environment. Hardness, reserve, and defensiveness are our armor, and yet this house connection can be full of possibilities if we have the courage to lay aside this armor. For then, the ability to explore and study things in depth can herald a really vigorous personal development without any striving for empty power.

Everything belonging to the 8th house can be used to define identity or as a means of securing our function in society. Therefore a position of authority can be regarded as important by people with this house connection, as can anything to do with life and death, from directing funerals to comforting the dying, or (para)psychology and so on. Usually, with this connection, we need recognition and support from the outside — at any rate in the beginning — in order to feel more secure on the inside. As a matter of fact, we often do receive this following and support because we put on such a show of confidence. The rest must come from us.

The Ruler of the 10th in the 8th

Here, just as in the previous connection, we are likely to undergo one or more far-reaching changes during our lives, because identity and crisis, identity and repression, but also identity and hidden gifts and talents are so closely bound together. I have observed more than once, with this connection, that the native had a craving for recognition because this was lacking in childhood, either through lack of encouragement from the parents or because he or she did not send out clear enough signals that encouragement was needed, or from some other cause. We keep looking for our identity and continually stumble upon all sorts of insecurities in ourselves. Time after time, whenever we form a particular self-image, we take it to the house of confrontations (8), where we come face to face with things about ourselves that we had (deliberately) forgotten, things that pose painful questions about ourselves and our lives.

Our responses can be exaggerated: we can perform some feat in order to give expression to an identity, both psychically and literally, or we can retreat behind an inner wall because we experience every external influence as threatening. And yet, in spite of all our retreating or exaggeration, we can certainly build a first-class career for ourselves; we are very good at keeping the inner life and outer conduct separate from one another. Here, too, we are inclined to pass ourselves off as powerful or self-sufficient, and to a large extent we can get people where we want them; but that does not satisfy us until we really come to terms with ourselves. For then we find the strength for which we have been seeking, and we can make balanced use of our hidden gifts and talents and win appreciation in the circles in which we move, whether large or small. Until this time comes, the outside world does not know us as we are, because our vulnerability makes us very reluctant to show ourselves in our true colors.

And so, with both 8th-10th connections, we see the conflict between our powerful stance in the outside world and our value as an adviser of others (because we are inclined to carry out a deep analysis of things), on the one hand, and the vulnerability and loneliness we feel because of a sense that no one knows us, on the other. Only a confrontation with ourselves—which seldom happens—can break the vicious circle and reveal hidden gifts and talents; and then in a very noticeable and intense manner.

The 8th and 11th House

The Ruler of the 8th in the 11th

Our need of intensity, our desire to dig deep to discover the core of things, our concern over complexes and neuroses, and our striving for power are an instrument here of the need to be in contact with kindred spirits, with friends, and with others who, in one way or another, are on the same wavelength as ourselves. We seek close contacts with friends and with others who share our outlook; and we want companions who are well-matched with us in character.

As with the ruler of the 11th in the 8th, we like sparring partners or, in other words, friends with whom there is such deep trust that we can say what we like without fear of causing offence or misunderstanding, even when we are being cynical or poking wry fun. But this necessitates the ability to take a frank look at ourselves; for, unless we can face our own weaknesses, we cannot make allowance for the weaknesses of others. We are liable to go to extremes (as we are with the ruler of the 11th in the 8th): on the one hand engaging in tremendous power struggles and jockeying for position with friends and associates, and on the other hand forging wonderful unbreakable friendships. Anything in between is also possible; but, with this connection, special importance attaches to the way in which we handle ourselves and the extent to which we are still playing hide-and-seek with ourselves and others. These factors are directly involved in our friendships — as they are invariably the building blocks of the latter.

Much of what we go through in ourselves is initiated by friends and kindred spirits, and the growth of our psyche can be largely dependent on them. Therefore, with this connection, it pays to be careful when we make friends, because their influence on us is greater than we might think. One good feature is that our friends will often help us out with problems, and will seldom desert us during hard times however prolonged.

The Ruler of the 11th in the 8th

Here too, friendships and the development of the psyche are closely entwined, and (as already mentioned) we need a sparring partner. Kindred spirits and people on the same wavelength as ourselves (the means) are very influential on our psychic growth (the end); but, with this connection, we are more in control. In fact sometimes we can make far-reaching changes in our circle of friends whenever we undergo changes in ourselves.

We do not refer matters to others, but (often unconsciously) take the line that if they will not go along with us they are welcome to leave. And with our powers of penetration, and our need to fathom everything to do with the psyche, we can go too far for some people. Thus our circle of friends evolves by "natural selection."

A negative trait is our endeavor to gain power over our friends, due to the fact that we need them to support us and to camouflage our insecurity. They must not have too much to say for themselves, because we have no intention of letting them put us under the magnifying glass. So the adverse side of the ruler of the 11th in the 8th is a preference for a crowd of followers to a few real friends. But, as with the ruler of the 8th in the 11th, we can certainly have true friends if we recognize our insecurity and dare to tackle it without reacting on them. So there is a contrast between psychological dependence on friends, disguised as far as possible by the use of power and authority, and very firm friendships that affect us deeply and are ended only by death. The 8th house always brings conflicting effects in its wake.

The 8th and 12th House

The Ruler of the 8th in the 12th

Our need for intensity, our desire to penetrate to the core of things and to tackle complexes and neuroses, and our striving for power, are concentrated on our need for detachment and isolation, and on a longing for a rich inner life in which material things have lost their luster. For the outside world, this is a rather incomprehensible connection; even for the native it is sometimes difficult, although it holds a lot of promise. For example, we can become intensely (8) involved in 12th house areas; possibly finding work in collective institutions such as prisons and hospitals, or seeking to make contact with the world of the collective unconscious through spiritual things, yoga, meditation, hypnosis, symbolism, and the like. An important point is that whatever we do we do with single-mindedness and intense application.

Often there seems to be some suggestion of a personal crisis or of personal problems (8) through which our eyes are opened to further possibilities, either in the sense of self-sacrificing service or in the sense of a conscious search for the solitude in which we are free to occupy ourselves with our internal world. Therefore, with this connection, even when the rest of the chart is very "open," it can be a long time before others really come to know us. Not that we are putting on act; no, we have something unfathomable in us that is very hard to place or to put into words even to ourselves. To the world it remains completely hidden. But we do need our quiet time in order to recharge our batteries and to remain ourselves. When in company, we can retain a sense of inner isolation, but this does not mean that we do not like having people around us. Certainly, the feeling of being alone need not be experienced as negative.

With the ruler of the 12th in the 8th, we find detachment and self-realization, but the relationship is reversed. When the ruler of the 12th is in the 8th, quietness and solitude (which are the instrument here) can assist the growth of the psyche and can contribute to the solution of problems. But, when the ruler of the 8th is in the 12th, we can have a sense (especially after a period or moment of inner disturbance) of approaching nearer to the universal source of things, of being joined to life in all its manifestations, and perhaps of entering into a deeper religious experience. Also, with the ruler of the 8th in the 12th, certain inner psychic processes and confrontations lead to an interest in dreams, the symbolism of fairy tales, hypnosis, and so on; while, with the ruler of the 12th in the 8th, we are already interested in such things and employ them for self-discovery and in tackling our complexes. With the ruler of the 8th in the 12th, we can prosper in any 12th house area where we choose to develop.

There is a danger of religious fanaticism as overcompensation for problems in the 8th that remain unassimilated; thus, even here, the 8th house craving for power can raise its head. Full of dedication, we apply ourselves to something that is not associated with our problems in order to avoid being sucked into them. We can behave, at first sight, in a perfectly acceptable social manner; by making it known that our ruling passion (8) is the selfless service of others (12). But anyone who takes a closer look at us will see that, in the long run, we are wolves in sheep's clothing. We manipulate those around us by playing on their sympathies or by aggressive service that actually serves no one. Other forms of fanaticism, in which we can be completely trapped, are even less rare with this placement. Nevertheless, the individual who is able to behave in a balanced way with this house connection effects such a union between two profound areas of life that the source of his or her creativity will never run dry. The native can draw from an all but inexhaustible reservoir and possesses great originality. This makes it possible for his or her life to be lived independently and non-provocatively and filled with personal symbolism — usually in a quiet and unobtrusive manner.

The Ruler of the 12th in the 8th

As we have already seen, with this connection we can use all kinds of 12th house matters in order to enter into confrontation with ourselves, to tackle our complexes, and to gain access to our hidden gifts and talents. Dreams, hypnosis, meditation, yoga and prayer, but also such things as quiet service and gazing out to sea, are helpful means of unlocking and developing the self. Quite often, paranormal abilities are found with this, and with the previous, connection; but there have to be confirmatory indications in other parts of the horoscope.

Often, with this house connection, we have to face a far-reaching change in our life that is typical of the connection. This can happen suddenly or may be very gradual. The source or cause of this psychic change, which can have the effect of waking from a dream, lies in the indefinable and spiritual 12th house. However, the ruler of the 12th house can also act as a bringer of pain and chaos, especially when we have been unrealistic and have set our sights too high, or when we try to escape from ourselves. In this respect, the ruler of the 12th in the 8th plays a remarkable Janus role[2] and has two aspects. Any planet or house ruler in the 8th can wake us up to ourselves, and the ruler of the 12th is no exception, as we have just seen. But we must not leave out of account that the 12th house offers us flight mechanisms in the form of illusions, aberrations, and addictions, which hush us asleep rather than wake us up. So we have to be careful when interpreting the ruler of the 12th in the 8th. This connection can be found in the drug addict who is trying to escape from himself or herself, but also in the psychiatrist who specializes in dreams and symbolism.[3]

As with the ruler of the 8th in the 12th, so here, when we have achieved balance, we have a never-failing source within us whereby the collective unconscious works in a fructifying way on the personal unconscious and both flow together to give positive results.

The 9th House

The Ruler of the 9th in the 9th

Our need for expansion and to widen our vision and our horizons, our love of physical or mental travel, and an interest in future possibilities and in justice, are a means and an end in themselves. With the ruler of

---

[2]Janus, an ancient Roman god with two faces, front and back. Tr. note.

[3]A quick check on some charts of famous people revealed this house connection in the charts of self-confessed drug addict Crowley, the unconventional French poet Baudelaire, three psychologists including Adler, but not in those of Freud or Jung. Tr. note.

the 9th in the 9th, there will be a tremendous desire to form our own view of people and society—a view that is the result of looking beyond the horizon, either literally by making a journey, or metaphorically by reading, studying, and researching. The welding of facts into a greater whole lies in the synthesizing and coordinating 9th house.

With the ruler of the 9th in the 9th, we are inclined to look for fresh data and to follow broad outlines; not so much to penetrate to the core of things as to accommodate our findings in our existing model of reality, and thus to strengthen this model, or—at least in principle—to modify it. Visiting other countries and seeing them with our own eyes can give us tolerance and understanding and can make us take a less parochial view of the society into which we were born. Study, religion, and the like, have a similar effect, each in its own way.

When we have made up our mind about things, which we will surely do with this connection, opinionatedness is frequently the result. Because, for truth-seekers like us, an opinion has more the character of a conviction. We are eager to propound our ideas to others as persuasively as possible. Since we are already convinced, all that remains is for them to be convinced. This sometimes makes us moralistic and pedagogic. And if people refuse to listen (perhaps because we are wrong), we still go our own sweet way; for venturing an opinion is quite different from submitting a conviction to discussion. In fact, the strength of our opinions can mean that we have no time for rules and regulations. Our self-justification may lead us to create and obey our own standards, which can be in serious conflict with those of society; so that problems are certainly not excluded. And yet, with this same strong-mindedness, the person who has the ruler of the 9th in the 9th can also serve loftier ends. If, with this placement, we are prepared to listen to the advice and opinions of others, and to give these a proper place in our thinking, then we can carry them with us and arouse their enthusiasm for such things as alternative forms of society, and more freedom for the individual, to name but two examples. Because we are able to see beyond the end of our nose, and take a long-term view, we can help to initiate new systems of education or to improve existing ones. The 9th house always involves looking ahead to the future, liberty, and possibilities for development. Our zeal for the things we discover and for the theories, ideas, and ideals we support, is often very great. We have it in us either to retire like a hermit into the convictions of a closed mind, or to go forth like a missionary in the service of the search for truth and wisdom.

The 9th and 10th House

The Ruler of the 9th in the 10th

Our need to expand, and to widen our vision and horizon, and to travel physically and mentally, and our interest in justice and in future possibilities, are used here, as an instrument for forming a self-image and identity for ourselves, on the basis of which we can function in the outside world and reach a certain social position and a measure of autonomy and authority. Quite literally, we can get a better look at ourselves through study, through travel, or from some other activity involving foreign countries. But other needs of the 9th house, not even in the professional sphere, can also contribute to the formation of an identity. We are thinking of the desire to express our sense of justice, to exercise free speech, to propagate our own opinions, and so on. Since the 10th house has to do with our career, 9th house matters can form an important part of that career, or can assist in its promotion. For example, an individual with the ruler of the 9th in the 10th will be prepared to take training courses for the sake of promotion, or will give up schoolteaching to become a scientific assistant at a university. There are many other possibilities: the native may become an ambassador, or someone with overseas interests involving travel (especially long-distance travel), or someone earning a living in an institution devoted to religion or to philosophical pursuits. These things can also be encountered with the ruler of the 10th in the 9th. However, there is the difference that, whereas with the ruler of the 10th in the 9th we concentrate on finding a synthesis, on travel, and on development when building a career and an identity, with the ruler of the 9th in the 10th we can do numerous other things—beside which we can use (and generally will use) the means offered by the 9th house.

With the ruler of the 9th in the 10th, we also have an urge to promote our religious or political beliefs. We want to convince others in order to become more convinced ourselves, and more settled emotionally.

The Ruler of the 10th in the 9th

The entire formation of our identity not only depends on, but is chiefly concentrated on, a philosophy of life and a vision of society. Everything we think of ourselves and everything that contributes to defining our identity, we place within the framework of the greater whole — the framework of society or the framework of life — according to whether we are politically or philosophically minded. With this connection, we are liable to become upset if anyone starts pulling our ideas to pieces or throws doubt on their value, because this pulls the (social) rug out from under our feet when we think we are safely standing on it. Our vision in any area, no matter what, is decisive for the way in which we present ourselves to the outside world in general and to society in particular. If we are very insecure, we can develop political, religious, philosophical, or some other sort of fanaticism, which is wholly in conflict with the real need of the 9th house, namely the development of tolerance in ourselves on the basis of knowledge and wisdom. With this connection, we can see much of the world, either literally through travel, or metaphorically through exploring the world of human knowledge; and this, on the other hand, puts us in a much better position to acquire tolerance, provided we preserve an open and honest attitude toward ourselves.

With the ruler of the 10th in the 9th we can become an outstanding teacher, stimulating and enthusiastic, or a scientist with the same qualities. But here too there is the danger we might turn into a fanatical propagandist or ride unbridled hobby-horses if we allow our sense of security or our identity to depend on the 9th house (the 9th is the end-point of the 10th here!). However, if we manage to curb this tendency a little, then open enthusiasm, flexibility in forming our opinions, and a willingness to let others stick to their own ideas, can be our badge of honor. And, with such obvious virtues, our love of freedom and our need to widen our horizons (9) may well find an outlet in our professional life (10) as we warmly recommend our idealistic vision.

The 9th and 11th House

The Ruler of the 9th in the 11th

Our need to expand and to widen our horizon, and to travel physically or mentally, and our interest in justice and in future possibilities, are concentrated here on the formation of a circle of friends and on making contact with kindred spirits. We want to make friends of people who have something to teach or tell us, with whom we can exchange experiences and ideas, and can travel, philosophize, or otherwise communicate on the same wavelength. We wish to share ideals and plans for the future with them, and find opportunities for doing so; and we look for enthusiastic and motivated individuals who can stimulate us with their ideals. However, in all discussions and conversations we can adopt other people's opinions or even pass them off as our own, because on the level of study and the formation of opinions, the need to share with and to communicate with others and to feel we are functioning as one of a group, is central for us. Certainly we put forward our own opinions and talk about them, but we are also prepared to water them down considerably. If we have very little self-reliance, we allow ourselves to be swayed by others and so lose ourselves, but this is by no means always the case. If the horoscope points elsewhere to a love of ease, then both with the ruler of the 9th in the 11th and with the ruler of the 11th in the 9th, we may be inclined to choose friends with whom we can travel for fun without bothering to evaluate our experiences, let alone make a synthesis of them in true 9th house style. Yet often the opinions of ourselves and others play a big part in our friendships. If there is some view we favor which we would like to propagate, then, with the ruler of the 9th in the 11th, we will first test it against the views of our friends. Once we feel sure of our ground from this angle, we can sally forth full of confidence, even though a plank may be completely missing from our argument. The knowledge that others are involved gives us reassurance.

The Ruler of the 11th in the 9th

With this connection too, friendship and the exchange of thoughts and opinions go hand in hand, but we are much less ready to let others get in a word, to listen to them, or to respect their views. The reason we need friends and kindred spirits so much, and we do need them, is to off-load our ideas and opinions on them. We are always eager to talk, but the danger of "one-way traffic" is great. Usually, as far as we are concerned, conversation means us doing the talking while others express enthusiastic approval of our findings. Therefore we often make others enthusiastic, but the other side of the picture is that our friends are not true friends on a basis of equality, but followers whom we lose altogether as soon as they wander off. A lot depends on how much we are in the clear with ourselves, for if we make a balanced approach to ourselves and others, we will not want followers as friends, but friends to whom we can keep presenting our ideas so that they can help us (friendships are always the instrument here) to improve, refine, and even (thoroughly) revise our vision.

With this connection, too, we like traveling with friends, both over the globe and in spirit (by studying with them, philosophizing with them about everything under the sun, and so on). Not seldom, with this connection, we feel the need to make our opinions common property, and so they reach a much wider (if not worldwide) public. This result can be achieved through lectures, publications, or via the media, or by introducing our views into the field of education, or in some other manner.

Nevertheless, in both connections between the 9th and 11th, there is a degree of conflict. Both houses favor freedom, and we should naturally expect that the two connections would be characterized by freedom and equality. Of course, freedom and equality play a significant role, but the extent to which we grant them to ourselves and others largely depends on the extent to which our insecurity will allow us to do so. In many horoscopes with these connections I have encountered extremes, such as a complete dependence on the opinions of friends, which with the ruler of the 9th in the 11th implies inequality in the relationship, and a complete dominance over friends, who are not real friends in the sense of companionship (again there is inequality) in the area of opinion-forming with the ruler of the 11th in the 9th. But, in all the cases concerned, the native feels very vulnerable and insecure. Persons who are more balanced are capable of showing true freedom and comradeship in a very heart-warming manner.

The 9th and 12th House

The Ruler of the 9th in the 12th

Our need to expand, to widen our vision and horizon, to travel physically and mentally, our interest in justice and in future possibilities, combine with a need for detachment and isolation, our longing to experience unity in diversity, and a need for a rich inner life where the material has lost much of its appeal. With this connection, we need studies, ideas, theories and opinions (our own or those of others) that lead us (whether we consciously intend it or not) to a deeper understanding of human existence, or to the realization that underneath our individual cares lies a deep union with our fellow-men and -women, or to more profound religious feelings, or to deeper, hidden layers in ourselves, through which we learn, for example, to interpret dreams, to gain insight into the working of archetypes, to use hypnosis or alpha-training, and much more of the same kind. The crux of the matter is that, by means of study and because of the urge to widen our theoretical and practical knowledge, we can penetrate to silent depths of our own psyche, where matter, space, and time coalesce.

This house connection can surprisingly be very concrete in its effects. The sea and the universe show a symbolic analogy to the depths of the psyche, and quite often we see that people with this connection are interested, for example, in space travel or marine navigation as a concrete expression of an archetype. And yet these interests are active in the psyche because the feeling they give us, which we can neither describe nor explain, unmistakably contributes to a sense of general well-being. Incomprehensible as this feeling is, it is hard to talk about it, which explains some of the reserve of the 12th house. In our minds we can be eagerly occupied with typical 12th house matters (dreams, hypnosis, myths, fairy tales, legends, the accounts of creation found in various cultures, and so on). But the 12th house also has to do with being of service and the need to deny ourselves; so, with the ruler of the 9th in the 12th, studies concerned with hospitals, institutions, and so on, are also possible.

The ideas of foreign lands (9) and oppression (12) are sometimes united in the desire to serve the third world, either actively or passively, either as a fund-raiser, as a worker in the field, as a member of committees or action groups, as a propagandist for this area of need, or as someone who helps behind the scenes. And the aim of all these activities is to learn to see ourselves in proportion, and to experience within us something of humanity in general.

The Ruler of the 12th in the 9th

With this connection, the need for isolation and detachment, the longing for unity and for a rich inner life (in which material things no longer play a part), are instruments for widening our horizon, for forming our own vision and opinions, and for study and travel. Certain feelings we may find hard to pin down, which come from somewhere deep inside us (12), and spring from an unconscious knowledge and the primary union with life, can influence our beliefs, our (social) vision, the studies we pursue, and our contacts with foreign countries. The emotional aspect invariably enters into this. Not, by any means, that we have difficulty with the rational side of our study (or studies), or that we study in a chaotic way (chaos, too, belongs to 12), but that we apply ourselves to our studies only when we are emotionally involved in them and are able to work alone at our own speed. Our preferred subjects are those dealing with 12th house matters: dream-interpretation, service to the third world, psychiatric nursing, work with or on water or space, or work having religious or occult connotations. The possibilities are many, but something with a 12th house flavor must come into our studies somewhere along the line.

Our desire to help the underprivileged (12) can motivate us to take up some study (9) that prepares us to assist them; but it can also motivate us to visit a third-world country. The development worker is a fine example of the influence of this combination. However, the background is different from that of the previous connection; because here the desire to travel abroad is satisfied through relief work, whereas there the desire to help is satisfied through travel.

With this connection, the desire to aid the needy or oppressed does not have to be felt in regard to material things alone: we can also be convinced that there are people in spiritual need requiring help. This, too, can induce us to study or to journey overseas (as a missionary, or a guru, etc.). In an unbalanced personality, connections between the 9th and the 12th house sometimes bring dangers, because outlandish ideas can steal into our philosophy of life and into our politics with the ruler of the 12th in the 9th, and certain ideas and opinions can lead to (self-)undermining behavior with the ruler of the

9th in the 12th and have physical, mental or social repercussions. And then we see the reverse of the true effect of this house connection: intolerance and lack of understanding instead of the deep human sympathy and insight and the level-headed tolerance to which this, and the previous house connection, can lead.

The 10th House

The Ruler of the 10th in the 10th

The need to define our ego and form a clear self-image, and our desire for a social position in which we can enjoy a measure of autonomy, authority, and power, are both a means and an end here. Everything reinforces this need and this desire, which can show up in various ways; but, first and foremost, we have a compulsion to prove ourselves in the community and/or in society at large, and also to discover for our own satisfaction what we can do. We are, so to speak (often unconsciously), in competition with ourselves—a mechanism by which we keep hoisting ourselves up the social ladder or increasing our kudos.

A lust for power is to be expected with this connection. Usually we cannot endure interference or contradiction; something in our attitude says, "I'm in charge," or, "I know what I'm doing, leave the organizing to me." At times we take too heavy a load on our shoulders, but nothing will induce us to admit it. We are continually spurring ourselves on, keeping ourselves on our toes, and, in the long run, we may become muscle-bound, metaphorically speaking. Even with a chart indicating that we are very retiring, we have a great deal of ambition if the chart contains this connection.

The truth is that we are constantly looking in the outside world for values to confirm our sense of identity and self-image, and it is this insecurity that lies behind the way we motivate and stretch ourselves. But, if we come to feel more assured and learn what we are able to achieve at a certain level, we can moderate our ambition. However, this does not prevent us, at every turn, from feeling that there is still more we can do. Our need to be an achiever (and often to win prestige) keeps us on the go. Another danger with this house connection is that (for a longer or shorter period) we overconcentrate on our role in society and in the outside world, at the expense of our emotional world, our inner world, and our family life. In the end this can take its revenge, and leave two courses of action open to us: either we can brush aside every reproach and every objection with the hardness of the 10th house, can see to it that they miss their mark, or can discourage them in advance, leaving us free to continue in the same old way, or we can learn that we could keep searching in the outer world forever, but true reassurance is available within us and only within. Certainly, we want to prove ourselves—and it does not matter if it's to ourselves, parents, immediate family, friends, or society. The more refined individual with the ruler of the 10th in the 10th can attain a certain degree of satisfaction with himself or herself by accepting and using limitations creatively. Frequently this does not happen until the person in question has been at the top (relatively speaking) for some time (whether in a small way or in a big way makes no difference), for only then can he or she see things clearly enough to get them into perspective.

The 10th and 11th House

The Ruler of the 10th in the 11th

Our need to define ego and form a clear picture of ourselves, and to achieve a position in society that carries with it a certain measure of authority and autonomy, is focused here on contacts with friends, kindred spirits, and others with whom we feel an inner bond in some way or other. Working with friends or in groups, or finding work through friends, groups, or organizations, has often been ascribed to this connection. Now, although they are very likely with this connection, we find the same effects with the ruler of the 11th in the 10th. With the ruler of the 10th in the 11th, friends, kindred spirits, and/or organizations do play a big part in our lives, however, because we are inclined, very largely, to see ourselves and society through their eyes. Even if the rest of our chart reveals pronounced egocentric tendencies, with this connection, we still have to have a lot of approval, help, and support from outside in order to feel comfortable. But it does not follow, by any means, that we surround ourselves with people we call our friends or soul mates. We can also find the desired affirmation by identifying ourselves in some way with a trend, a cultural group, a group with spiritual aims for society, or something of the sort, without taking the trouble to meet those involved or even to find out who they are. The point is that how we look at ourselves depends, more than we may be willing to admit, on the attitude and judgment of our friends, because this gives us a sense of certainty.

Although, with this connection (and with the ruler of the 11th in the 10th, as already said) we can be helped socially by our friends, we are also prepared to use our own position and means to help them whenever necessary.

Because the 11th house also has to do with breaking old molds, we are liable, with this connection, to undergo a significant change by coming to see ourselves in a completely new light as a result of our functioning in society and in our circle of friends. And we will try to introduce a touch of unconventionality and humanity, something fraternal and a flicker of freedom, into the work we do and into the social position we occupy. Quite often I have seen people with this connection engaging in spare-time activities that are humanitarian or promote solidarity, and this has contributed to their status and role in society.

The Ruler of the 11th in the 10th

With this connection, contacts with friends and kindred spirits assist in the formation of our identity. This was also true of the previous connection, but there the role of friends and kindred spirits left a deep impression on our identity. With the ruler of the 11th in the 10th, our own social status and self-image are the deciding factors. In other words, we welcome contacts with friends and others when they are broadcasting on our wavelength, but not when they expect us to "tune in" to them. Here, too, we have the need to season our social position with the spice of humanity, and with something mold-breaking, libertarian, and consultative (which is why the ruler of the 10th in the 11th and the ruler of the 11th in the 10th are good house connections for members of Congress).

When the effect of this house connection is harmonious, we are able to formulate the aims of our group (11) in such a way that it makes a bigger impression on society (10). Frequently we make our friends while building our career and, as a rule, they help us to build it. Lack of balance can lead us to abuse our friends by keeping them harnessed to our little chariot; but with a balanced approach there can be mutual respect in the relationship and mutual help.

Traditionally, the 11th house represents hopes and wishes in regard to contacts with others, but it also embodies a kind of ambition, namely the freedom we use to be ourselves when we are with other people, and our desire to let others be given consideration. Therefore the ruler of the 11th in the 10th can make us ambitious in a way that says: "Everyone is free to be themselves, and I am going to be as free as they are!" This can make us wayward but also resourceful enough to cope when times are hard.

The 10th and 12th House

The Ruler of the 10th in the 12th

The need to define ego and form a clear self-image, the desire for a social position that carries with it a certain measure of authority, autonomy, and power, are both focused on some form of detachment and isolation, on a longing for unity and for a rich inner life in which worldly aspirations have lost their appeal. In many ways, the 10th and the 12th house seem to be at odds with one another: the 10th is intent on forming an ego and on manifestation in the outer world, while the 12th is concerned with disassociation and with the inner world, and shuns the outer world.

The ruler of the 12th in the 10th and the ruler of the 10th in the 12th frequently occur in individuals who have lived through a period of insecurity (especially in their very early years). This may be no fault of the parents. Internment in a camp during a war, or some other unavoidable hardship, can very often be indicated by this house connection. Owing to a lack of security when we are so young, we can keep looking for something most of our lives, often with absolutely no idea what this something is. We seek security, but immediately undermine it with doubt; then we try to find certainty elsewhere, but simply start doubting again. Even when we have built up a certain identity, we are liable, both with the ruler of the 10th in the 12th and with the ruler of the 12th in the 10th, to disbelieve and undermine that identity. In confrontations of all kinds, in and with the outside world, we feel unsure of our ground because we allow ourselves to be influenced far too quickly, and our uncertainty makes us even more impression-able. (The ruler of the 12th in the 10th also gives this feeling of uncertainty).

However strong our character may be in other respects, we can display a great deal of docility and servility toward those who have managed to influence us. Nevertheless, the 10th house has to express itself in the area of life represented by the 12th house. Therefore, with the ruler of the 10th in the 12th we have to learn that we cannot find security in externals, but can find it only in our own inner source. Those who have learned to put some trust in their own feelings, their inner voice, their dreams, and so on, can actually develop very strong personalities, even if they prefer to keep out of the limelight. The outside world does not matter to them in the ordinary way; they feel the glory of it all when they are helping behind the scenes, and their sense of unity helps them to share in it in their own special way.

However, many concrete expressions of this connection are possi-ble, such as a career in an area that bears some analogy to the indefin-able qualities of the 12th house. Thus the native might become a physician, a medium, a sea captain, or a hypnotherapist, for example. The crux of the matter is that the experience of unity, whether or not in symbolic form (e.g., the universe or the sea), is indispensable to us in our search for a personal identity.

The Ruler of the 12th in the 10th

I have met even greater insecurity in this connection than in the previous one. Here chaos and disassociation are always an instrument for our identity, and this can be very undermining. We are so uncer-tain of ourselves that we tend to accept what others tell us we are like, and are susceptible to all sorts of reactions and opinions impinging on us from the outside world. In fact we are probably rather hard for anyone, including ourselves, to understand. But this is usually because of unsettled circumstances in early youth, such as given by the ruler of the 10th in the 12th. However, it is noticeable that, when we no longer look for security and stability in the outside world, but in ourselves, in dreams, in our feelings, and so on, our uncertainty in the outside world will gradually disappear and we shall start occupying ourselves with a 12th house interest of some kind.

What we need with this connection is work where we can use our feelings (of sympathy) and can be intuitive and empathic. Whether we become a social worker, doctor, nurse, probation officer, or yoga teacher, our aims will be to use and give shape to the 12th house in order to define our identity. If we learn to handle the elusive side of our nature, and if we are able to find a measure of stability in it, then we can achieve a great deal with this apparently chaotic house connection. There is only a slim chance (in spite of what some books say) that we will become alcoholic or a drug addict, or otherwise land in the gutter, with this connection. Our inner resources generally bring out our good side, if our ego is prepared to stand back a little.

The 11th House

The Ruler of the 11th in the 11th

With this house connection, we need contacts with friends, with kindred spirits, and with others to whom we feel inwardly united in some way, and we need to break through established patterns in order to give everyone the same chance. Exchanges with others are very important, and often we are active in one way or another in societies, clubs, or other (formal or informal) groups. We do not strive for a position of power but, on the contrary, value democracy and equality. However, this does not mean that we are never guilty of a certain form of discrimination: even while promoting equality within our own group, we can be dismissive of other groups. Such behavior is sometimes intensified in proportion as other trends in the chart indicate our identity (and not only that part of it involved in the 10th house) is adopted from our friends.

In the circle in which we feel at home, we like to hobnob with folk who have something wayward, individual, or distinctive in their makeup; and the friendly iconoclasm of the 11th house shows itself here. Certainly we have a passion for equality, but we are in no way prepared to let it stand in the way of diversity where friendships are concerned.

What often escapes notice is that the 11th house has a confrontational side. Not only do our friends reflect traits and preferences of ours that we find pleasant, but through their involvement in our lives they can form a clear mirror for other things going on inside us, too. It is not possible to tell from the 11th house alone what our friends will be like externally, but it does show what we want from them and how we interact with them. On the one hand, Saturn in the 11th can mean no friends or older friends, and on the other hand it can mean a close bond in which few words need to be spoken or in which serious conversations can prove very stimulating to both parties. Filling in the details depends largely on us and on the extent to which we can accept ourselves and can allow others to be themselves. With the ruler of the 11th in the 11th, the confrontational activity of friends and kindred spirits is unusually great. Therefore a very sudden or very far-reaching change can take place in our circle of friends after a lot has happened in our own psyche. And so, with the ruler of the 11th in the 11th, friends and allies are important in many respects: without any conscious intention on our part, they help us to settle down and to look ourselves squarely in the eye.

The 11th and 12th House

The Ruler of the 11th in the 12th

Our need for contacts with friends, kindred spirits and others with whom we feel united in one way or another, is focused on detachment and isolation, on experiencing the unity of all things and on a rich inner life in which material values have lost their appeal. This means that we badly need friends with whom to share an interest in one way or another on an emotional or other indefinable plane—from music, poetry, and art, through religion and spiritism—in order not only to experience unity in diversity but also to give it expression.

As with the ruler of the 12th in the 11th, we are inclined to idealize our friendships, and so lay ourselves open to the chaos and disappointment of the 12th house. We invariably see others not as they really are, but as they fit into some picture in our dreams, fantasies, and ideals, and so we seldom do justice to our friends or to reality. Therefore, with this connection, we must take care in choosing our friends. Otherwise we can be disappointed, or we can make so much of our friends that we let ourselves be used by them and always put their interests before our own.

On the other hand, we may just as easily use our friends for the sake of our ideals, probably without meaning to do so. The fact of the matter is that a degree of estrangement, disappointment, abuse, or advantage-taking can creep into a friendship with this house connection. Both with the ruler of the 11th in the 12th and with the ruler of the 12th in the 11th, I have more than once observed third parties trying to undermine a good friendship by gossip; so there is every justification for warning the native to look out for this.

With this connection, too, the possible effects can fall outside the world of the senses; that is to say there can (virtually) be a telepathic link with friends, and something very valuable but impossible to describe in the way of an atmosphere or shared environment. Friendships can be essential in helping us look deep into our soul, to analyze dreams, or to share in Bible study or in the investigation of Eastern religions or of anything else in the realm of the collective unconscious.

The Ruler of the 12th in the 11th

With this house connection, our need for isolation and detachment, plus the desire for unity in diversity and for a rich inner life are focused on our need for friends and kindred spirits. As in the previous connection, this means that we are looking for a certain emotional tie with friends. Whereas, with the ruler of the 11th in the 12th, friends have to fit our ideal image of them, with the ruler of the 12th in the 11th we are much more inclined to allow this ideal picture to be determined by what is customary or approved in our group. There is a danger that friendships will be abused by others, but also by us, because friendships are the outlet for our service, our (at any rate partial) dependence, and our need to give shape to the 12th house.

What is more, our behavior can have a rather chaotic and unpredictable tendency, in keeping with similar behavior in the circles in which we move. This can create doubts in ourselves and others, making us either more and more withdrawn or more and more subservient, and carrying us round and round in a vicious circle. Only by acquiring insight into our activities (and in this we can be helped by dreams, daydreams, fantasies, word association and many other 12th house energies) can we break a vicious circle such as this. Then we can realize other possibilities, for example: we can share some ideal with friends and also make it more widely known; we can help friends and others behind the scenes in order to foster the life of the community and encourage people to accept one another for what they are; we can set up parapsychological experiments with our friends; or we can share with others a love of the sea, or of music, or of some other 12th house interest. In this way we are strengthened in our inner depths and feel we are immersed in the unconscious current that flows through all, as well as in the consciously experienced stream that joins us to kindred spirits.

The 12th House

The Ruler of the 12th in the 12th

One of the most subtle and sensitive house connections, and one that runs to extremes, is the ruler of the 12th in the 12th. Our need for isolation and detachment, and our desire to experience the unity of things and to have a rich inner life, are reinforced so that our susceptibility, which can show itself as empathy and intuition, is greater than average. Our sympathies, too, are quickly aroused by those who play on them.

If the desire for isolation gets out of hand, we shall long for peace and quiet in one form or another, but we shall not find it because the search becomes never-ending. Then there is a danger that we shall finally take up with all sorts of outlandish ideas, which block balanced functioning in the physical world. But this is not inevitable.

A very different form in which our (over)sensitivity can express itself is the ability to intuit things or have presentiments of situations; in other words, clairvoyance and direct knowledge. Many individuals with the ruler of the 12th in the 12th seem to have more than their fair share of paranormal gifts (when the rest of the horoscope points in the same direction, of course). If we learn to recognize and use these gifts, we shall find that we have tapped into an inner source that will never dry up. We can keep drawing that source of security that is so characteristic of this house connection that it astonishes and puzzles the outside world.

And so we see the extremes of a deep union with ourselves and others, and of escapist tendencies. Quite often we are kept going by some belief or faith, which need not have anything to do with religion. On the quiet, this can motivate a great deal of that part of us that is represented by the rest of the horoscope. We are not motivated by enthusiasm or by the prospect of conscious gain; no, the motivation provided by the 12th house lies in the often scarcely conscious "knowledge" that life is good the way it is, whether or not it meets our wishes and desires. The motivation provided by the 12th house can also take the form of an unshakable faith in the meaning of life, in the sense that we are all small cogs in the big wheel.

Frequently, these underlying motivations can be symbolized in the conscious by something very concrete. Thus someone with the ruler of the 12th in the 12th can be stirred by the sight of the national flag, and can feel ready to fight for it, not realizing that the feeling has nothing to do with some entity known as the "fatherland" or so on, and that the "fatherland" carries the projection of a need of unity, in this case unity with one's people. With the ruler of the 12th in the 12th, we can be prepared to efface and sacrifice ourselves completely in all possible ways. On the other hand, we can become idle dreamers living with our thoughts in a different world.

The need to experience unity is strong, and we can find a feeling of unity in social activities on behalf of the needy, because they are people just like ourselves; but we can experience temporary unity in the abuse of drugs and other addictive substances which blur the edges of our personality and engulf us in a collective fantasy.

It is most important to help children who have the ruler of the 12th in the 12th to express in some way, at an early age, the rich feelings that they themselves cannot understand or put into words. For example, we can teach them to make music, to paint, draw, recite poetry, etc. The earlier in life we learn to express our feelings, the better we shall understand them later.

Bibliography

Hamaker-Zondag. *Aspects & Personality*. York Beach, ME: Samuel Weiser, 1990.

_____. *Elements & Crosses as the Basis of the Horoscope*. York Beach, ME: Samuel Weiser, 1984.

_____. *Foundations of Personality*. York Beach, ME: Samuel Weiser, 1994. Combines *Elements and Crosses as the Basis of the Horoscope* and *Houses and Personality Development* into one volume, to be published in the fall of 1994.

_____. *Handbook of Horary Astrology*. York Beach, ME: Samuel Weiser, 1992.

_____. *The Houses and Personality Development*. York Beach, ME: Samuel Weiser, 1988.

_____. *Planetary Symbolism in the Horoscope*. York Beach, ME: Samuel Weiser, 1985.

_____. *Psychological Astrology: Astrological Symbolism & the Human Psyche*. York Beach, ME: Samuel Weiser, 1990.

_____. *The Twelfth House: The Hidden Power in the Horoscope*. York Beach, ME: Samuel Weiser, 1992.

Maternus, Firmicus. *Matheseos Libri VIII*. Translated as "Ancient Astrology Theory and Practice," by Jean Rhys Bram, Park Ridge: New Jersey, 1975.

Morin de Villefranche, J. B. *Astrologiae Galleicae. Liber Vigesimus Primus*. Translated as "The Morinus System of Horoscope Interpretation," by R. S. Baldwin, Washington, 1974.

Index

I

J

K

Karen Hamaker-Zondag started her astrological practice in 1975. She is a founding member of two schools in Holland: an astrological school, Stichting Achernar, and a school of Jungian psychology, Stichting Odrerir, with a current enrollment of over 200 students. She is a graduate of the University of Amsterdam with doctoral degrees in social geography and environmental engineering. Her post-graduate study of psychology, astrology, and parapsychology inspired a full-time counseling practice. A leading astrologer in Holland, she publishes a quarterly astrological journal, *Symbolon*, with her husband Hans. She lectures extensively throughout the world, traveling to Russia, Japan, Canada, the USA, and all over Europe, where she has been enthusiastically received by the astrological communtiy. She has written thirteen books including, *Foundations of Personality*, *Handbook of Horary Astrology*, *Aspects & Personality*, *Planetary Symbolism in the Horoscope*, *Psychological Astrology*, and *The Twelfth House*, all published by Samuel Weiser.